SOLDIER FIVE

This book is dedicated to the memory of Vince, Bob and Steve, and to my ever-loving wife Sue, who made it all worth coming home for.

THE BOOK THE BRITISH GOVERNMENT TRIED TO BAN

SOLDIER FIVE

THE REAL TRUTH ABOUT THE BRAVO TWO ZERO MISSION

MIKE COBURN

MAINSTREAM
PUBLISHING
EDINBURGH AND LONDON

First published in Great Britain in 2004 by
MAINSTREAM PUBLISHING COMPANY (EDINBURGH) LTD
7 Albany Street
Edinburgh EH1 3UG

ISBN 1 84018 866 9

The publishers have made every effort to trace the owners of photographs
used in this book. In cases where they have been unsuccessful, they invite
copyright holders to contact them directly

A catalogue record for this book is available
from the British Library

Typeset in Futura and Garamond

Printed in Great Britain by
Mackays of Chatham plc

CONTENTS

FOREWORD

This is not only Mike's story; it's mine.

I could not have related the events more truthfully and objectively myself. Mike captures the feelings of frustration, betrayal and self-doubt we experienced in the ill-fated mission code-named Bravo Two Zero. Although we had been given up for dead, we made it home against all the odds, not unscathed, but able to tell the story. And it was a story that needed recounting, to one another, to the regiment and, not least of all, to the families of those who had died.

Many of us were shocked when the details of this operation escaped from the confines of the proper regimental forum and spilt into the public domain. However, over ten years on, the issues surrounding the demise of the patrol have yet to be put to rest. For those of us who have until recently remained serving with the SAS and therefore bound by its code of silence, this has been frustrating, to say the least.

Now I can endorse this credible account of the events as they happened. While it is hard-hitting and uncompromising, there is an intelligent analysis of events as they developed. Mike has not shied away from relating some of the more unpalatable incidents, neither has he painted the men involved with qualities greater than they possessed. To have done otherwise would have gone against everything the Special Air Service stands for. In this, he has upheld the ideals of David Stirling, in particular those of professional integrity and humility. Mike is an SAS man who stands tall and is not afraid of the truth, and his gripping account is an impressive reflection of the man himself. Above all, it is a fitting tribute to 'the only real heroes of Bravo Two Zero', our comrades who did not beat the clock, our friends we shall never forget: Bob, Vince and Legs.

Mal

AUTHOR'S NOTE

Soldier Five was born out of frustration more than anything else: years of frustration at being forced to keep quiet and not pass comment, at not being able to respond in kind to allegations or distortions regarding Bravo Two Zero, the events and its personalities, years of being without a voice.

The aftermath of the 1991 Gulf War saw a steady erosion of the secrecy surrounding SAS operations in Iraq. While it is not necessary to list all these, suffice to say that for those who remained with the SAS regiment and kept their silence it was a very troubling period. With the Bravo Two Zero operation in particular, revelations became more and more outrageous, culminating in the book and film of *The One that Got Away*, which saw one of the deceased patrol members, Sgt Vince Phillips, portrayed in an unfair and undignified manner. A former CO (Commanding Officer) of 22 SAS described in open court the vilification of Sgt Phillips as 'a most disgusting act', a comment that reflected the view of the majority of the SAS at the time and a sentiment recognised by the High Court some years later.

In 1996, the three surviving members of the patrol who had not published their version of events (Mal, Dinger and myself) felt the 'no comment' policy of the SAS and the MoD over Bravo Two Zero had reached the point where it was actually detrimental to the reputations of both the regiment and the Bravo Two Zero patrol, and subsequently requested that the regiment officially answer the mistruths and misrepresentations now circulating in the public domain. While the then current CO 22 SAS agreed that something more substantial needed to be done, MoD refusal to support such action precluded any comment. The regiment in general, and the three still-serving patrol members in particular, were hugely disappointed by the MoD's refusal;

however Mal, Dinger and I were permitted to write personal letters to the Phillips family expressing our support for them and the memory of Vince. Some years later, this incident, along with several others, formed part of a 'slow burning fuse' that finally prompted the writing of *Soldier Five* in 1998.

There have been several accounts written on what has now become an infamous tale, so before I start I would say the following: *Soldier Five* tries nothing more than to provide a realistic view of the events that led to the deaths of three, and capture of four, of the men of Bravo Two Zero. In the course of writing, some events and personalities have been altered to preserve their security.

Unfortunately, however, and a little unexpectedly, in the telling of this story I put myself once more into the breach. I thought that my major battling days were long gone when I put pen to paper, but alas, events proved me wrong. While I realised that in submitting my manuscript to the British Ministry of Defence I would provoke a reaction, the actual response was quite removed from that which one would have anticipated under normal circumstances. Common sense suggested that the MoD would want to enter into practical dialogue and negotiation, something that hopefully would lead to a sensible conclusion acceptable to both parties. The reality could not have been further from this: draconian threats, intimidation and overwhelming hostility ensued, something that did not diminish over the four and a half years of litigation that followed.

And during those years more revelations (referred to in open court or in later publications) about Bravo Two Zero came to pass along with expert commentary: commentary more often than not by people who were never there but still felt they had a valid opinion to offer. To have to sit in silence, gagged while all this went on, has been at times exasperating to say the least.

However, and despite the best efforts of the MoD's legal army, the courts have now at last given me the opportunity to have my say. Ironically, the further spilling of information by others has afforded the opportunity to expand somewhat the tale of Bravo Two Zero, to the extent that the new revelations can allow, and in so doing produce a more complete and accurate documentation of the events that surrounded the ill-fated mission.

Looking back on the events that have shaped my life, and in particular my time in the Special Air Service, I often find it hard to associate those happenings with myself. As far as I am concerned, more often than not, there was never anything special about what I did, or how I went about my work; it was just part of the job, an extension of my training. Now, as a civilian, my priorities have changed and perhaps that is why I have found it possible to recount the story of my involvement.

Actually sitting down to pen an account of one's own life is not an easy thing to do: the knowledge that your actions, emotions and perspectives will be judged publicly is extremely daunting. But it could also be said that for me this has been part of the healing process, for certainly writing this account was a cathartic experience that unlocked long-suppressed memories, memories both good and bad. At times it was emotionally very draining.

However, in the writing of *Soldier Five*, and the subsequent fight for its publication, I have been fortunate enough to have received support along the way from many close friends and family, both old and new, from Auckland to Hereford, and had it not been for them I no doubt would have given up on this a long time ago.

Finally, it could be said that it is the story of courage in the face of adversity, mishap and circumstance, for ultimately all these factors conspired to rob three families of their husbands, fathers and sons. Vince Phillips, Bob Consiglio and Steve Lane are the heroes who never made it back: gone but never forgotten.

ACKNOWLEDGEMENTS

A great many people have given me assistance in writing *Soldier Five* and also in the fight to see it published.

To my good friend and comrade in arms, Mal, many thanks. Without your support, input and contribution in both the writing of the book and at trial, this project would not have got off the ground.

I'm also indebted to Warren Templeton, our knight in shining armour. Without his advocacy skills, vision, strength and patience, combined with our passionate belief in the moral justice of this book, I doubt that we would have ever won in court, let alone seen the book published. Thanks to his unflagging enthusiasm, ably supported at home by Barbara, what once seemed a remote possibility finally became reality.

Paul Rishworth, Raynor Asher, Rick Bigwood, Julie Maxton, Peter Twist and Grant Illingworth all made significant contributions to the cause quite apart from many other friends and colleagues of Warren's. To you all, my enduring gratitude.

To Dinger, whose silent support was known but could never be acknowledged, and Ken, whose show of support and testimony came through when it was most needed: cheers, guys.

I am also indebted to the New Zealand Legal Aid board, who put the issues to test and concluded that this was a fight worth funding.

To all the unmentioned friends who helped simply ease the stresses and strains of the past years, my thanks. Your unfettered friendship went a long way to making everyday life as normal as could be under the circumstances.

Last but not least, I wish to thank my wife Sue, who has had to put up with more in the last few years than I am sure she ever bargained for when we exchanged vows in church. Through all the twists and turns, her support and encouragement have helped provide the focus for us all to carry on.

'It is not the critic who counts, not the man who points out how the strong man stumbles, or where the doer of deeds could have done better. The credit belongs to the man who is actually in the arena . . . who strives . . . who spends himself . . . and who at worst, if he fails, at least he fails whilst daring, so that his place shall never be with those cold and timid souls who know neither victory nor defeat!'

Theodore Roosevelt

PROLOGUE

UK, MARCH, 1991

I stared out of the rain-blurred window of the Augusta 109 as it flew on towards Hereford, passing over seemingly endless miles of flooded pasture land, a reminder of what was proving to be one of the wettest winters on record. My brain was registering the progress of the aircraft, but the fact that I was actually back in the UK hadn't really sunk in yet. The cramped confines of the helicopter made it easy to cast my mind back to another helicopter journey, a trip that seemed so long ago, but which in reality occurred only eight weeks previously. The sheer ferocity and pace of the Gulf War had compressed into a few short months a conflict that might have gone on for years. The legacy of that conflict, however, could never be erased in so short a period.

I shot a quick glance over my right shoulder at Mal, who also appeared to be lost in his own thoughts. Considering what we had been through, one might have expected non-stop banter and boyish enthusiasm to be the order of the day. After all, we had survived and made it home; we had beaten the clock, just. Yet it seemed we were withdrawing into a protective cocoon of silence. If we didn't talk about it, maybe it never happened. Perhaps this was the guilt of the survivor?

The 20-minute flight from Lyneham Air Force Base seemed to take only seconds. I had so many thoughts flashing through my mind that the passage of time never registered. An unexpected change in engine pitch and bank of the heli brought me back to the present. Suddenly I caught a glimpse of my rain-swept adopted city and recognised the impressive outline of Hereford's famous cathedral, a landmark and welcome home sign to all who know this sleepy town.

Our speed decreased as the tall communications mast that dominates the camp, red warning lamps aglow, guided the pilots in for their final approach. The Augusta 109 jockeyed for position before settling down on the pan at Stirling Lines; its sister aircraft with Dinger and Andy on board landed a moment later.

Off to one flank a small welcoming committee was assembled, patiently waiting for the rotor blades to power down. I could see the unsmiling face of the adjutant amongst the group, the Yorkshireman's tall, stocky frame unmistakable, despite the layers of camouflaged windproofs which were protecting him from the elements.

We began to climb down from the cab, Mal assisting me as I fumbled my way out, trying to get a grip on the slippery tarmac. I wasn't used to the luxury of freedom yet, let alone the awkwardness of trying to manoeuvre a plastered leg on crutches. The adjutant closed in and shook each of our hands in turn, his stoical expression never altering as he moved from one man to the next. Pausing, he surveyed us all for a moment: four gaunt, pale figures who barely resembled the men who had left Hereford some two months earlier.

'Welcome back, lads,' was the only comment that escaped his lips, before he spun on his heels and told us to follow him to RHQ (regimental headquarters), where the Commanding Officer (CO) of 22 Special Air Service Regiment was waiting.

PART I
INTO ACTION

CHAPTER 1

FORWARD OPERATIONS BASE, SAUDI, 22 JANUARY 1991

I heaved a sigh of relief as Dinger and I dumped the last of our stores onto the tailgate of the camouflaged Chinook. Although I had recently passed selection, Dinger and I had met previously when I was in the New Zealand SAS. His squadron had turned up for a two-month exercise the year before in New Zealand, and in between work, skydiving and getting drunk, we had got on very well. Dinger's credentials were impeccable. He was tall, rangy and deceptively strong, an ex-para, Falklands veteran and an absolutely suicidal rugby player to boot. He couldn't play to save himself, but he would put his body in front of anything that moved. If it wasn't for the constant smouldering rollie in his mouth, it might have been possible to understand what he said when he spoke.

'Right, you useless Kiwi twat, let's get the hell out of here before somebody else decides to give us another 50 lb of kit!' he cursed, at the same time taking a deep drag from his cigarette. I didn't mind the derogatory tone – we all spoke to each other like that; in fact, had he been civil, I would have been worried.

I stood away from the heli for a moment and surveyed the amount of equipment we were going to be carrying. Our own personal bergens must have weighed somewhere in the region of 150 lb. On top of that there were other specialist stores, extra rations and water, all items necessary for a deep penetration OP (observation point) mission. It certainly looked a daunting load.

My gaze turned to the rest of the blokes milling to one side of the airstrip. Andy, the designated patrol commander, was talking with the loadmaster. I had met Andy briefly in New Zealand as well, and he seemed a sound enough guy. He was a cockney through and through, with the accent and mannerisms to match. If there was something to say, no matter what the subject, you could guarantee that Andy had an opinion on it.

Next was Vince, 2IC (second in command) of the patrol. Vince was actually senior to Andy, but this was a B Squadron operation and Vince and myself were on secondment from A Squadron. Vince was a tough old nut who had been in the regiment for years. A mountaineering and diving specialist, he had a lot of SAS experience behind him, along with quite a volatile temper.

Aussie Mal and Bob were standing together laughing their socks off at the sight of one of our pilots doing his pre-flight checks. The RAF squadron leader wasn't the largest of men, but he had on a bulletproof kevlar flak jacket, with ceramic plates included, which gave him a Humpty Dumpty appearance.

I wandered over towards Mal. 'What do you reckon, Squeezer, does he know something that we don't?'

'Who are you calling Squeezer, you Kiwi hick! You're the only Squeezer around here,' came the usual retort. Now I have to admit that this 6 ft 6 in. tall monstrosity was a brilliant bloke, even given his Aussie roots, but natural trans-Tasman rivalry dictated that we were always on one another's case.

We all reckoned that Mal could easily pass a James Bond audition if he had the inclination. He had the looks, mannerisms, dress sense and 'gift of the gab' to bullshit himself out of any dodgy situation, especially if it involved women. The national and international trail of broken hearts that lay strewn in his wake was testimony to this.

Once Mal stood up he absolutely towered over Bob, who was about 5 ft 6 in. tall if he was lucky. We had all had a great laugh at Bob's expense earlier when, after putting on his bergen, all that could be seen of him from behind were a two-foot pair of booted camouflaged legs. The size of his bergen was nearly the full length of his body. Nevertheless, what Bob lacked in size, he more than made up for in strength and courage. An ex-Royal Marine commando, Bob had chosen to leave the corps and try his hand with the SAS.

Geordie (Chris) was making a final inventory of his belt-order, ensuring that he had all the items necessary for not only his own survival but also a basic medical drama if one occurred. Quiet and softly spoken, he always gave the appearance of being deadly serious, unless of course you bumped into him on the town after five bottles of Newcastle Brown.

Legs Lane was the final member of our motley crew. Like Dinger, an ex-para and Falklands veteran, he had transferred to the engineers before ending up in the arms of the SAS. Legs was the signals guru of the patrol, and most of the time he could be found ploughing through code books, instruction manuals or checking frequency antenna lengths. Professional at all times, Legs would never leave anything to chance.

* * *

By now, everyone in the patrol was gathered together. Dusk was fast approaching; it wouldn't be long before the rotors were turning and we would be off. As I looked down the length of the air base, I couldn't help but be struck by the sheer scale of it all. Having come from a country where you are lucky if you can find two Hercules C130s serviceable at the same time, to see the almost limitless expanse of armaments and air-frames stretched the entire length of the runway made me feel very insignificant in the grand scheme of things. Row upon row of Apache strike helicopters, fighter bombers, F111s, F15s, A10 tank busters, tanks, artillery, anti-aircraft batteries – it would have had the editors from *Jane's* drooling at the mouth. I found myself actually pitying the Iraqis, for I doubted that they had any inkling of what their leaders had got them into.

It seemed an age since I had walked into the B Squadron lines at the mounting base, lugging all my kit and cursing the powers that be for transferring me from my squadron.

Four days earlier, Regimental Mounting Base, UAE

I was chatting with Pete, another Kiwi who had passed selection with me and come to A Squadron. Pete was a mate from old. An ex-RNZIR and NZSAS soldier, he and I had followed remarkably similar paths in our army careers, even to the point of leaving the NZ Army on the same day to travel to the UK and join 22 SAS. Initially, we met in Singapore, while stationed with 1RNZIR, and formed a friendship that was cemented with our time in NZSAS. His battered boxer's face and greying hair belied the fit, intelligent and professional soldier that he was. He had, however, turned into a right anorak out here amongst the array of helicopters, especially the gunships, on display. A private helicopter pilot himself, he couldn't shut up about the hardware on the tarmac.

We were sitting on his camp bed when the SSM (Squadron Sergeant Major) walked on over. One look at his face told me the news was bad; it was simply a matter of whether it was bad news for Pete or me.

Mac, an ex-army boxing champ, was never one to mince words, but even so, his tidings came as a complete shock.

'Mike, pack up your kit. You're off to join B until the rest of their squadron arrives in theatre. Meet up with Vince, Bob and the other lads, and report to SSM B at 1400 hours.' Without another word, he turned on his heel and disappeared to inform someone else of his good news.

Pete turned to me with a look that said, 'Bad luck, mate, but I'm chuffed it wasn't me.'

A Squadron had been ordered by the Regimental Headquarters to furnish B Squadron with eight men. B was already under-strength, as half their number were still in the UK and some had been dedicated as the in-theatre hostage rescue team. So, being as I was just off selection, I found myself transferred along with five other junior members of A and two patrol commanders.

Moving around the hangar, collecting all my equipment, I could see the looks on the other blokes' faces: sympathetic to my plight, but at the same time relieved that they had not been transferred.

'That sucks, it does,' one of the lads commented as he helped me unload my bergen and ration box from what only a few minutes before had been my Landrover. 'Taking guys from the squadron just before we're due to move out. What a bone call.'

As I lugged my kit towards my new quarters, Pete came running up. It wouldn't be long before he was off over the border. 'Mike,' he said, a little out of breath. 'Glad I caught you in time. We're getting ready to go, so I'll see you when I see you.'

I stuck out my hand, jealously wishing our places were reversed. 'Keep your head down, mate.'

'Kia, Kaha,' he replied, shaking my hand. 'You too, mate.'

As I watched him run back in the direction from which he had come, my wave of jealousy subsided. 'Look after yourself, Pete,' I said to myself, a pang of concern pricking my conscience. It would be many months before we saw each other again.

* * *

Feeling dejected, I found a bed space in the B lines, and mulled over what the rest of A would be doing now. Not that there was anything wrong with B Squadron; in fact, on the contrary, it was arguably the strongest squadron in the regiment at that time. However, I had been with A for four weeks now, all of which had been spent doing build-up training for that night's vehicle mounted insertion. I didn't fancy my chances of getting back on board with my lot once they were in Iraq – unless there were casualties, I severely doubted that anyone would want to change places for some considerable time.

To make matters worse, I had seen the heavily laden pinkies (110 Landrover specifically designed for SAS use) being loaded onto a Galaxy Transporter that afternoon, my ex-call sign included, and by nightfall the boys would be preparing to go over the border. The only job I could see myself doing for the foreseeable future was camp patrol and radio watch.

I was in the process of rearranging my kit when Bob pulled up a chair for a chat about organising some heavy weapons training for the squadron. Bob, a regular PSI (Permanent Staff Instructor) staff sergeant attached to R Squadron, had been in charge of organising the logistical, administrative and training requirements for the part-time squadron. He had set both Pete and myself up in R Squadron on our arrival in the UK, and then had promptly beasted us stupid all over the Brecons on every training weekend that followed. 'As you train, so shall you fight.' Bob lived and breathed that phrase, always leading by example. Although now in his 40s, he was fitter and stronger than most blokes half his age, and had the benefit of a wealth of experience to draw on.

He had managed to bung a lift out to the Gulf on the back of A Squadron in the hope of seeing some action, and being transferred to B as one of the patrol commanders had not been part of his plan.

'Listen, Mike,' he began in his strong Scottish accent. 'These lads haven't done any heavy weapons training whatsoever since leaving the team [Counter Terrorist Team]. The boys are keen to get up to date, but their SSM doesn't want to know so I'll organise something for them. You're current on the .50 and mortars, aren't you?'

This was typical of Bob, seeing a problem and getting stuck straight in to sort it out. 'Yeah, mate. I can help with those, no probs.'

'Good, between us we can bring those who need it up to speed.'

'What do you reckon the chances are of us getting across the border with B then, mate?' I asked, bringing the question that was most pressing on my mind to the fore.

'Not too good at this stage. I've heard a rumour that a couple of OPs might be going out, but the chance of us getting on one of those in front of the B boys is small.'

He stood up to leave, slapping me on the back at the same time. 'Don't worry, Kiwi, I'll keep pressing the head-shed [commanders] to get us involved in something. Whether they listen or not is another matter . . .'

He disappeared into the maze of bodies, kit and camp beds, to search out the other A Squadron blokes to give a hand with the training, leaving me to ponder what the future would now have in store.

* * *

I was watching the demo on how to strip and assemble the M19 40 mm grenade launcher when Vince appeared beside me, grinning like a Cheshire cat. This was unusual, as Vince was not known for such displays of emotion. 'Look lively there, Kiwi, we've got a job, a fucking big one!' Instantly my mood changed – maybe I wasn't going to miss out after all.

We quickly made our way over to the improvised operations room, which had itself been divided into various sections by the cunning deployment of hessian sheets. Vince led me through a curtain labelled 'Map Room', where we found the rest of the patrol gathered around a huge map of Iraq.

No sooner had I got into the room than the slagging started. 'All right, you Kiwi tosser, come to do some real soldiering now, have you?' Such was the warm welcome out of Dinger's mouth, quickly followed by various other unrepeatable quips from most of the others. I managed to get a few digs back in myself, before Andy brought the briefing to order.

'Close in, lads, and listen up.' The noise quickly subsided. 'This is a warning order for an OP mission on this MSR [main supply route].' I craned forward to see where he was pointing, as did the rest of the blokes. The line that Andy's finger was resting on stretched from Baghdad, north-west to the Iraqi–Syrian border, and the area indicated was most definitely a long way from friendly territory.

Bob spoke aloud what we all were thinking, 'Christ, any further north and we'll be in Syria. I hope we're not tabbing [forced marching].'

'No choice, mate,' Vince interrupted, 'we're last on the list. All the pinkies have been allocated to other patrols and squadrons. It's going to be a case of using the good old size nines.'

At that moment the OC (Officer Commanding) B Squadron walked in, closely followed by the yeoman of signals. OC B looked ill at ease in his desert camouflages; I suspected that he would have been more at home with a shotgun tucked under one arm, pipe in mouth and a Labrador at heel.

'B Squadron has been allocated some important tasks at last,' were the first words out of the OC's mouth. 'We'll be the deepest squadron, and you the furthest patrol, in Iraq.' He paused significantly for effect.

'There will be two other patrols operating in your area, one each on these MSRs,' the yeoman chipped in, gesturing towards two other lines on the map immediately below ours. 'All will have squadron call signs, yours is Bravo Two Zero.' He turned towards Legs. 'I should have the comms plan from RHQ for that area by this evening, so come and see me about 2000 hours, and we'll get it sorted out.'

'Now I know it looks like you're out on a bit of a limb,' OC B continued, 'but if another Scud lands in Tel Aviv or somewhere similar, and the Israelis enter the war, the coalition could collapse. The fall-out would probably destabilise the whole region. RHQ put forward the plan to observe the northern MSRs, with the hope of catching a TEL [transport erector launcher] on the move. Preventing the launch of one Scud could prove vital. Any sightings of a Scud are to be reported on the SATCOM [satellite communications] immediately, and you will have fighter bombers on "no notice to move" readiness 24 hours a day.'

He looked at us all briefly before carrying on. 'AWACS [airborne warning and control system] is also providing 24-hour coverage of the AO [area of operations] for any major problems. If all else fails, a call on the TACBE [tactical beacon] using your call sign will be intercepted immediately. You will have a reply within 20 seconds and CSAR [combat search and rescue] will deploy to your assistance. As you are over 350 clicks from the Saudi border, I have decided that your E & E [escape and evasion] plan should take you north to Syria. It is a lot closer, and the CIA have safe houses manned in the populated frontier villages. They will be identifiable by white material draped from the windows.

'Your cover story, should you require one, is that you are a pilot rescue team, sent into Iraq to search for, locate and recover downed coalition pilots. That gives you a plausible reason for being so far behind enemy lines.'

The OC looked at the assembled faces and continued.

'As of now, you are in isolation; OPSEC [operational security] is to be maintained at all times. I expect the squadron to move forward to the FOB [forward operations base] in the next day or so, and once we are located there, you will be on 24 hours' notice to move.'

Once again he paused. 'Questions?' It was a statement more than a question. 'Good. Andy, carry on.' And with that, he left.

'White material draped from the windows – is he serious?' I asked after he had left the room.

'Don't worry about it, Kiwi, I've got no intention of having to go anywhere near Syria. If we are in the shit, a quick blast on the TACBE and the boys will come roaring in to get us. What could be simpler?'

Andy then turned to Vince. 'I know there aren't any 110s, but I'm sure there are some dinkies [short wheelbase Landrover] floating about.'

'There are,' Vince replied. 'Three of them. Problem is that one of the other patrols has nabbed two already, and I doubt we can fit eight blokes plus kit into a three-quarter-size Landrover.'

'Where would we hide the bloody thing, anyway?' said Geordie. 'This is an OP task, not a recce.'

The debate continued in this vein for a couple of hours or more, as various plans, options and contingencies were thrashed out amongst the patrol (a process known informally in the regiment as 'the Chinese parliament'). Once the debate was concluded, everyone had a general idea of their tasks and how the patrol would be conducted. The detail of the plan would be left for Andy to cover in his orders.

* * *

'Isolation' was a term used to describe the administrative, logistical and planning phases of a patrol prior to its insertion behind enemy lines. This usually entailed the patrol being separated from the rest of the squadron, thus maintaining the concept of OPSEC.

In reality, however, the constraints that not only the patrol but also the squadron were under at the time meant that OPSEC in its traditional form went out the window and was necessarily modified to allow those that could give a hand the opportunity to do so.

The next 36 hours were hectic. The shortage of pinkies meant that the only equipment we could take would be what the patrol could carry on its back. Bob and I were put in charge of the SATCOM/TACSAT, a device neither of us had seen before, let alone operated.

This unit was one element of the patrol comms structure. The PRC 319 was earmarked as the principle means of communications – a high-frequency encoded burst transmitter that was very secure. We also had TACBE emergency beacons; small hand-held units that operated on unencrypted, international frequencies.

However, the TACSAT itself was a real-time comms device,

something that was supposed to provide field and rear commanders alike more flexibility and greater accuracy over battlefield reporting.

Due to its bulky nature – it consisted of two large separate units plus ancillaries – it was decided that Bob and I would split the load between us and somehow squeeze the parts in amongst the rest of our kit. We were forced to take a crash course on the mechanics, theory and operational procedures necessary to make the satellite communications system work. This would normally take a week; we could spare only a few hours.

'Right,' the B Squadron's yeoman of signals began. 'The first thing you have got to realise with this piece of kit is that it gives off a signature footprint when you transmit that tells the whole world where you are. Anything over 15 to 20 seconds and the enemy will DF [direction find] you bang to rights.'

DF was a term used to describe the ability of the enemy to locate the source of your radio transmissions. Typically, this involved the use of various listening stations that continuously scanned the full spectrum of radio frequencies searching for enemy communications. Once a station has located a frequency, it tries to direct other listening posts onto the same band and thus begin to triangulate the origin of the broadcast. The more stations able to receive the transmission, the more reliable the fix.

'So, you only use this in an emergency, or if you sight a Scud. Is that understood?' We nodded our heads in agreement.

'Now, when the antenna is tuned in to the correct frequency you will get a series of bars reading off this display' – his finger pointed to a small grey LCD – 'and you will hear quite a lot of traffic on the net. Your codes are listed in the back of the aide memoire.'

After a couple of hours of this we simply went off and practised with the thing. If we could get it working, that would be all that mattered. That was, of course, as long as there was a chopper coming to get us not long after.

* * *

Dinger and Mal were busy rehearsing the construction of a desert OP hide, endeavouring to keep it as basic and functional as possible. Rehearsals form an important part of any pre-operational administration, and as we would have to carry all our equipment, it would be essential to try and minimise the stores. By pre-constructing the hide, they would be able to determine the most efficient way to achieve this.

Geordie, a mountaineering specialist, was the patrol medic. Every SAS patrol carries a comprehensive medical pack, which is equipped to deal with most medical emergencies encountered in the field, from diarrhoea to a sucking chest wound. The idea is to keep the casualty alive, by whatever means available, until higher medical treatment can be arranged. All members of the patrol are trained medically to a basic standard, but designated patrol medics have undergone an intensive three-month course on anatomical and physiological theory, and advanced trauma life-support protocols. They also have to do a minimum six-week accident and emergency hospital attachment. Patrol medics at the end of their course walk away with a reputable qualification, easily equivalent to that of an advanced paramedic.

Once again, it was necessary for Geordie to try and keep his medical stores to a minimum, to check that all the drugs were in date and serviceable, and to take note of every patrol member's medical history.

Legs was in deep consultation with the yeoman of signals most of the time, sorting through the complex series of code and frequency changes that would be vital to not only the success of our mission but also to our safety in the event of an emergency.

The PRC 319 was particularly susceptible to changes in ionospheric conditions, and therefore frequency prediction for the operations area would have to be irrefutably accurate. This, thankfully, was not the problem of the patrol, but that of the signallers at RHQ. The difficulty was in testing the communications, for as we were so far south of our objective, there was no sure way of determining if the frequency predictions were accurate or not. Trust in the system was paramount in this situation.

As the 2IC, Vince was the logistical and administrative co-ordinator of the patrol. Any item of equipment, all the ammunition, rations, explosives – it was Vince's job to beg, borrow or steal it.

The rapid pace at which the war, and SAS operations in particular, was moving forward meant that a lot of stores, normally regarded as fundamental, were in short supply, for example, claymore anti-personnel mines. The usual case was that each patrol member could expect to have at least one of these little beauties in his possession for a patrol.

Small, compact and lightweight, the claymore was what is known in the business as a shape charge. It was a mixture of explosive and hundreds of small ball bearings, encased in plastic and moulded in a slight arc designed to project the mine's explosive force in one direction. It has proven its value as both a defensive and offensive weapon many times over since its introduction by the Americans during the Vietnam War.

Vince's solution to this particular deficit was simply PE4 explosive, empty ice-cream containers, nuts and bolts, and detonating cord. Within no time, he had us constructing 'improvised claymores', which were the next best thing to the real McCoy.

Andy was oblivious to this activity most of the time, needing to concentrate on the actual mission mechanics and preparation of patrol orders, which he would be expected to give to the patrol and squadron head-shed very shortly.

Mission orders are an intricate part of any military operation, be it a simple road move from one location to another, or a complex multi-fronted assault on a huge battlefield. Orders are passed on down the chain of command, from the CIC's initial concept of operations, through the various brigade, regimental, company/squadron commanders, until finally the filtered individual unit tasks are allocated. Once a unit commander receives his task, he then goes away and plans for that particular objective, and once completed gives his orders to his men. Due to the strategic importance placed on SAS operations, patrol orders are also attended by the squadron head-shed, who in turn report back to RHQ; thus the system is replicated in reverse. This ensures that there is no ambiguity or misunderstanding in the application of the task both up and down the chain of command.

Andy would occasionally get the patrol together to go over certain points in the plan, to gauge our opinions and, where appropriate, to adopt the general consensus. However, as time was of the essence, these meetings were few.

* * *

The period prior to the squadron's move forward was complete bedlam. Frustration and irritability could easily have boiled over, yet despite this, amidst all the disorganisation, guys in the squadron pitched in to help where possible, and the constant banter and slagging went a long way to easing the tension. Somewhere in amongst all this activity, we managed to fit in intelligence updates, target briefs, squadron parades, meals and a bit of sleep. War was proving to be chaotic, to say the least.

Our day and a half came and went with frightening speed, and we were forced to call a halt to the proceedings as the needs of the squadron and the move forward took precedence. Vehicles, motorcycles, stores of all description . . . the list of equipment was endless, and it all needed palletising and loading into the Hercules.

We soon found ourselves jammed into the back of a C130, perched atop a mountain of explosives and ammunition destined for Saudi Arabia, and the regimental Forward Operations Base.

Dinger, never one to miss an opportunity, lit up one of his ever-present rollies and sat astride a box of 81 mm mortar rounds.

'Bloody hell, mate, the crabs [RAF] will go ape if they see you doing that in here,' I said, a little uneasy myself at the idea of a naked flame being so close to all that ordnance.

'Mate, if you look at the mixture of stuff they've got in this crate, my smoke is bugger all. What's the matter, getting a little windy, are we?'

'You can piss right off and all, the only wind around here is the shit coming out of your gob!'

Dinger just grinned at me and took a long leisurely drag on his cigarette before pulling out an old paper and settling down for the flight.

LAST LIGHT, 22 JANUARY

'Right then, chaps.' An extremely posh-sounding voice broke through my thoughts. 'We're all go in about ten. Same drill as before, stop at the FARP [forward air refuelling point] to refuel and confirm deconfliction, then it's full steam ahead.'

It was fingers crossed now, as 24 hours previously the mission had been aborted due to deconfliction problems. Hopefully there would be no issue this time.

The loady walked on over. 'I need those bergens on the back now.'

At the same time a jeep pulled up, and out jumped Fred, the previous B Squadron sergeant major, and a couple of the boys, Paul and Mick, one of whom sported a battered-looking camera.

'Give us a minute,' Dinger said, moving towards the recent arrivals. 'Hey there, Fred.'

Fred walked on over and shook hands with both of us. Almost shouting over the noise of the massive twin-engined Chinook's turbines winding up, he said, 'Keep your heads down, lads, good hunting,' in a voice that was full of pride.

I could see that his presence meant a lot to the B Squadron blokes, and I was surprised that the other members of the B Squadron head-shed were not there.

'You all right, Kiwi?' Paul asked, shaking my hand. 'Got to watch out for these suicide missions. I had the same when I first joined the squadron: straight out to the Falklands for a C130 infil and squadron attack on mainland Argentina.'

I looked at him, not quite sure if he was joking or not, and replied, 'Yeah, no worries, mate. Cheers for the morale boost.'

He laughed and slapped my back. 'You lot will be all right.'

'C'mon then, guys,' chirped Mick, camera in hand. 'Let's get one for the record books.'

We all manoeuvred ourselves onto the rear of the tailgate, Andy sounding off constantly, Mal and Geordie preening themselves as though it were a beauty contest, all of us fighting to get into the frame. Then, without warning, click, it was done, and for a couple of seconds after, no one said a word. Perhaps the significance of that photo was felt by us all, who knows? But prophetically, it was one for the record books, for that picture would never be re-created in real life. Five days later, Vince, Bob and Legs were dead.

CHAPTER 2

FORWARD AIR REFUELLING POINT, SAUDI, 22 JANUARY 1991

As the Chinook touched the pan, the loadmaster jumped out and raced toward the bowsers to co-ordinate the refuelling. I wandered to the rear of the aircraft, where I could get a good breath of fresh air. This may sound ridiculous, but I have always suffered from terrible travel sickness, and low-level tactical flying, mixed with the stench of aviation fuel, was doing my system no good whatsoever. (On my NZSAS freefall course, after two and a half hours of low-level flying, and about the same amount of time spent being sick, I was so relieved to get off the aircraft at 3,000 metres that I lost all fear of jumping. The end result was a perfect textbook descent and landing; however, the slagging from my mates is still ringing in my ears to this day.)

I took a few deep breaths and immediately the nausea abated. The engineers were nearby, battling with the huge bowser hose. In the half-illuminated night, it had the appearance of some great black anaconda, and due to the downwash of the rotors, was giving them just as much trouble. Finally, they were able to secure it to the side of the Chinook, and almost immediately the hose flexed and straightened under the enormous pressure, as avgas poured through it into the fuel tanks.

It was about 2100 hours, and as I looked skywards, I witnessed a most incredible sight. The heavens were filled with groups of assorted aircraft – bombers, fighters and tankers – visible only due to their landing lights. The sole planes identifiable were the American B52 bombers, their vast size making them unmistakable. As the first wave of aircraft approached overhead, they suddenly disappeared in unison, as their synchronised watches and voiced commands told them to 'go dark' and extinguish all lights. Wave after wave reached the same point and all carried out the identical procedure on cue.

Initially, watching this huge parade of aircraft fly by, I couldn't help but feel pitifully unimportant to the outcome of this war. With the air, land and sea superiority enjoyed by the coalition forces, one had to wonder what a small SAS patrol in a hole in the middle of the desert could really achieve. However, if we managed to prevent one Scud from being launched, we could possibly save countless lives. It generates quite a sense of pride in both yourself and your regiment to know that someone has placed that kind of responsibility and faith in you.

It must have taken a good seven or eight minutes for the last of the aircraft to pass overhead, and soon all evidence of their crossing vanished, as the full expanse of the night sky came back into focus. Five minutes later, the loadmaster clambered on board, and we too were airborne, and Iraq bound.

* * *

It was approximately two hours' flying time from the FARP to our designated DOP (drop-off point), the pilots needing to employ a serpentine flight plan in order to avoid all the known anti-aircraft positions en route. We approached the border at about 150 metres and 120 knots. Suddenly the aircraft went 'black', all illumination extinguished save for the deep crimson glow of the interior ops lights, designed to protect night vision but still allow reasonable function aboard the helicopter.

I looked over towards Andy, who was sitting with a set of headphones on, plugged in to the aircrew's communications. He leaned forward and yelled over the noise of the engines, 'We're over!'

The craft levelled out at about 30 metres, with no discernible decrease in speed. Looking out the porthole, I could see the eerie shape of the rotor blades glowing yellow and silver in the dark, as their downwash kicked up vast quantities of sand and whisked it all around.

My heart was racing, adrenalin pumping through my veins. This was it, we were in Iraq. Years of training would now come into play; this was no longer a fictitious exercise, this was the real thing. I looked at Dinger, a stupid grin on my face like some schoolboy off on a great adventure. Dinger just smiled briefly and nodded his head, once again taking a deep drag on that ever-present rollie. He had been here before.

The flight had seemed to drag on forever. After the initial buzz of crossing the border, the lack of activity made me feel that it was 'just another taxi ride'. About an hour and a half into the flight, though, we were all brought back to earth with a jolt.

The pilots swerved left and right, blew chaff and took the Chinook as low to the ground as possible in order to lose the radar signature. Suddenly, however, lights started to blink, the loadies (loadmasters) were shouting God knows what as they clambered all over us, and the heli bounced all over the place – it looked like total chaos. Now, if you are flying at around 30 metres and at 100 knots in enemy territory, and you find yourself illuminated by an anti-aircraft radar, you are in deep shit, for there are not a lot of places to go.

Meanwhile, the rest of us passengers prayed for forgiveness, knowing that the situation was totally out of our control. After what seemed like an age, but in reality was only a minute or so, the heli levelled out onto its normal track. No sooner had the crisis started than it was over.

My only thought after that was 'Get me the fuck off this thing ASAP!' If I was going to get whacked, I would rather have it done standing on terra firma than flying along in a blacked-out coffin. Better to have some chance than no chance at all. I certainly did not envy the crew the return flight, even if it was on a different route.

All three patrols were inserting on two Chinooks that evening. Bravo One Zero, split between the two aircraft, was the first to be dropped off. Their task involved the southernmost MSR, and they had the good fortune of being able to use two vehicles, dinkies as they were known. Smaller than their big brother, the pinkie, they had nowhere near the load capacity of the modified 110 Landrovers, but they were better than nothing.

The Chinooks, flying in formation, descended rapidly, and ours struck the hard desert surface with a resounding jolt. The guys were already seated in their wagon, and as the tailgate lowered, the vehicle shot out into the sand and dust storm thrown up by the rotors, to be lost from view in seconds.

'All clear.' The loadmaster gave the signal and shouted into his head-mike. The helicopter was climbing and away even before the tailgate had begun to rise – a very slick despatch.

Watching them depart, although I knew it would be my turn soon, it still seemed a little surreal. I found myself trying to imagine what was going through their minds now: were they afraid, exhilarated, or simply too preoccupied to notice any emotion at all?

Quarter of an hour later we received the ten minutes out call, and I would soon have my own answer to those questions. I took the soft sponge ear protectors out of my ears, and, what a surprise, there was bugger all difference. Frisking pocket and pouch for the thousandth time, reassuring myself that everything was intact and secure, I pulled my *shamag* (Arab headdress) out of my pocket and wound it tightly around my head and face. This pre-landing routine had been rehearsed hundreds of times before, in many different environments, on countless other missions, missions that had only been exercises. Make-believe had been left behind at the Iraqi border. The difference this time was palpable.

I pulled a set of ski goggles down over my eyes to protect them from the minor sandstorm the rotors would be stirring up when we landed and checked that the Minimi's safety was on. Finally, there was no more time for thinking; it was time for action.

* * *

The tailgate was already lowered to hasten our exit from the aircraft as the Chinook flared into its hover position just prior to landing. Bob and myself were crouched as close to the edge as safety allowed, ready to dive off as soon as we touched down. My concentration was so intense that I could only just hear the noise of the engines over my pounding heartbeat. I could see the dull outline of the loadmaster against the dim red interior of the heli, craning his neck, counting down the feet.

Thump. We had barely touched the surface before Bob and I were off like sprinters out of the starting blocks, racing through the sea of whipped-up sand, looking for a vantage point to secure the LZ (landing zone). Legs and Mal weren't far behind, each pair taking up a point on the high ground above the wadi to observe the surrounding area and provide cover while the rest of the patrol unloaded the helicopter.

The wadi itself was about 20 metres wide and 7 metres deep, with gently sloping shingle sides. We had been at the top of the wadi only a matter of seconds when the deepening throaty pitch of the Chinook's engines alerted us to its departure. It rose slowly out of the dry riverbed, gradually increasing speed and height, until its blackened features blended with the night. It took a couple of minutes for the drone of the engines to finally disappear, and once it had, the silence was deafening.

There·was a surprising amount of ambient light about, thanks to a full moon and one of the most awesome starlit skies I had ever seen. All this, however, was doing us no favours at all, for the night was supposed to be our co-conspirator, aiding our movement and hiding our presence. In these conditions, it could easily do the opposite.

I wriggled my torso slightly, trying to make myself more comfortable on the rock-strewn ground, my eyes continuously sweeping the terrain around me for any unusual feature or movement that might indicate danger. At the same time I activated the handheld Magellan global positioning system (GPS) to confirm our position and to estimate the distance to our pre-selected LUP (lying-up point).

Methodically, below in the wadi, the remainder of the patrol were organising the stores for caching, the folds in the rock supplying natural concealment for the excess rations and water. This was to be only a temporary hide until a more suitable one could be found.

The Magellan finished downloading the information from the satellites and computed our location. The expected result should have been only a few degrees out from what I already had committed to memory, which would put us about 12 kilometres south of our objective. To my surprise, and alarm, the respective co-ordinates did not correspond at all; in fact, there was such a discrepancy that I couldn't even begin to make a mental estimate of the positional error. I heard a slight slip below and watched Andy make his way slowly towards me.

'Got a fix yet, Kiwi?' he whispered as he knelt down beside me.

'Yeah, and you're not going to like it,' I replied. 'I think the crabs have dropped us in the wrong place, but I'll have to check it out on the map first.'

'Oh, fucking great,' cursed Andy immediately. 'Trust the RAF to fuck up on a real job, and leave us in the lurch.'

I whispered quietly in his ear, 'Take over here, and give me a few minutes to plot these co-ordinates. We can't move anywhere till we know where the fuck we are!'

Andy shuffled closer to the top of the bank, and I moved off the skyline, pulled out the map and sorted out roughly where we were. Within minutes a quiet little 'For fuck's sake' slipped out of my mouth. The RAF, bless their cotton socks, had ruined all their good work getting us here in one piece by plonking us almost on the target, about two kilometres short of the actual MSR – and a damn sight closer than was tactically sound.

Vince gave a low whistle from below, indicating that all the stores were cached and the remaining kit was ready for the move. Slowly, we all converged on the bergens.

My eyes were now accustomed to the area, and as I made my way over to the others, I was shocked to see that we had landed in the middle of some sort of makeshift graveyard. There were mounds of small rocks everywhere, the length of human bodies, tucked tight into the sides of the wadi. In the rush to exit the aircraft I had completely ignored them, not recognising their form.

'Must be the local village burial ground,' Vince whispered as we moved in. I hoped that this wasn't some kind of omen.

'That's the least of our worries,' Andy continued, turning towards me. 'Right, Kiwi, where have they put us this time?'

I gave everyone a quick brief on our location. Legs piped up immediately with another gem of information.

'That's not the only good news. There are lights about 500 metres over to the west, and it looks like a sizeable habitation.'

'Military Intelligence strikes again,' Bob interjected.

According to our intelligence brief, the nearest habitation to this area was supposedly 15 kilometres away. From what Legs had described, there appeared to be a small village no more than a couple of minutes' walk from our position. More of a concern was the fact that it would have been impossible for someone not to have heard the Chinook. The question was: would they ignore it?

It had just gone midnight, which gave us about five hours of darkness to play with, and it was essential to find a good LUP before first light. After a quick discussion, it was decided to send two recces out, one north along the course of the wadi, and one following the wadi south. Andy and Dinger took the northern route, while Vince and Geordie took the southern one, the remainder of us staying with the bergens and stores.

Within the hour both groups had returned and we quickly gathered to hear the results, but, unfortunately, both the terrain and the news were bleak.

Vince spoke first. 'Well, there's sweet fuck all in that direction, it's as bare as a baby's bum.' His whisper didn't hide the obvious frustration in his voice, frustration that we were all beginning to feel.

'Well, I guess we'll have to go towards the MSR then,' Andy replied, looking around the assembled patrol for any further comments.

From Andy's report, the most promising position sounded about 1,200 metres to the north, up a small ravine, which would offer some cover from view. The problem was that we would be moving towards the head of the wadi, which was at the foot of the high ground next to the MSR. The closer you moved towards it, the shallower the wadi became, and the chances of finding a decent LUP were thus severely diminished.

The decision was basically made for us. Given the time constraints, we couldn't afford the luxury of another extended search for a better position. We had too much kit to lug around, and the ravine was the best option available. I had just learnt my first lesson in war: nothing goes to plan.

The decision made, everyone retrieved their bergens and made ready for the move. Down on one knee, while Bob covered me, I hefted my 150-lb pack onto my back, feeling body and soul attempting to revolt at the outrageous weight. It would take a few minutes for the muscles, limbs and mind to become accustomed to the additional load they would be expected to carry.

Once the bergen was in place and adjusted, I picked up my weapon and covered Bob while he did the same, the identical procedure being carried out by the remainder of the patrol. Pairing off in this manner ensures patrol security and is a process that becomes automatic with time. I couldn't help but grin again as I saw those booted trouser legs of Bob's just managing to beat the bottom pack to the ground.

Bob caught sight of my amusement and mouthed a very deliberate 'Fuck off!' as we shook out into patrol formation, Bob and I the tail-end charlies.

Geordie took the lead, as he had on the recce, because he was the only one of us with an NVA (night vision aid). The rest of us silently slipped in file behind, eyes and weapons moving together, never focusing too long on one point, just constantly traversing the terrain.

Patrolling was deliberately slow, about 500 metres an hour with frequent halts, not only because of the bergens but also with the tactical situation in mind. The last thing you need is to be racing along into unknown territory at night; stealth was the order of the day.

Every step seemed to echo, the very still of the night appearing to increase the almost silent slight crunch of crushing sand and gravel as boot met ground. From time to time, the wadi all but disappeared and the patrol was left standing high and dry on an open alluvial plain, desperately seeking the track of the wadi, which, usually, would start again within 100 metres or so. Despite the cool temperature, I found myself bathed in sweat barely 20 minutes into the patrol, a combination of physical exertion and pumping adrenalin totally eradicating any sensation of cold.

After a couple of hours we arrived at the proposed LUP and it became painfully obvious that the eight of us with all our kit would have severe difficulty in concealing ourselves in that space. Consequently, Andy took another two-man recce out to try and improve on the position, and within 30 minutes he returned with good news.

'Right, we've found a good position at the head of the wadi. It's a small overhang in the wadi face with a huge fuck-off boulder concealing it. It's brilliant!' Finally, lady luck had decided to shine some fortune down on us.

We reached the position about an hour later, and it looked too good to be true. We could easily conceal ourselves and our equipment, had good cover from fire, and even had room for all the cached kit. Things were definitely looking up.

Time was of the essence. Half the patrol prepared the LUP for occupation, setting out the improvised claymores, establishing the observation point, organising the equipment storage and maintaining sentry watch. The other half, myself included, returned to the drop-off point to retrieve the excess stores. Moving in light order proved considerably easier, and as the route back to the cache had already been cleared to some extent, we were able to proceed with a little more haste, reaching the burial ground within half an hour. We immediately set to ferrying the stores back to the LUP/OP.

The stores had been prepared for carriage by grouping them in two hessian sacks, linked together with rope, thus fashioning a type of truss. There were four sets of hessian sacks pre-assembled, along with two jerry cans of water.

Taking turns at carrying the stores, we moved up to the forward position as a patrol, with two blokes providing front and rear protection, and the other two, initially Aussie and myself, acting as coolies, a role that Dinger found particularly suitable for us 'fucking foreigners'.

The return leg was hard going and, once again, painfully slow, but thankfully we made it to the LUP without mishap, Vince guiding us the last 50 metres or so through the treacherous maze of improvised claymores and 'Elsie' mines he had laid.

Legs gave us a nod as we passed his position, which guarded our route in. Geordie and Andy were already in place observing the general area, trying to identify the actual MSR.

'Right, dump that lot behind the boulder, then close in for a brief,' whispered Vince as we moved up to the rock face.

With Legs and Geordie on watch, we huddled together at the base of the boulder as the dim glow of first light cast eerie shadows about us. Andy started proceedings.

'Right, Vince has made up the stag list, two-hour stints. It's pretty exposed up there, so once the sun is up, we will all move into the lee of the wadi and basically keep out of sight.'

The intelligence brief we received at the FOB on Scud activity indicated that they were only being moved at night, so there was no point in exposing ourselves to possible compromise during daylight hours.

'Make yourself comfortable, we're going to be here for a long time,' Andy continued, before turning to Legs. 'Get the comms set up, I'll have a message for you in about ten.'

In turn we all saw Vince, took note of the stag times, and then those who were lucky enough got comfortable with a bivvy bag and had some much-needed sleep.

AL JOUF, SAS FORWARD OPERATIONS BASE

Al Jouf was in total darkness, the self-imposed black-out in place to protect the base from Iraqi attack. But those inside the sand-bagged buildings that made up 22 SAS RHQ were oblivious to the fact. The operations officer and B Squadron OC stood over the radio operator waiting intensely for some news from the three IR (information reporting) patrols inserting that evening.

'That's Bravo One Zero safely away, sir,' the radio op reported excitedly, covering his mouthpiece with one hand. 'The pilot is estimating 28 minutes to Bravo Two Zero drop-off.'

'What about Three Zero?' OC B eagerly enquired.

'No report as of yet, sir.'

Within the hour, confirmation of Bravo Two Zero's successful dispatch came through. 'That's Two Zero out and away, Three Zero reports no drop-off yet.'

'What the hell is going on? Three Zero should have deployed 20 minutes ago. Ask for a status report.'

'We won't get much from them at this stage, sir, they're still minimising with code words. Wait one . . .' The operator pushed his headphones tightly to his ears, before turning back to the two officers. 'Aborted drop-off. Three Zero is returning to base.' B Squadron was now down to two patrols.

CHAPTER 3

IRAQ, DAY TWO, JANUARY 1991

I awoke, shivering and disoriented, to the urgent whispered voices of Dinger and Andy above me on the wadi ledge, and I knew immediately by their insistent tone that something was up. I hadn't noticed the cold much during the night's march, but now, no longer warmed by physical exertion, I was only too aware of the frosty conditions.

The sore, gritty 'I need another eight hours' sleep' feeling under my eyes told me it was early, removing the need to consult a watch. Rolling off my sleeping mat, careful not to disturb the others still asleep, I made my way cautiously toward the brow of the wadi, the conversation becoming more intelligible the closer I neared.

'Well, I never fucking saw them last night,' Andy hissed, peering over the ledge at some unseen object.

'It's too late now, we couldn't move until dark anyway,' Dinger replied. 'They've got the whole of this wadi covered.'

Both turned as they heard me approach, careful not to break the skyline unnecessarily.

'What's up?'

'There's what looks like an S60 Triple A [anti-aircraft artillery] position on the high ground directly to our north, about 800 to 1,000 metres away,' Andy explained, indicating the position with a slight movement of his head.

'I can see a couple of trucks and the outline of the guns themselves, but there is no indication as to the amount of troops that may be escorting them.'

'You've got to assume at least platoon strength, on top of the actual Triple A operators themselves,' Dinger interjected.

I slid up to the wadi's edge and took a cautious peek in the general direction Andy had indicated, immediately spotting the man-made shapes, skylined on the high ground in the middle distance. Two dark-green canvas hulks were close together, obviously the canopies of four-ton trucks, or the Iraqi equivalent, their definitive lines blurred at this distance, along with a radar platform and the artillery pieces themselves.

I could just make out the tiny shape of a man walking between the vehicles, his nonchalant manner indicating that he had no knowledge of our presence a kilometre to his south. 'Well, at least they haven't got a clue that we are here,' I ventured, moving back away from the edge. 'Which is a miracle considering we almost landed on top of them.'

'Yeah,' Dinger continued, 'but their radar must have tracked our flight path. Even they couldn't be that thick!'

Andy ended the conversation abruptly, 'Well, there's no use bitching about it now, we can't do anything at the moment anyway. Just pass on the info to each of the sentries as they come on stag, and we will reassess the situation tonight.'

With that he slid down the slope back into the wadi, waking up Legs as he passed. 'Get the 319 booted up, Legs. I need to get a sitrep [situation report] off to SHQ [squadron headquarters] ASAP.'

I turned to Dinger. 'You may as well get your head down, mate, I'm on stag in ten minutes anyway.'

Dinger rolled onto his side so he could face me, his blond-stubbled face breaking into a wry grin. 'You offering to do extra work?' he scoffed sarcastically. 'This must be a first.'

'I'm feeling sorry for your ageing old body, and, besides, you look like you need a nicotine fix.' Dinger incoherently mumbled something abusive under his breath, at the same time pointing a finger skywards, which was definitely intended to complement the comment, before moving off back into the wadi, leaving me in peace.

Returning to the wadi's edge, I began scouring the general area, trying to locate the tarmacadam hard-standing and other features with which to orientate myself. It took a couple of sweeps for me to realise that there was no hard-standing. In fact, the whole MSR was in reality a huge desert track system spanning some 600 metres.

There appeared to be no discernible pattern, simply a flat desert plain, the tracks themselves meandering alongside the ridgeline to the north. Considering that the two southerly MSRs were tarmacadam and had the same map designations as this one, it came as quite a surprise to find that it was unsealed. Furthermore, this would also cause us problems in our secondary task of locating and disrupting the fibre-optic communication cables that were supposed to run parallel to the road.

I didn't dwell on this too much. No doubt there would be a patrol going out at some stage charged with various tasks, one of which would be a recce of the MSR.

My two-hour stag passed without incident, the only problem being the biting cold, despite the early morning sun. It was certainly a lot warmer than this in Saudi and the UAE.

Vince crawled up next to me, the ever-present Omani shamag wrapped around his head and face, concealing all features apart from his steely brown eyes.

'Morning there, Kiwi, I hear we've got neighbours to share this shithole with now.'

Carefully placing his M203 beside me, he inched his way forward to the brow, conscious of the possibility of exposure, even at this distance.

I pointed him in the right direction. 'Just one o'clock of the sharp escarpment on the high ground.'

'Yeah, seen,' he replied. 'What the fuck are they guarding all the way out here? There's not supposed to be any military installations around for 20 clicks.'

'Well, whatever it is, it must be reasonably important, because there are enough of them moving about up there. They've been up and about for the last half-hour or so. Can't make out exact numbers, but there's at least a dozen.'

Vince grunted an acknowledgement, before moving back to my side.

'So, apart from the fact we've got an Iraqi platoon bashered up a squirrel's fart away, is there anything else I need to know?'

'That's the score at the moment, mate, and I'm off to do a few jumping jacks to warm myself up. It's bloody freezing.'

'Fucking antipodeans. You need a couple of good English winters and a Norway trip or two under your belt, then you'll have something to moan about.'

I quickly disappeared before Vince started to recount one of his war stories; otherwise I would be up there for another two hours.

No sooner had I reached the wadi floor than Andy pounced on me. He was looking rather agitated.

'You're signals trained as well, aren't you, Mike?' he blurted at me.

'Yeah, why, what's the problem?'

'Go and see if you can give Legs a hand. He's having a major problem with comms at the moment.'

I thought this a bit strange. Legs was by far the most proficient signals operator among us, and if there was a problem with the comms that he couldn't solve, I was damn sure I wouldn't be able to.

I made my way over to where Legs was, propped up against a boulder, staring intently at the EMU (electronic message unit) on the 319.

'All right, mate,' I said, crouching next to his inert figure, 'anything I can do to help?'

Legs didn't look at me, he simply shook his head in confusion, checking his frequencies and looking bemused.

Finally, he turned to me. 'I'm not receiving any messages, nothing at all.'

A headset was attached to the radio, the hiss of background static softly emanating from its tiny speaker. However, the static lacked one essential component, the high-speed dots and dashes that characterise burst-Morse data transmissions. These two sounds should have accompanied one another, the burst transmissions providing a conduit for the receiving station to home in on.

More disturbing still was the fact that the data transmissions were supposed to be a constant, and, assuming that we had been given the correct frequencies of course, there seemed no logical reason for their absence save a major mechanical malfunction of some kind.

The only way to approach this type of problem is to start from the beginning and work it through methodically, hoping that the solution is simple – a loose antenna wire, or perhaps something equally as mundane.

'I've checked all the connections over and over again, run the test, changed antenna direction and length, but every time it's the same result: sweet fuck all!'

'You give it a rest for a few minutes, mate, and I'll do the same. If there's still no joy, at least we know it's not our fuck-up.'

Legs passed the set over to me, slowly getting to his feet and moving off to revive his circulation after the period of sustained inactivity. I wasn't hoping for much. If Legs had been trying since I went on stag, I doubted that there was much he would have missed, but double-checking was the name of the game in our business, so I got on with it.

Half an hour later I gave up, totally bemused as to why the set could not receive a message. It didn't make sense. In theory the only reasons left were: (a) the set was knackered, but the internal test mechanism on the EMU and 319 would indicate if that were the case; (b) the transmitting station had gone down; or (c) we had been given the wrong receive frequencies, which was highly unlikely.

By now, everyone was awake, and those who were current gathered round the radio. A brainstorming session ensued, each person trying to add his weight to the problem.

At one stage, Mal and myself stood on opposite sides of the wadi, the antenna strung between us, held full stretch above our heads for over 20 minutes (the maximum time between messages should have only been a matter of minutes). All this was to no avail; the screen remained blank.

Towards midday, the patrol convened a Chinese parliament in order to weigh up our options and formulate a new plan of attack. Andy opened proceedings, directing his first comment at Legs.

'I assume there is still no joy with the comms then?'

'Sweet F.A., and everyone who has an inkling of signals training has had a go. I've even tried Morse on the guard net; the set must be shot.'

'We've still got the TACSAT, though,' Vince joined in. 'If the shit hits the fan, we can use that.'

The problem with the TACSAT, or SATCOM as it was also known, was that it gave off a huge signal 'footprint' when transmitting, thus increasing its susceptibility to enemy intercept, and therefore multiplying the risk of compromise tenfold. Hence the strict caveats on its use: Scud sightings and in deep shit only.

'About lunchtime tomorrow the lost comms procedure is initiated, isn't it, Legs?' Legs nodded in agreement. 'So therefore, we can't realistically expect the heli to bring a new set until midnight tomorrow, at the earliest.'

Lost comms procedure was an 'in case of' scenario, normally given in orders, whereby a patrol specified a predetermined time and place to either receive a new radio, or, if the situation required, extract. If a patrol had not been heard over a certain period of time, the lost comms procedure was implemented.

I decided to add my ten cents' worth. 'Yeah, but which rendezvous point will they go to? The one they were supposed to drop us off at, or the one they did drop us off at, or even better, now that we've experienced their navigation first hand, somewhere completely different!'

Nobody spoke for a minute, taking in what I had just said. It sounded like a gripe, but the fact of the matter was we couldn't guarantee where the crabs would show up.

Vince broke the silence. 'If it comes to that, we'll have to split up the patrol to cover both RV points, but we'll also have to decide if we will maintain this position or not. I don't like the thought of having three separate groups of us wandering about in the desert with no way of keeping in contact with each other. Besides, we got away with a heli landing close to the target once; I wouldn't like to chance that a second time.'

The gathered heads bobbed up and down in agreement, digesting all the information and trying to come up with a suitable solution. No matter which way you approached the problem, the end result was the same: we would have to strike this position and move further south to establish a secure rear location. Even if the heli did arrive at the original drop-off point, we could never re-occupy this location after having left it vacant; the compromise risk would be too high.

'Right, then,' Andy continued. 'The decision is really made for us. If we still have not established comms by midday tomorrow, we will prepare to evacuate this location and head south at last light to the co-ordinates where the crabs were supposed to drop us. Once there, secure and cache the stores, then myself and one other will return to the actual DOP, and between us, hopefully, we should be able to RV with the heli, and get our new radio. In the meantime, we carry on with the OP routine and keep trying the comms. If this thing fucks up and we end up pulling out, at least no one can say we didn't try.'

I left Andy and Vince deep in discussion, returning to my bergen, ready to indulge in some mouth-watering freeze-dried rations prior to recommencing the communications effort. Between Bob and myself, we had organised it to give Legs a break from his radio stag. In truth, we were more worried about the safety of the radio than relieving Legs – if looks could kill, then that radio would have been murdered several times over.

The remainder of the day passed reasonably uneventfully. The only movement observed on the MSR was civilian traffic, the odd battered pick-up or four-wheel-drive bouncing along the rough terrain, their dust wake viewable for thousands of metres in each direction. Yet even these sightings were few and far between.

A long-forgotten adage sprung to mind: 'War is 99 per cent boredom and 1 per cent sheer terror.' Well, the boredom aspect was certainly evident at that moment.

Towards late afternoon, the patrol was stood-to, alerted by the sound of small bells jangling from the necks of some unseen animals in the dead ground just to our west. Sure enough, one of these animals, a goat, made its way over to the edge of the wadi, eager no doubt to find some scrap of food, desert brush or the like. We all held our breaths as the goat stared into our position, cocking its head at an inquisitive angle, surprised by the sight it encountered.

The immature voice of a young boy could be heard in the distance, shepherding his flock, cajoling them along their meandering course, probably back to the village some two kilometres distant. The goat, meanwhile, refused to listen to its master, preferring to remain at the lip of the wadi, enjoying the unusual interruption in its daily routine.

It didn't take a genius to realise that unless the goat buggered off, the boy would also come on over, and then the situation could very rapidly change from one of potential compromise to one of certain compromise.

Geordie initiated the attack first of all; he threw a small stone in the general direction of the animal, not trying to alarm it too much, just to get it to move off. It didn't budge. Andy, who was slightly closer, then joined in the fray, lobbing a quite large missile at the annoying beast, but was hopelessly inaccurate. Finally, Bob let go a humdinger, which smacked right into the goat's side, promptly initiating a hasty retreat, with indignant bleating to boot.

We waited to see if there was any reaction, ears straining for the slightest hint that something might be amiss, but luckily the boy had remained some distance away, and probably never even noticed the deviation of his charge.

With relief we listened to the ever-decreasing sounds of the herd and their guardian as they continued eastward toward the village, until, at last, the jangling bells could be heard no more.

The patrol stood-down with fears allayed. The incident had passed without any visible repercussions. What never entered anyone's head, however, and should have, was the fact animal herders normally followed the same well-established routes and routines, and there was therefore a better than even chance that this occurrence would be repeated. Perhaps next time, fortune would not be so kind.

CHAPTER 4

IRAQ, EVENING DAY TWO, JANUARY 1991

We embraced evening like a long-lost relative, thankful for the temporary protection it afforded. The moonless night cast a black shroud over the entire landscape, something that we particularly welcomed after the incident with the goatherd earlier. As dark descended, we were able to venture further out from the wadi warren, allowing a more uninterrupted view of our temporary home.

Apart from the wadi itself, the surrounding desert was a flat featureless plain, broken only by the high ground to the north. The harshness of the terrain, accentuated in darkness, reminded me of photographs from the moon surface, a rock-and-sand-strewn wasteland.

It quickly became apparent that, apart from the hills already occupied by Iraqi troops, our position was the only one within kilometres that afforded any semblance of cover from fire or view. But we were also like rats in a trap. The nature of the wadi system had funnelled us into a dead end, the only exit being either back down the gorge or over the top onto the surrounding billiard table. If circumstances turned against us and forced a rapid evacuation – worst-case scenario during daylight – the prognosis for a successful escape did not look good. These factors were being taken into account as the patrol huddled together for another head-banging session.

Andy started proceedings, reiterating what we all already knew. 'Still fuck all on the comms, so if it stays that way, we are out of here tomorrow night, back to the drop-off.'

'Vince and I have been having a chat, and we think it wouldn't be a bad idea to recce that enemy position to the north, at least if we get pulled out it will look as if we have achieved something while we were out here.'

'If we get pulled out, they better send us back to the UK,' Dinger interrupted. 'The slagging the boys will give us will be legendary.'

'At the very least,' Andy continued, 'we can plot the position accurately for an air strike later on if the head-shed see fit, and who knows, maybe we've stumbled upon a Scud command centre or something equally important. Unless we take a look, we'll never know.'

Andy glanced around the group for any opinions to the contrary, but all the heads were bobbing up and down in agreement. The patrol was already halfway to being a cock-up; any chance at retrieving something from the situation would be a blessing.

'Fine. I will take Dinger, Aussie and Mike with me tonight.' Andy looked directly at me. 'I want that position stored in the Magellan, along with any other possible targets we come across.'

'No worries, mate. I'll set it up so that we can take co-ordinates on the move, and not be searching for satellites as the system initialises itself. That will use a lot of battery power but will save us heaps of time.'

'Right, then,' Andy continued, 'I'll give a set of orders at 2200 hours for those concerned.'

* * *

At five minutes before the appointed hour, we all assembled in a corner of the wadi around a makeshift model of the ridgeline and surrounding areas. Andy, Dinger, Mal, Vince and I closed together while the remainder either rested or provided sentry.

Vince needed to be aware of exactly what the half-patrol's intentions were in order to avoid a possible 'blue on blue', or friendly fire, incident, something that could all too easily happen in the dead of night in a hostile environment.

As before, Andy commenced proceedings by describing the 'model' of the area in front of us, complete with bayonet north indicator. It was perfectly adequate for the task at hand.

The 'Ground' and 'Situation' paragraphs were quickly dealt with, really just confirmation of the facts as we all knew them. Andy briefly summarised the facts relating to the enemy and our present situation before moving on to the meat of the orders.

'Mission, to carry out a recce of the enemy position at co-ords, Lat. . . . Long. . . . for possible future exploitation.' Andy repeated the mission statement twice.

'Execution, General Outline.

'This will be a five-phase operation: phase one, preparation and rehearsals; phase two, move out to the FRV; phase three, FRV to target; phase four, target to FRV; phase five, FRV back to OP.'

And so the process continued, until every aspect of the night's task had been covered and each individual knew what his responsibilities entailed.

The departure time had been set for midnight, which allowed us about one and a half hours to make any final adjustments to our kit and deal with a few bodily functions. I even managed to slip in 20 minutes of shut-eye. (I remembered the old soldier's adage: always take the opportunity to grab some sleep if you have the time. You never know when you might next get the chance.)

As midnight approached, the patrol shook itself out into the allotted formation: Andy in front, myself, Mal, and then Dinger bringing up the rear as tail-end charlie.

We looked decked out more for a direct action attack than a recce. Our camouflaged desert combats, veiled shamags and cam-cream smudged faces blurred into one in the dim Iraqi night; the weapons made the scene all the more sinister. Andy, toting an M203 with 40 mm bombs strapped all over his belt-order, looked like something out of a *Rambo* movie.

The rest of us carried Minimi light machine-guns, with boxed 200-round 5.56 mm magazines underslung. The Minimis had been chosen prior to insertion in preference to the more famous and long-trusted predecessor, the GPMG (general purpose machine-gun). The GPMG had been proven time and time again in countless conflicts, but its weight and the logistical problems of carrying countless amounts of belted 7.62 mm ammunition had determined its fate as far as small tactical patrols were concerned.

By comparison, the Minimi offered a lightweight, robust and highly efficient alternative, with the added bonus of using 5.56 mm ammunition that was both lighter and (more importantly for the MoD bean-counters) cheaper to produce. Hence, soldiers were able to carry more, and because the standard round of the British Army (and NATO for that matter) was 5.56, rounds were interchangeable with the other weapon systems used in the patrol.

The boys milled around at the wadi exit point, making final checks to their equipment, jumping up and down to check for noise or loose objects.

Dinger moved on over to me, pretending to be interested in the system boot-up of the Magellan. 'You know what you're doing then, do you?' was his helpful comment as I waited for the system to initialise and pick up the satellites. The regiment had only recently acquired these hand-held versions of the Magellan GPS, and therefore only a few blades had received training on their use.

Lightweight, portable and accurate to within ten metres, the Magellan was an invaluable aid in the desert, especially where dubious mapping quality was prevalent. It was basically a small receiver that scanned the heavens for a number of the many satellites that continuously circumnavigate the earth. Each of these satellites send a signal to earth which obviously also reveals their own position. By acquiring the information from three or more satellites, the Magellan simply interprets the data and triangulates it to give an extremely accurate positional fix on the ground. The more satellites contacted, the more accurate the fix. I had never seen their like anywhere in my previous travels, and I most certainly knew it would be a few years before the New Zealand unit would be fortunate to benefit from their use.

I programmed in the relevant information to allow the GPS to work continuously, thus allowing us to plot and record in the Magellan's memory 'waypoints', or positions of importance, on the move that could be referred to at a later date. The last thing that was needed on patrol was to have to wait ten minutes for the GPS to boot up and find satellites every time a positional fix was required.

'You could probably buy half of New Zealand with that, eh? Not that anyone would want to.'

I cast a wry glance at Dinger's smug grinning face, surprisingly bereft of the long thin rollie usually associated with it. Dinger was one of the more 'switched-on' soldiers around, but you could never let on that this was the case. Furthermore, if your retorts weren't quick enough, he could get on a roll and leave you standing speechless. In other words, attack was the best form of defence.

'Yeah, well, that may be the case, but I don't see one in your future. You have to be capable of at least some semblance of reading and writing before you can get your hands on one of these.'

'You've got some neck. Kiwis can barely speak English, let alone read and write it!'

'Yeah, I can vouch for that,' Aussie piped up as he muscled in on the conversation.

'Hark, a profound statement from the Squeezer in the corner. You must be feeling pretty sad and lonely to want to side with a Pom!'

'Everybody good to go?' Andy interrupted, just as things were starting to warm up.

On the stroke of midnight the patrol climbed its way out of the wadi onto the open desert plain to the north, the only noise a slight crunching of gravel and sand underfoot.

Bob was on stag at the top of the wadi, the Minimi propped by his side, scanning the area with the NVA for any sign of movement. Andy paused beside him briefly, dropped to one knee and whispered quietly, 'All right there, Bob, anything of interest?'

'Haven't seen or heard a thing since I came on at 2300.'

Andy moved his head slightly to acknowledge the statement. 'Crack an infra-red cyalume once we have moved past to mark your position, and make sure there is an infra-red torch handy for the recognition signals.'

Bob passed over the NVA as Andy got back up and looked back to check on the rest of us. A quick nod of the head and he was off, moving slowly onto the plain. I allowed Andy to move a couple of metres ahead before I followed, the amount of spacing between patrol members dictated through both experience and the prevailing conditions.

I drew level with Bob as he lay prone on the desert floor and slipped my foot between his legs to give him a quick kick up the backside. 'Not like a Marine to leave his back door exposed like that,' I whispered. 'Or is it?'

I moved on past Bob as he slowly removed the sight from his eye and rolled onto his side to glare up at me. 'Fuck off, you antipodean knob, before I shoot you,' was the last thing I heard as we disappeared into the night.

Slowly, almost hesitantly at first, we made our way northwards towards the ridgeline some 1,000 metres distant, all conscious of the fact that we were terribly exposed out on the plain. This uncomfortable feeling subsided very quickly, however, when it was realised that that very same exposed desert expanse appeared to absorb all the ambient light around. It was difficult to see further than a few metres in any direction.

Within a few seconds, not only the wadi, but Bob also had disappeared from view, emphasising the fact that although the openness of the desert gave the impression that all things were visible, at night the opposite was the case. The night light played tricks on our eyes: there was an optical illusion in so much as the darkness appeared to vary in intensity. From ground level to about head height, in all directions it was pitch black. You could see only a metre or so before shape and substance disappeared into the gloom. Yet, as we gazed above that height, the visibility was quite considerable, so much so that it left us feeling vulnerable to detection.

We continued for no more than 100 metres or so before Andy halted to check our position in relation to the OP. He raised his weapon to the shoulder and peered through the night sight, searching for the infra-red cyalume that would be our homing beacon on the way back.

'C'mon then, Bob, where the fuck are you?' escaped from his mouth as the M203 scanned a few degrees left and right.

A few more seconds passed then, 'Gotcha. Bloody hell, that's weak. You sure that you've got the OP co-ordinates in the GPS, Kiwi?'

I gave him a quick glare. 'Chill out, Andy, of course they're in there. The Magellan will bring us back no worries, have faith.'

'Hrmph,' he grunted at me, turning on his heel and moving off in the original direction once more.

I turned towards where Aussie and Dinger were kneeling, each facing outwards observing their arcs. A quick, near inaudible double-click of my tongue got their attention and indicated that we were moving off northwards once more. As I turned and followed Andy's slowly receding silhouette, they silently fell in line behind me.

It took only a few minutes for us to strike the first deeply rutted tyre marks that marked the border of the MSR, if you could call it that. The more distance covered and the closer we got to the high ground, the more numerous and congested the tyre tracks became until they converged as a mass of ruts covering the hard gravel and sand floor.

Every now and then the patrol would stop for a listening halt, a pause of no more than a couple of minutes, ears straining to catch wind of any possible danger. The flat open terrain contributed considerably to the distance that sound could travel, especially at night. This could therefore be exploited to give the patrol fair forewarning of any possible complications, be they human or otherwise, ahead. On the other hand, it also made it imperative that our own noise was kept to a minimum. This advantage could very easily be turned into a disadvantage: a cough or a careless knock of metal objects could spell disaster.

Methodically, we continued towards the ridgeline, cautiously making our way across the indented ground. The ridge loomed ever larger ahead, its presence making us all the more conscious of the known enemy emplacement above and equally aware of the sound of our own barely audible footfalls.

The base of the ridge was finally reached, and above us rose a sheer 40-metre wall of compressed sand, rock and gravel. The shadow cast by it created an impenetrable wall of black around the patrol, giving rise to an impression of invisibility and security after the openness of the plain.

The patrol closed to assume a defensive posture at our predetermined FRV (final rendezvous). Each man moved in till we had formed a small cross, with each patrol member facing out covering an arc of responsibility. With our shoulders almost touching, it was easy to communicate without having to raise the voice above a whisper.

We had been advancing to a high point on the skyline over the past hour, and we were now directly below it. I entered the exact position into the Magellan's memory, storing it as a waypoint.

'Listen up,' Andy whispered. 'This is now the ERV. We'll have a five-minute listening halt, and then continue east with the recce, following the ridge. See what it turns up.'

The ERV (emergency rendezvous) was a designated recognisable point which the patrol members would be able to return to in the event of being separated or lost, something that could easily occur in a contact at night. There could be many ERVs, but the last one designated always had priority over the rest.

'Kiwi, get this position down on the GPS.'

'Done, mate.'

'Good. A couple of more minutes and we're off.'

Everyone settled down, resting on one knee, eyes constantly scanning the blackness and ears tuned, ready to pick up the slightest noise, anything out of the ordinary.

The minutes passed quickly, and Andy signalled that it was time to carry on by slowly rising to his feet. We all followed suit, then peeled off into patrol formation once more as soon as Andy moved forward.

We cautiously patrolled eastwards following the base of the ridge, straining to catch any hint of activity, all the while searching for a practical and covert route that would give us access to the ridgeline above. It didn't take long for the first signs of human habitation to become apparent. Discarded water bottles, multicoloured plastic bags and various other pieces of flotsam littered the area, tell-tale signs that the enemy military presence was not unique to this part of the desert. The further east we continued, the more it appeared that there was some form of substantial habitation nearby, discarded oil drums adding to the general rubbish strewn about.

Suddenly a burst of guttural laughter broke out from above, followed by a rush of Arabic. We all halted and immediately closed into the lee of the ridge, hugging the wall, at the ready for any reaction to our intrusion.

I opened my mouth to clear my eardrums and increase their sensitivity. We stayed there motionless for what seemed like an age, trying to absorb as much information as possible on the activity above.

The banter continued unabated, drifting in and out with the night air. Sometimes, as if right next to us, the conversation could be heard clear and distinct, at other times it was just a faint, barely audible noise in the background. This gave some indication of the direction, distance and size of the encampment, but further investigation would be necessary to confirm all these details.

Placing my weapon carefully beside me, I cautiously reached into my belt-order and removed the Magellan. Covering the GPS over with my shamag to hide the illumination of the display, I then punched in our position as a waypoint, thus ensuring a reference point for future use.

We had yet to discover a viable approach route to the top of the escarpment. In fact, the whole feature was proving to be somewhat more of an obstacle than first imagined. The sheerness of its banks coupled with the loose gravel and sand would make a covert ascent almost impossible and most certainly not quiet.

Andy nudged his way carefully toward me, placing each footfall as delicately and deliberately as possible. Leaning close he whispered, 'There's been no reaction to our presence, so let's move on. Give the others the heads up.'

Nodding my head in acknowledgment, I turned towards Mal and relayed the message, which he relayed on to Dinger. Once again, as Andy rose and moved stealthily off, the patrol did likewise, perhaps a little more cautiously than before, and carried on east.

The task had now taken on a new sense of urgency. Although we always expected and prepared for an enemy presence, the knowledge that the enemy was literally right on top of us added a new dimension to the equation.

I could feel the tension amongst us. It was one thing to talk about a close target recce, but actually doing it was an entirely different matter. What's more, the only CTRs that I had been involved in previously were conducted in the jungles of Malaysia and Brunei, or the thick bush of New Zealand. This was an entirely different kettle of fish, and the lack of cover was quite disconcerting.

Skirting the escarpment, we began to find small re-entrants hewn out of the rock face, ancient weathered watercourses unused for centuries.

Each one that we encountered was summarily searched for any sign of the enemy or possible access to the plateau above.

Exiting one of these re-entrants, we came across the camp, indistinct in the black of night. Andy stiffened and halted in front of me, immediately initiating the same reaction from the rest of the patrol. He began to move his head from side to side, trying to get a focus on something at the very edge of his vision. Once again he put the night sight to his eye, adjusting the focusing ring to get a clearer picture.

A dim glow from a dying camp fire could be seen some 50 or so metres ahead. Occasionally it would flare up slightly as a gust of wind fanned the smouldering embers, illuminating the outline of a number of ragged tents about the place.

We all sank to one knee, contemplating the pros and cons of moving forward for a closer inspection. The distance coupled with the lack of ambient light made it impossible to determine whether or not the habitation was civilian or military.

His eyes scanning the tents before us, Andy slowly rose to his feet once more and began a cautious move forward, trying to reduce the distance between the tents and ourselves. The dwellings didn't appear to be military, but that did not necessarily mean that soldiers weren't living in them.

The new sound of voices stopped the patrol dead in its tracks. Even at this late hour the occupants were still not bedded down for the night. Andy turned to me once more and, putting his mouth near my ear, began, 'We'll circle around to the south and try to approach from the east, out of the glare from that fire.'

We cautiously moved forward once more, stealthily placing our feet using the outside of the boot to minimise any noise, fingers resting lightly on the triggers of our weapons. Keeping the fire and tents on our left, we slowly began to circle the encampment, careful not to concentrate simply on tents but on all about us. Target fixation could be a costly mistake.

A movement by the fire caught our attention and once again the patrol froze. Somebody was either standing guard or couldn't sleep. Sentry or shepherd, it made no difference – it was the enemy.

We remained silent and still for a good five minutes, just listening and observing, assessing the situation and gleaning as much information as possible, all our senses stretched to the max.

The reduced distance now allowed us to see that there were four large tents tucked close into the cliff, not dissimilar to the standard British Army 11 by 11s, with a pick-up or Land Cruiser parked to the side. It was looking more like a military camp. Four tents, six to eight soldiers in each: platoon strength.

Satisfied that it was safe to move on, Andy gave a quiet double-click of his tongue. Nodding my head in acknowledgement, I was about to turn to Mal when a slight movement caught my eye; a small shape was bounding out of the darkness toward us.

Now, apart from the target itself, there is one true enemy of a covert reconnaissance team that has proved the downfall of many a mission: animals. In this particular case it was the worst kind, a dog.

We probably all recognised it for what it was at the same time, as the mutt approached from a flank. Nothing needed to be said; we were fucked if this thing started to yap.

The dog drew up about ten metres short of us, trying to work out if we were friend or foe, no doubt. Andy had already made the decision by then, and we began to retrace our steps in the direction we had come. Sure enough, the dog began to growl and, as if on cue, five or six more of the beasts appeared out of nowhere, the pack closing in for a kill.

'Let's head straight out into the MSR,' I whispered to Andy, as our pace increased somewhat. We were conscious of the fact that on this track we would head right back to where some known enemy were housed.

'Those mutts aren't going to stay silent forever, and if they let loose while we are near the Triple A position, it could make life interesting.'

Andy had obviously been thinking along the same lines as he altered course without pausing, taking a bearing south across the MSR and towards the open desert.

It was too good to last. We had only moved about 200 metres from the tented site when one of the dogs let out a bark, the call of which was naturally taken up by its mangy companions. Our pace increased accordingly, so that we trebled the distance between the habitation and ourselves in a matter of minutes. All the while, at a discreet distance, the pack of baying mutts accompanied us, refusing to get bored with this particular game.

The dogs stopped barking quite rapidly, obviously happy that we had left their territory and were no longer a threat. That did not prevent them, however, from following us for another good couple of hundred metres, the last one finally satisfied and giving up the chase three-quarters of the way across the MSR.

With the last of the dogs out of sight, the patrol halted and settled down to take stock of the situation.

'Probably a fucking Bedouin camp,' Dinger cursed. Bedouin, tribal nomadic Arabs, commonly kept dogs to both safeguard their property and keep pests at bay.

'You know, if you were paranoid, you could get the feeling that we are jinxed,' I began as I squatted down on my haunches. 'I have never had so much bad luck in the space of a couple of days, it's ridiculous.'

'You could look at it from the other perspective and say that we have had a run of very good luck not to have been compromised by now,' Mal countered.

Andy finished scanning the ground with the Kite sight. Satisfied that the dogs hadn't alerted anyone he added, 'Well, I agree with Aussie, because it looks like no one has taken a blind bit of notice. Perhaps the dogs go off like that every night. I think that we have pushed it enough tonight anyway, best to quit while we're ahead.' Those words echoed everyone's sentiments.

'You took a fix at the base of the ridge, didn't you, Mike?'

'Yeah, and I can plot those tents no problem.'

'So that gives us a point of reference to bring in the jets if needs be.'

Andy put the NVA to his eye once more, searching out the infra-red cyalume that marked our OP.

'Well, it was worth a try. Let's see if your gizmo works then, Kiwi. Give me a direction and bearing to the OP.'

'Two secs, mate,' I replied, placing my Minimi down once more. The patrol fell silent, each man left to his own thoughts as I worked through the GPS menu and plotted our course back.

'650 metres south-west bearing 240 degrees,' I finally whispered across to Andy and watched him set his compass accordingly.

As I replaced the Magellan, Andy gave the nod for us to move out, taking up the direction indicated by the compass.

'We'll take it nice and easy. Last thing we need now is a blue on blue.'

Every few minutes the patrol paused to check for the sentry's infra-red cyalume, which would give us the point at which to direct our recognition codes.

We were right on top of the sentry position before the cyalume was visible. The patrol halted immediately, going to ground, while Andy moved forward slightly with a small torch equipped with a filter. Using Morse code, he flashed a 'Bravo' in the direction of the sentry position, and then looked through his Kite sight for the sentry's infra-red response signal, receiving a 'Bravo' in return.

With that, Andy moved forward and confirmed his identity with the sentry, while we continued to wait some 50 metres away.

Andy returned within minutes. 'All right, guys, let's go. I can hear my pit calling me.'

We all filed past Vince, who had drawn the graveyard stag, and headed down into the wadi for a quick debrief.

Removing the Magellan from its pouch, I shut the system down, conserving what was left of the current battery power. There were enough spare batteries to keep us going for a week or so, but having the system on continuous operation would reduce that projection dramatically.

'Don't all these Arabs know that there is not supposed to be any habitation around here for 20-odd clicks? I mean, don't they listen to the intelligence reports?'

'Maybe we should demand the slime [intelligence corps] come here and give them one of their bone intelligence briefs. Then they would have to move on and leave us in peace,' Dinger added, at the same time pulling out a canteen for a swig of water.

Andy finally joined us in the wadi. 'I briefed Vince on the goings-on tonight, and he will pass it on to the others as they come on stag. I said to be that extra bit vigilant; we can't assume that the dogs didn't cause an alert, or that somebody won't investigate it further in the morning.'

Andy looked for any comment then continued. 'Anyway, we managed to get a rough fix on the enemy position, certainly more accurate than off the map.'

'Yeah, and we also know that every man and his dog live around here, literally!' Mal interjected disgustedly.

'I never saw a route up to the ridge. Did anyone else?'

We all shook our heads.

Mal added, 'I would think by the terrain their access must be from behind the encampment, further to the north or east.'

'Yeah, the ground flattens out onto a plateau on the northern side, and runs down east to the MSR about five clicks from here according to the map.'

'Fuck knows, we could speculate all day,' Andy continued. 'I will simply put it down as what we did and didn't find, and let the slime interpret that as they like.

'Anybody got anything else to add?'

Andy looked at his watch. 'It's 0410 hours. Vince and the rest of the lads will continue with the stag until 0900. After that we will kick in again. Go and get your heads down.'

Turning to me, he finished with, 'And Mike, can you give me the co-ordinates for the enemy camp? That way I won't have to bug you for them in the morning.'

'Sure, mate, I'll have them for you in a couple of minutes.'

I retrieved the GPS and jotted the position down. Hopefully those few numbers would mean that this patrol had achieved something, a little success, possibly a decent target for an air strike at the very least. It could have been our one saving grace, seeing that nothing else seemed to be running according to plan.

After passing on the information to Andy, I returned to my bergen and slipped gratefully into my bivvy bag. I descended into a deep sleep, my mind blissfully unaware of the trauma and anguish that lay in wait.

Chapter 5

Iraq, day three, January 1991

Once again, the early morning chill ate its way through the bivvy bag and the layers of clothing that covered me, the biting cold forcing me awake. Glancing at my watch, I inwardly groaned, as the three hours I had just managed were not enough to replenish the batteries.

A slight snore emanated from the dishevelled lump a few feet opposite, the top of Dinger's black beanie peaking out from under his camouflage blanket. The thought crossed my mind to throw something at him; I was jealous of the fact that he could still sleep on oblivious to the conditions. But then, I suppose that these were positively luxurious compared with what he had been forced to put up with in the Falklands.

I was well awake by now, and trying to convince my body otherwise would have been pointless. Taking care not to disturb the others, I quietly packed away my sleeping kit, first rolling the bivvy bag into a tight ball before forcing it into a stuff-sack. What little personal equipment/clothing I had was kept like this, as the stuff-sacks were able to reduce the size of items considerably, meaning that they occupied less space in the bergen. Making myself comfortable at the base of a large rock, I tore open the top of the vacuum-sealed foil bag that constituted my breakfast and began hungrily spooning the cold fruit salad into my mouth.

'You're awake early there, Kiwi,' Vince whispered as he moved over beside me. 'What's the matter, not sleeping?'

I nodded my agreement in between spoonfuls of peach and pear.

'Don't worry, a couple more days of this routine and you'll be out like a light, cold or not.'

Licking the remnants of the syrup from my spoon, I queried Vince on his view of last night's activities.

'Andy pass on last night's sitrep to you, did he?'

'Yeah, could be bloody Bedouin, they get everywhere. Scrounging nomads of the desert. But with the military-style tents and the Land Cruiser, not really their style.'

'What do you reckon about the dogs, then?'

'Well, chances are that they will have been ignored. Same as over the water – dogs are a good deterrent, but most of the time people just dismiss their barking because it happens so regularly, that is unless it carries on and on, of course.'

'Over the water' was a term that the guys used to describe Northern Ireland. I was the only one of the patrol who hadn't been on active service there; even the Squeezer had been deployed to Northern Ireland on a short trip. It really brought home the fact that I was the 'cherry' of the bunch.

We chatted on for a few more minutes, before I excused myself for a call of nature. Now, one of the less pleasant things about OP assignments is that everything that you carry in with you, you take out, and I mean everything.

The art of manoeuvring oneself into such a position that you can deposit the contents of your bowels into a small plastic bag was an act that had neither grown in appeal nor proficiency for me over the years. After finding a not-so-conspicuous spot, I was in the process of completing such a contortionist's act when there was a worryingly unnatural click. Looking up with dread, my worst fears were realised. There, a few feet away, smugly waving a small disposable camera in his hand, was the testosterone-heavy Aussie.

'What do you reckon, mate, worth a few beers?'

Still busy trying to rearrange myself, I cursed in Mal's general direction, referring to his dubious parentage and the wrath that he would incur if the pictures ever came to light. 'What the fuck do you think you are going to do with that?'

'I think this will put the page three *Sun* girl to shame, but everything is negotiable,' Mal replied, replacing the camera in his belt-order.

I made a mental note of the pouch into which it had disappeared and then immediately responded, 'You've got no chance if you think that you are going to get out of here with that intact, Squeezer. You've got to sleep sometime.'

Mal just laughed quietly, carefully moving off out of my reach and back towards the others.

AL JOUF, SAS FORWARD OPERATIONS BASE, 1230 HOURS

The Communications Centre (COMCEN) was a hive of activity. With two and a half squadrons in the field, this was the largest regimental deployment since Dhofar 20 years earlier.

'Sir.'

The officer turned and looked up from his desk.

'We have now gone over the lost comms threshold without contact from Bravo Two Zero. Do you wish to instigate the patrol's lost comms procedure yet?'

'They have a SATCOM, don't they?'

'Yes, sir, but they also have strict instructions not to use it unless there is an emergency or if they sight a Scud.'

'Were their radio checks with us OK before they deployed?'

'Yes, sir, but they could only confirm with the squadron base station direct, not with Forest Hero.'

('Forest Hero' was the call sign of the regimental base station; as such, all communications in the region were supposed to pass through it before being relayed on to the FOBs.)

'All right, I will get back to you.'

The signaller turned on his heel, relieved that the decision was now out of his hands.

Turning to the adjacent desk where his colleague was seated, the officer began, 'We've got one patrol on the move back to the Saudi border, mission aborted, a second that didn't even get on the ground, and now a third that I can't get in contact with. B Squadron will be the laughing stock of the regiment!'

'Well, they obviously haven't any problems or you would have heard on the SATCOM, and there is no way I can task the Chinook for them tonight anyway; they are resupplying A and D squadrons in the field.'

'Well, then, that's the matter out of my hands. Once they come up on the SATCOM, we will have a better idea of their situation and can work on it from there. How soon will you have a heli available?'

'Hard to say at this stage, they are definitely tasked up for the next 48 hours. Don't worry, you'll probably get a call on the SATCOM in the next few hours saying they are in Damascus on the town and can we get them next week.'

Both men chuckled at this thought before the two were interrupted once again by the yeoman, who now looked decidedly anxious.

'Yes, what is it, man?'

'Sir, we've just been going over the frequency prediction charts again for our area, and one of the lads noticed an anomaly. It doesn't match those that were given to Bravo Two Zero. They've got the frequencies for the border area around Kuwait City.'

'So what are you saying?'

'Basically, sir, with those frequencies, they haven't a hope in hell of getting through to us.'

* * *

Midday came and went, and with it the automatic decision to strike the OP that evening. It would be a long hard slog back to the ERV, but there was no alternative, we needed a new set.

'Bob.' Andy called him over. 'Get the SATCOM set up and see if there is any traffic on it about the Chinook's arrival tonight, or anything to do with us. Just keep monitoring it.'

Bob came over and said, 'Andy wants the SATCOM set up and monitored.' I nodded my head in acknowledgment and proceeded to remove the necessary components from my bergen, Bob doing likewise from his.

It took us about ten minutes to assemble the radio. It consisted of two large black boxes, one the actual radio and the other its encoder/decoder, which were joined together by a series of cables. Along with this there was the antenna, housed in a tube-like container complete with 20-odd metres of coaxial cable, which unfolded umbrella fashion into a small wire-framed satellite dish.

I adjusted the antenna according to the bearings Bob read out, and then looked to him to give me the directions for fine-tuning. By bringing up the LCD (liquid crystal display) in receive mode, the SATCOM could lock onto a satellite and give a display of signal strength. You could therefore use this to fine-tune the antenna: the more bars that appeared on the LCD, the better the reception.

'Try left, that's it, more, more,' Bob persisted until the maximum amount of bars were consistently displayed. 'That'll do you.'

Careful not to dislodge the light aluminium antenna, I climbed down from my perch to join Bob at the base of the wadi. 'Hear anything, then?'

We had set the SATCOM up on numerous occasions since arriving at the OP location and, as of yet, had heard nothing on the net. This was particularly disconcerting, as we had been led to believe that many different agencies were operating on the frequency given to us, and therefore somewhere along the way we should be hearing other communications.

The soft crackle of static was all that emanated from the handset, which did nothing to increase the confidence in our ability to operate it.

'Maybe we're in the Bermuda Triangle of Iraq,' Bob whispered at me. It certainly was strange that none of our communications wanted to play ball.

I moved off to report to Andy, leaving Bob in place to maintain the listening watch.

'SATCOM is set up, mate, but there is still no traffic on the net.'

'Right, fuck this. Do a radio check. See if anybody is listening.'

'What about the DF? We've got that enemy position right on top of us. If they have anybody monitoring the area, we could be fucked in minutes.'

Legs interrupted us before we could go any further. 'I just received a partial message on the guard net. We should be able to transmit back.'

'OK, get our locstat [locations statistics] off and tell them that we are moving to the ERV tonight to receive a new set. Make sure that message about the enemy position goes as well.'

Turning to me, Andy finished by saying, 'You and Bob keep listening out. I want to know as soon as anything pops up on that net.'

I gave Andy the thumbs up and moved back over to Bob, explaining the situation.

'Thank fuck for that,' Bob exclaimed vehemently. 'At least they will know we are still alive now.'

An almost tangible feeling of relief swept the patrol; such was the stress that having no comms had placed us all under. Suddenly, we were not so alone. If the shit hit the fan, we could at least ask for help now.

'It will be good to get out of here tonight as well. Pick up the new radio and find somewhere to start the OP over again. This place is bad karma.'

Unfortunately the air of optimism was short-lived. Word returned that, although Legs had got his message away, he had not received any acknowledgment of its receipt, something that should happen automatically within two minutes of a message arriving at base.

And, more frustratingly, once again it appeared as if the patrol had been dropped into the comms abyss. Legs had lost contact on the guard net.

Andy moved on over to us, now even more stressed out than before. 'Make a radio check on that thing, I want to know what the fuck is going on!'

I didn't hesitate, simply picked up the handset and began to transmit, 'Zero Bravo, Zero Bravo, this is Bravo Two Zero, Bravo Two Zero, radio check, radio check, over.' Releasing the transmit button, I waited for a response. That call had taken about ten seconds. Andy watched me intently as I kept the handset to my ear. Shaking my head, I said, 'Nothing.'

'Try again.'

'Zero Bravo, Zero Bravo, this . . .' Bob grasped my arm tightly, causing me to stop in mid-sentence.

Chink, chink. The sound of a small bell could be heard above, followed very soon after by the bleating of goats.

'Shit!' Andy swore. 'Get everybody under the lee of the wadi.'

I could see Vince already making his way across from where he had been on stag, coming to warn us of the impending danger.

'That fucking boy is back with his fucking goats,' he hissed. 'Only this time he is coming directly toward us.'

We all scrambled to the base of the wadi, trying to squeeze in behind a large boulder that sat there, hoping it would hide us from the herder. But if he ventured that close, we were stuffed.

There was no way all of us could hide from him, and in any case he would see our claymores and antennas long before that. So the question was, should we take him out right under the noses of the troops above, or should we risk leaving him and make a run for it?

I hoped to God that I wouldn't be the one to make that decision. I didn't fancy having the death of a nine- or ten-year-old boy on my conscience.

* * *

'Sir,' a young signaller thrust a piece of message page under the officer's nose. 'It's from Bravo Two Zero, we managed to make contact on the guard net briefly, but they haven't acknowledged our message with their new frequencies on it.'

'They still don't realise they have the wrong frequencies, then?'

'Exactly, sir.'

'This says that they are withdrawing from the OP tonight and moving to pick up a new set from the ERV. Is that their lost comms procedure?'

'Yes, sir, we are supposed to send a chopper from this location at last light with either a new set or reinforcements.'

'Well, that won't be necessary now, will it? They have established communication.'

He passed the communiqué over to the other desk. 'Take a look.'

His colleague read it through carefully. 'It says here that there is an S60 anti-aircraft emplacement by their position. I wouldn't authorise a heli anywhere near that anyway.'

At that moment Harry, one of the B Squadron patrol commanders, walked over. 'All right there, Boss,' he barked across the desk, 'what's the score?'

Harry was an ex-Marine commando, full of the fierce aggressiveness and hot blood that younger years encourage. Over six foot tall, lean and mean, he was always looking for action of one kind or another.

'We've just managed to hear from Bravo Two Zero. They're OK but are having some comms problems.'

'So are we going to send out another set to them, then?' Harry continued. 'I could do with a heli flight to get out of this place.'

'We are just discussing that at the moment. Your volunteering is duly noted.'

Another signaller came rushing across, bursting in on the conversation, his hands shaking as he handed the officer the flimsy piece of paper.

'Sir, message from Bravo Two Zero.'

The officer looked down at the message and felt his blood run cold. Written beneath the coded transmission was its translation:

COMPROMISE. REQUIRE IMMEDIATE EXFIL.

* * *

There was no way we could all squeeze in behind the rock. Four would have been no problem, five could just about do it – eight was hopeless.

I was lying on my back, Minimi across my chest, looking straight up to the top of the wadi. I could hear the boy quite clearly, talking in the high immature octaves of pre-pubescence. The goats were clearly visible now, their inquisitive nature making them automatically peer over the lip of the wadi, searching for anything remotely edible.

'Shoo, shoo,' the boy was saying as he tried to move them from the edge and towards some unknown objective.

Geordie and I were exposed on one side, Vince and Andy on the other. I could just make out the top of his curly black hair as it bobbed in and out of view between the uneven rock formations that littered the edge above. All it would take was one curious glimpse over the ledge and he was guaranteed to see some of us.

His continuous stream of chatter ended abruptly, as if someone had grabbed him by the throat. Out of my view, I couldn't ascertain why he suddenly shut up, and before anyone could even think of a reaction he started on again, exactly the same as before.

We could see the goats meandering around the edge of the wadi, not in any great rush, and slowly but surely they and the boy continued on their way, finally out of earshot.

'Right,' Andy started as soon as the boy's voice could no longer be heard, 'did he see anyone?'

'He definitely didn't get a look at us on this side,' Geordie quickly stated.

Andy turned. 'What do you reckon, Vince?'

'Hard to say. I could see the whole side of his face at one stage, but if he saw me he showed no recognition of the fact.'

'Shoot on up top and see if he is in a hurry.'

Vince nodded his head in agreement and slowly climbed up to the wadi edge.

Bob whispered across, 'I don't think we can risk it. You have to expect the worst.'

'Yeah,' I added. 'From where he was, he would have to be blind not to see the claymores and the antenna wires. You've got to assume that that is a compromise, whether he saw somebody or not.'

A small avalanche of gravel preceded Vince as he slid back down the slope. 'I don't like it; he is heading towards the high ground, which could mean the Bedouin camp, or the soldiers, or both. Who the fuck knows!'

Andy looked around the patrol, gauging the consensus of opinion. 'What do you reckon, Dinger?'

'I think it's time to didi-mau and get the fuck out of here. Dump all the non-essential kit and make like racing snakes. It's still an hour before last light, and I don't fancy trying to hold off the Republican Guard in this wadi in daylight.'

Most of us nodded our heads in agreement; it was better to get some distance between the OP site and ourselves while we still had the luxury of choice and opportunity.

'Let's do it, then,' Andy finally decided. 'Dump everything that isn't needed and prepare to move out.'

The decision made, there was no more concern about being quiet. Bergens were ripped open and anything that wasn't needed was thrown into the crevasse behind the large boulder. Wire detector, OP stores, NBC (nuclear, biological, chemical) suits, extra rations and jerry cans of water – in they all went.

I had moved over to the SATCOM to begin dismantling it when I heard a noise that no foot soldier in these conditions would ever want to hear: tank tracks. For a moment nobody moved or said a word; the shock of hearing the tank stunned us into temporary immobility.

But the noise was getting ever nearer, and we were soldiers. If this was where we had to scrap it out, so be it. The professional in us all took over. Firing positions were taken up behind what limited cover was available. Ripping an M72 anti-tank rocket launcher from my bergen, I slung it over my shoulder, hoisted the Minimi and ran over to the boulder, the most solid piece of cover about, Dinger doing the same on the opposite side.

The roar of the engine was almost deafening now, the clatter of its tracks as they crunched their way over gravel and sand drawing ever nearer. As I extended the rocket launcher and prepared it for firing, I hoped to God it wasn't a T72 or something similar coming toward us. If it was, this rocket would be as good as throwing a stone at it, so thick and strong was the armour of an MBT (main battle tank).

'Watch it, Mike,' Geordie suddenly piped up as I settled the launcher on my shoulder. 'This face has still got to score down Sticky's, you know.'

Sticky's was one of the clubs down Hereford, and Geordie was referring to the fact that the back blast from an M72 at close range was just as dangerous as what came out the front.

'Best you get your fucking head down then, mate, because I sure as hell ain't going to be worried about your looks when that tank pops around the corner!'

A hint of black nudged around the bend in the wadi some 60 metres distant, and as I closed one eye and concentrated on the sight, it registered in my brain that something here was amiss. The shape of the tank was nothing like I had ever seen before.

Soon it dawned on me that I wasn't looking at a tank, but a bloody bulldozer, and one upon which sat a very confused-looking Arab driver, obviously trying to make his way out of the wadi. Even at this distance, I could see the shock register on his face, eyes bulging from sunken sockets at the picture presented before him. Panicking, he immediately turned the bulldozer off to the right and disappeared from our view, engine over-revving at full pitch.

'Well, if we weren't compromised before, we certainly are now,' Mal laughed, breaking the tension. 'Best we get moving, I think.'

A real sense of urgency gripped us now. There was still probably about half an hour till last light, and the troops above were definitely not a half-hour's drive away. I immediately got onto the SATCOM, trying one last time to raise base and relay our predicament. 'Zero Bravo, Zero Bravo, this is Bravo Two Zero, Bravo Two Zero, over.' Nothing but the steady crackle and hiss of static.

At the same time Legs grabbed the 319 and sent out our pre-arranged code word for a compromise on the guard net, pressing the transmit button over and over again.

'Zero Bravo, Zero Bravo, this is Bravo Two Zero transmitting blind, patrol compromised, require immediate exfil, repeat patrol compromised, require immediate exfil.'

'Mike, Legs, sack it,' Vince yelled across to us. 'We're out of here.'

Bob and I quickly dismantled the set and stowed the pieces between us, Legs doing the same with the 319.

Dinger was racing around the wadi, defusing the claymores and destroying their detonators so they would be of no use. Last but not least, Vince booby-trapped the abandoned stores.

'Right, you fuckers,' he murmured to himself, delicately placing a white phosphorus grenade amongst the kit. 'Here's a little present for you.'

Emptying a bottle, I gorged myself with water before replenishing it from a jerry can. From now on, the only water available would be what we were carrying.

'Throw me your bottle, Mal, I'll fill it now.' Mal tossed over a half-full container and finished off sorting his bergen.

'Everyone ready?' Andy asked.

'C'mon, then, get your bergens on and let's move out.'

We headed south, following the meandering path the wadi took that afforded us temporary cover from view. Vince and Andy led the patrol out at a steady pace, Dinger and I at the rear with two Minimis, the rest strung out between in single file. As we withdrew from the OP site, we took turns at facing back to the north, the 'one foot on the ground, one moving' principle automatically taking over. I would take a position to cover the rear of the patrol and call Dinger on past me, and he in turn would do likewise.

Although our bergens were considerably lighter now, they would still be too much of a burden if we ran into a contact. We were in desperate need of darkness to cover our tracks.

'Not long now till last light,' I thought to myself. 'Another quarter of an hour or so and we'll be safe.'

Getting up from my firing position as Dinger whistled me through, I noticed that the patrol was now spread out over a considerable distance, probably nearly 100 metres between the front and rear man. Suddenly I saw Vince and a couple of the others waving their hands in the air as if greeting someone, and thought to myself 'What the fuck?'

I had the answer all too soon as the first distinctive crack and thump of rifle fire whistled overhead, and I saw the front part of the patrol breaking right in a contact drill.

'Contact left,' I yelled at Dinger and immediately swung my Minimi in that direction to cover the threat, but there was none. As of yet, the intermittent volley of shots that were coming the patrol's way were only directed 50 metres to my front. I was simply staring up at a three-metre sheer rock face, still hidden from view.

Whack, thump, whack, thump, whack, whack, whack. The rate of fire was beginning to increase rapidly, as the unseen enemy managed to get more rifles to bear.

'Come on, you Kiwi twat, break right!' Dinger screamed at me as the others disappeared from view. Dinger was on the opposite side of the wadi, kneeling down with a Minimi at the ready, covering my retreat across the divide. I raced on past him, the bergen on my back forgotten as if it was no weight at all, and took up a position about 15 metres behind.

'Go, Dinger!' I screamed, urging him to leap-frog past me for the next bound.

'Go!' Dinger responded a few seconds later, at the same time letting rip a burst from his weapon.

Turning and moving towards Dinger, our predicament dawned on me. We were suddenly becoming visible to the enemy on the opposite side of the wadi, and the forward slope we now had to negotiate was bare as a baby's backside. It was turkey-shoot time.

My mind vaguely registered the bursts of Minimi fire from further on up the wadi that now began to overlap the incoming racket. Mal and Bob were bringing their weapons to bear, but the terrain was such that they were completely blind to me, as I was to them.

Thud, thud, thud, thud, thud. A new, deeper and slower tune rose above the incessant clatter of machine-gun and rifle fire as the booming notes of a 12.7 mm DSHKA heavy machine gun began to join the fray.

My lungs burned as they strained to suck in air, blood pounding like a sledgehammer in my ears. I struggled past Dinger, his machine gun firing off rhythmic four- to five-round bursts as he covered my extraction. The bergen was now taking its toll as the incline of the wadi bank increased, at the same time presenting the enemy opposite a much easier target.

This was like some bad dream – one of those moments when you feel like you are running through water. I tripped and stumbled to the ground. All around me bits of gravel and stone were being thrown up as invisible missiles struck the surrounding desert with deadly intent.

Rolling over onto my back, I tugged at the quick-release strap on my right shoulder strap, but the catch was under such tremendous strain that it refused to release. Time appeared to stand still as I lay there struggling to free myself from the pack. Almost transfixed, I watched a stream of white tracer track its way toward me, the distance between myself and the firer such that the deadly burst arced inward as if in slow motion, accelerating with frightening speed at the last moment.

Ironically, I had spent some time firing the DSHKA in the UAE as part of A Squadron's deployment preparation, and being on the receiving end of one had never been in my plans.

A tracer round crunched into the gravel beside me, this guy was getting bloody good. The worry was, however, that for every one tracer round you could see, there were four other unannounced rounds hurtling behind. Where they were landing didn't bear thinking about.

'Dump your fucking bergen,' Dinger yelled at me as he bounded past, dropping to release his load at the same time.

'What the fuck does it look like I am trying to do!'

I could get a clear look at our foe now, and there sure as hell were plenty of them.

The DSHKA was sat atop an armoured personnel carrier about 600 metres distant, the steady rhythmic beat of its burst slightly behind the flashes of light flaring from the barrel. About 100 metres in front of that were two white Toyota pick-ups, which had obviously also been carrying loads of troops, all of whom were lying prone, firing in our direction.

I finally freed myself and sprinted past Dinger a few metres to take up a firing position, ready for his bound past me.

The lines of dark-green soldiers were still about 400 metres away at this stage, their small-arms fire very inaccurate at that distance, but I continued to let short bursts go in their general direction. This wasn't going to be all one-way traffic.

Boom. A dark black cloud appeared above us.

Looking up, I said, 'What the fuck was that?'

'I don't fucking believe this,' Dinger yelled, 'not again. That's the fucking S60s shooting at us.'

Pulling a White Phos (phosphorous grenade) out of his pouch, Dinger threw it just to our front, the slight pop as it ignited practically lost in the din.

Immediately clouds of thick white smoke began billowing out, providing us with a temporary shield from view behind which we could make good our escape.

'Go, go, go,' I yelled at Dinger, not that he needed any encouragement, and together we sprinted the remaining 50 metres to the crest and relative safety.

* * *

Harry raced into the B Squadron lines, grabbing available bodies as he passed. 'Listen up!' he yelled at everybody and anybody he saw, 'Two Zero's in the shit. We're taking a few of you and going across to get them. You, Mick, grab that GPMG! Scouse, you, John and Taff with me on the chopper. Get your kit, fucking move it!'

'Get this thing wound up,' Harry said, pouncing on the unsuspecting RAF flying officer. 'We've got a patrol in the shit and in need of immediate exfil.'

The B Squadron lads came over in a rush, strapping on their belt-orders and cocking weapons on the trot. At the same moment an SAS officer appeared, looking none too pleased.

'What do you lot think you're doing? That chopper is going nowhere.'

All movement ceased and the men turned to look at the officer.

'What the fuck is that supposed to mean?' Harry retorted, giving the man such a stare that he was forced to take a step backward.

'You can't just go flying off across the border like that. Deconfliction has to be sorted out, routes submitted to HQ. What's more, there's an S60 battery right on top of their position. I will not subject an air-frame and crew to that type of known risk.'

'Two Zero's ERV is ten clicks south of that position, that's a load of bollocks,' Harry counted.

'Listen you lot, you are all ordered to stand down. The situation is in hand. We will get someone out to them.'

The Chinook pilot kept his distance, not wanting to be part of the stand-off. If six heavily armed SAS soldiers told him to fly into Iraq to get their mates, he most certainly wasn't going to argue with them. The SAS officer was the one paid to do that.

'We are monitoring the situation carefully. They've got plenty of rations, comms and ammo. Let's all just calm down and let Two Zero report and give us more information. Then we can organise something rationally.'

The impasse lasted for another 30 seconds or so before Harry finally spoke up. 'Stand down, lads.' It was the hardest thing he had ever had to say in his life.

The malice in the soldiers' eyes burned bright as they backed down. They were, after all, in the army, and orders were orders, whether you agreed with them or not.

'What a load of piss . . .' The grumbling continued all the way back to the lines.

* * *

The mad dash ended at the crest of the wadi, and both Dinger and I threw ourselves over like sprinters diving desperately for the finishing tape. The crest was actually higher than the surrounding desert, and so we lay there briefly, tucked away temporarily out of harm's way, our heaving chests gasping for breath and thankful for the respite.

'I have got to give up smoking. I am definitely too fucking old for this shit.' Dinger's rasping voice sounded the way I felt. It took me a good half minute to even get my breath back enough to reply.

'Is that all you are worried about? I should be at home catching rays on a beach, not getting ten barrels of shit shot out of me in the middle of some godforsaken desert. I intended the odds to be a bit better than this when I had my first contact!'

This attempt at frivolity was probably a way of expressing the relief we both felt at making it thus far intact, the realisation that we weren't full of bullet holes giving rise to an elated feeling of accomplishment – as if we had just won a competition.

With each less violent intake of air, the burning sensation in my chest diminished, as did the adrenaline-enhanced pounding within my ears. I thought I was fitter than this.

Dusk was descending rapidly now; the barely visible Iraqi troops opposite in their drab green uniforms were blending in with the night. They had lost that race by a whisker. At least in that respect we had come out on top.

The noise of the vehicles moving forward accompanied by heavy bursts of machine-gun fire interrupted our brief rest. Although it wasn't that accurate, it was directed well enough to remind us we weren't quite out of the woods yet.

'Where the fuck are all the others?' Dinger said, scanning the ground about us.

'Buggered if I know, mate, but we better get a move on before someone offers us a lift.'

Half crouched, we moved off on a westerly bearing, the sounds of sporadic gunfire still cracking overhead. In theory, the patrol should have rallied a short distance from the contact point; well, that was the theory in the jungle anyway. What I wouldn't give to have thick green vegetation about me now. I had spent 90 per cent of my military career training to fight in jungle environments, and the first time I get a chance to have a scrap, there is not a tree in sight for hundreds of kilometres. Fucking great.

'What were you on about back there, Dinger, when you said not again?' I questioned him as we trotted side by side, looking for any sign of the others.

'In the Falklands, the Argies had S60s and brought them into the ground attack role during our assault. Scared the shit out of me then, and I didn't need to see that happening again this time.'

'Over there,' I pointed at the shape of a man in the half gloom.

Increasing our pace, the enemy vehicles left well behind in the deepening darkness, we caught up with Bob and Mal, also minus bergens. They both looked OK and in one piece.

'What the fuck happened back there?' Bob asked breathlessly as we drew up, still panting from the exertion.

'I think everyone got malleted in the open and split up. Mike and I were lucky that the ground paired us off and allowed us to fight out of it.'

'Yeah, that's generally what happened to us as well,' Mal added.

'Did you see anything of the others?'

'I saw Andy and Geordie take off in that direction,' Bob said, indicating the general bearing that we were all headed on.

'Well, let's get moving then,' Dinger replied, taking control of the situation. 'They'll be holed up waiting for us somewhere.' He took the lead as we moved off again to the west, searching for some sign of the others.

Within a few minutes we heard a soft whistle, and on drawing closer found Andy, Geordie, Vince and Legs holed up at the base of a small escarpment.

'Is everyone OK?' Andy asked, checking us all off as we moved in.

Geordie was watching the distant enemy headlights that bounced up and down across the uneven terrain through the NVA, as they searched desperately for some trace of us, letting off bursts of red and white tracer indiscriminately every now and then.

'They're heading generally south-west, obviously trying to sweep the area and direction we initially took. We've got some time to re-org here.'

Dinger flopped down next to Andy and immediately asked, 'What the fuck happened back there, Andy? We were well isolated.'

'We ran out of wadi. You know, that bit where it disappears for 100 metres before starting again. We'd got about halfway across when the two pick-ups and the APC [armoured personnel carrier] pulled up. Tried to bluff our case with a wave, but the incoming 7.62 put paid to that. The rest is history.'

I glanced around the group, not a bergen in sight. Obviously everyone had been required to ditch their kit as well. Well, it wasn't too much of a problem, the chopper would be here in a few hours, and we still had the TACBEs to communicate with.

'Legs,' Andy whispered. 'Did you manage to bring the set?'

'You're fucking joking, aren't you?' Legs responded. 'I only just got myself out, let alone the bloody radio. I have got the codes and EMU, though, always keep them on me.'

The EMU was the 319's electronic brain that controlled all of the burst communication and message encoding. Without it, the radio was just a basic Morse and voice transmitter/receiver.

'Best I get on to AWACS, then, and make sure help is on the way.'

Andy ripped the TACBE out of his pouch and withdrew the pin that prevented unintentional transmissions. A steady squelch of static emanated from its small speaker, which broke up the minute he depressed the transmit button.

'Hello Starlight, hello Starlight, this is Bravo Two Zero transmitting on Turbo, over.' Andy tried using the pre-arranged code sequence for the patrol. As he released the switch we all listened intently, expecting to hear a friendly, English-speaking voice reply.

Ten, twenty, thirty seconds passed with nothing but the hiss of static to break the silence.

'Hello Starlight, hello Starlight,' Andy started again, somewhat more urgently. 'This is Bravo Two Zero, this is Bravo Two Zero, transmitting on Turbo, transmitting on Turbo, do you read, over!'

Once again, the same result.

'Fuck! Someone else have a go. Maybe my battery is flat or something.'

There were four TACBEs spread amongst the patrol, and those

carrying the remaining three immediately rushed to retrieve theirs and establish contact with AWACS, but there was no response.

'AWACS will respond within 20 seconds,' Mal said. 'Does that ring a bell? What a crock.'

We could now see four or five twin sets of headlights about a kilometre distant, crawling slowly across the desert scouring the area. It was time to get a move on; before long those sets of headlights would double as more and more Iraqi troops were called in to assist.

'We'd better get a plan of action sorted, quickly!' Bob urged, eyeing the distant vehicles warily. 'They aren't going to let us sit here and have a smoko break all night.'

'Well, what do you reckon, then?' Andy asked nobody in particular.

'The chopper should have left at last light, maybe before if our compromise message got through.' Legs glanced at his watch before continuing, 'So we can assume that it should be at the ERV point at about 2300 hours latest.'

'Yeah, but the fucking enemy are also moving that way. The ERV is only ten clicks away,' Vince added.

The Magellan had finished plotting our position as I pulled my 1:250,000 scale map from my trouser pocket. Careful to shield the tiny light I played on it, I suggested a course of action that would at least get us going in the right direction.

'We're here,' my pencil indicated a point on the map, 'and the ERV is here. We could continue moving south, paralleling the wadi and carry on past the ERV, maintaining the same bearing to the secondary RV, here.' Once again my pencil stabbed the plastic-coated map at a point roughly 25 clicks south.

'The Chinook should maintain a basic northerly course to run over the two RVs, and as the TACBEs have a range of about 70 clicks ground-to-air we can bring him on to us and authenticate, no problem.'

'We can't head too far south, though,' Vince stepped in again. 'They will be using that hard-top MSR as a natural barrier flooded with troops. Keeping up the pressure on us this end, they will try and herd us toward the waiting force. Just like a pheasant beat.'

Dinger brought the discussion to an end. 'Look, we haven't got a lot of choice. Let's head south like Mike said. By the time we reach the secondary RV, the Chinook should have arrived. No heli, we box west for a few clicks, then north again and make for Syria. That's what the E & E plan calls for, doesn't it?'

Andy glanced around the patrol once more, looking for any other comments but, as Dinger had so rightly pointed out, we were fast running out of options. Better to make a decision and act on it, than flounder around out here and wait for events to take their course.

'Right, let's move out, then. Geordie, you've got the NVA so take the front and head on a direct southerly bearing. The rest follow on behind, two Minimis at the rear.'

FORWARD OPERATIONS BASE, AL JOUF, SAUDI / SPECIAL FORCES GROUP HQ, VICTOR, UAE

The Commanding Officer of 22 SAS strode into his FOB headquarters and made directly for the signals room. 'Get me Victor on the TACSAT,' he ordered the duty signaller, 'I need to speak to the Colonel ASAP.'

The signaller acknowledged the CO's directive and turned to the array of communications in front of him. Grasping one of a multitude of handsets, he quickly established secure voice comms with his opposite number at the SF War Operations base in UAE.

The link established, 'Afternoon, sir' was the sole formality passed as the CO opened the dialogue with his superior, the Colonel replying in kind. Dispensing with any further pleasantries, the CO moved straight to the point: 'We have a slight problem.'

'Oh, what's that, then?' the distant voice enquired, slightly delayed by the complicated uplink-downlink mechanics inherent in satellite communications.

'Bravo Two Zero: they've been compromised and are requesting immediate exfil.'

The silence that followed, whether a result of the enforced transmission delay or through deliberate consideration, continued for several seconds before the response was heard. 'I would have thought that's a bit premature, isn't it?'

'The Ops O made a similar conclusion, and I concur. B Squadron QRF [quick reaction force rescue team] have been stood down until further information comes to hand.'

'Well, then,' the Deputy Director interrupted, 'seems like the decision is out of our hands anyway. Keep me posted, won't you?'

The CO returned the handset to the signaller and moved off, ignorant of the fact that their routine operation evaluation of military circumstance had now been instantaneously elevated to something much more. In the space of a few short hours, a point of no return had been reached and passed, and decisions made that would irreversibly seal the fate of the eight men of Bravo Two Zero.

CHAPTER 6

IRAQ, EVENING DAY THREE, JANUARY 1991

Free of our cumbersome loads, we moved swiftly southward at a cracking pace, eager to rid ourselves of our unwanted pursuers. Metres turned into kilometres and the enemy vehicle lights were soon swallowed up by the darkness. Their search was a lost cause in the night that had come to our rescue, hiding our escape.

Confident that the Iraqis would have been unable to co-ordinate a suitable response to the south so soon, we drove ourselves on incessantly, stopping for a quick listening halt and Magellan check every 20 minutes or so. Just over an hour after setting off, I passed on to Andy the Magellan's information. 'The ERV is about 500 metres to our east. If we hang a left now, we should hit the wadi in a couple of minutes.'

'Cheers, Kiwi,' Andy replied.

Without halting the patrol, we changed direction and slowed to a more cautious speed. Approaching RVs was a dodgy procedure at the best of times, let alone under conditions such as these. Within minutes we were at the edge of the wadi once more, having checked the ground around and satisfied ourselves that it was devoid of enemy.

'It's 2210 hours,' Vince stated. 'I reckon that we are better off heading on south to the secondary RV. It's a safer option than hanging around here. Ten clicks is nothing in this terrain, the contact point is still too close.'

The secondary RV was a further 15 kilometres to the south and, although we had never seen it, it was a recognisable feature on the map, shown as a point where a number of large wadis met.

'Yeah,' Andy agreed. 'I don't feel too comfortable with this location now, either. By the time we make the secondary, it will be midnight and there should be no reason that the chopper ain't there. He knows to fly over both RV points.'

'Geordie, give your TACBE a blast here. You never know, we might have been in a dead spot earlier.'

The patrol settled down in all-round defence and waited patiently as Geordie tried to call in AWACS. But our trust in that particular piece of kit was fast becoming non-existent – it came as no surprise that there was yet again no reply.

'Fuck 'em,' Andy cursed, 'I'm going to kill somebody over this when we get back. C'mon, let's move out.'

Once again, we began the trek south. At the very least, it felt good to be doing something for ourselves, to be making proactive decisions. It kept the nagging doubts at bay.

The secondary RV was reached in good time, well before midnight. Following the same routine as before, we closed in and, once the security of the area had been established, settled down to wait for our aircraft.

An hour later, everyone was starting to feel very uncomfortable.

'Where the fuck is that chopper?' Bob whispered to me as we lay against the slope of the wadi, watching the desert plain about us.

'Tell me about it. How long can we afford to wait?'

A low whistle interrupted our discussion, obviously someone else was having the same thoughts.

'This is shit!' Geordie spat out. 'What the fuck is going on back there?'

There seemed to be no logical explanation as to why the heli hadn't arrived, especially as now it was approaching one o'clock in the morning.

'Andy,' I said, 'the longer we sit and wait here, the less distance we can put between ourselves and the contact point. It's going to be light in a few hours' time, and I don't fancy being just 25 clicks away.'

'This place will be crawling with ragheads at first light,' Dinger continued. 'Maybe the chopper got shot down or something. Fuck knows, but it's time to head for Syria.'

I could see that Andy was racked by indecision: stay and hope the chopper would turn up, leaving us in a severely vulnerable position if it didn't; or cut our losses now, and make for the Iraqi–Syrian border some 200 kilometres distant.

It was one thing to talk about E & E, even to formulate a plan to cover that eventuality, but to actually have to carry it out was something else altogether. Once you headed down that route, you really were on your own.

'Andy, that chopper isn't coming, mate,' Mal quietly prompted. 'Let's go.'

Andy nodded his head in agreement and we shook ourselves out ready to move. 'Geordie, you've got the front.'

'We'll head west for ten clicks, then box back north. I want to be well over that MSR by first light. Five-minute halt every hour. Questions?' There were none. 'Let's do it, then.'

If our pace was fast before, it was positively racing now. Our single-minded purpose was to get as much distance between ourselves and where we perceived the Iraqi troops to be concentrated.

By 'boxing' our route, we hoped to throw our pursuers off the trail, though I doubted they would be expecting us to head for Syria anyway. But even heading those necessary few kilometres west was a cause for concern, burning up precious time that could have been spent reducing the scores of kilometres that stretched out to the northern border.

The ground we were covering now was a complete contrast to what we had been used to. A warren of steep wadis, rock-strewn plains and the odd steep falaise made it good country to hide in, but unfortunately, that was not our aim. We were still within easy striking distance of the enemy, and no doubt this ground would come immediately to their attention.

'That's ten clicks,' I passed on up the line to Andy.

'OK. Take five.'

I took the opportunity to rest, as I felt as if I had been on the go non-stop for days. Taking my water bottle from its pouch, I began to quench my thirst when suddenly it dawned on me that the three half-litre water bottles I was carrying were the sum total of all the water available to me for the foreseeable future. My gulp immediately turned into a small sip; the body could go weeks without food, but water was a different matter entirely, and we were a long way away from an accessible water supply point.

Without warning, the distant eastern night sky was lit up for all to see, as if some great explosion had occurred, followed closely by a bright fireball that tracked upwards into the heavens at a terrific speed.

'Fucking get a load of that,' Bob whispered in awe. 'That's got to be a Scud, eh?'

'Yeah, well, fat lot of use that does us now,' Geordie answered. 'We couldn't have reported it anyway. You need radios that work to do that.'

The bitterness in Geordie's voice was there for all to hear and was something we all felt. But those were the cards we had been dealt – nothing could change them now.

'C'mon, then, let's get going. Four hours left till first light, and we've got plenty of ground to cover.'

We saw another two launches that night, proof that although we had been given a shit brief on almost all aspects of this mission, at least they had got one thing right, we were in the middle of 'Scud Alley'.

The patrol assumed its formation once more and we quickly hit our stride, moving rapidly across the blackened landscape, ever northwards, towards Syria.

However, another half-hour later, the pace began to slow considerably and Mal was beginning to falter. Geordie called a halt, concerned at Mal's lack of co-ordination. The patrol took up a defensive posture with Mal and Geordie in the centre.

'What's up, mate?' said Andy, as Geordie hovered over Mal's heavily breathing form.

'I think he's suffering from heat exhaustion,' Geordie replied. 'The forced tab, his layered clothing, including thermals, coupled with lack of fluids, is sending his temperature through the roof.'

Without being asked, Bob handed one of his precious water bottles to Mal, saying, 'It's got rehydrate in it.'

Mal downed the contents in seconds.

'We'll take 20 minutes out here, give Mal a chance to recover, then press on,' said Andy. 'When we kick off again, drop the pace a bit, Geordie.'

We were all very tired now, the toll of the last few days – and the last few hours in particular – beginning to take hold, but rest wasn't a luxury we could afford. Time wasn't on our side.

As it was, ten minutes later Mel felt strong enough to carry on once more. 'Let's get on with it, guys. I'm good to go now.'

The patrol shook out again, Mal immediately behind Geordie so he could set the pace.

Taking up the position of tail-end charlie, I kept sweeping the area to our rear, ever mindful that a set of headlights could appear from nowhere at any minute. Not long into our new direction, I noticed figure-of-eight vapour trails in the sky to our south-east, the signature of a jet maintaining a holding pattern while waiting its turn to begin an attack run-in.

'Bob,' I hissed urgently, 'get Andy to halt.'

Bob nodded his reply and passed the message up the line.

Andy came towards me at a steady trot. 'What's the matter?' he asked, his head darting from side to side, looking for the unseen threat.

'Look up there.' His eyes turned to where I was pointing. 'There are jets over there in a holding pattern.'

'Yeah, so what?'

'Well, they're no more than 70 clicks away. You'll be able to get them on the fucking TACBE, won't you!'

I could see the realisation twig in his face, and he immediately put down his M16 and wrestled open a pouch.

Crump, crump. The pounding of 1,000-lb bombs impacting on their intended target could be heard in the distance now, their huge flashes lighting up the sky temporarily.

'Hello FGA call sign, hello FGA call sign, this is Bravo Two Zero calling on Turbo. Do you read, over?'

We both listened intently to the steady hiss of static, almost begging it to talk to us. Silence.

Andy tried again. 'Hello FGA call sign, this is Bravo Two Zero calling on Turbo, do you read, over?'

'Bravo Two Zero this is FGA, you are very weak, over.' A glorious-sounding Texas drawl answered back.

'Fucking yes!' I punched the air with delight. At last, help was at hand.

Andy could barely keep the excitement out of his voice, gone was the whisper. 'FGA this is Bravo Two Zero on Turbo. We are British Special Forces and require immediate assistance, over.' He shouted into the small hand-held set.

'Acknowledge Turbo, you are breaking up, repeat your me . . .' the pilot's voice broke off.

'Turn north, turn north!' Andy was nearly screaming now. 'Hello FGA, do you read, do you read?' The deathly hiss of white noise returned, our call unanswered and, more importantly, the vapour trails had disappeared along with it.

'FGA, FGA do you read, over?'

'Andy, look, mate. He will report the contact, either now or on his return to base. Either way, CSAR and AWACS should be alerted.'

'Yeah, fucking great! We'll be out of here in no time. C'mon, let's tell the others.'

We turned north again expecting to see the rest of the patrol, but there was just bare desert and blackness.

'Fucking hell,' I said. 'Where are the others?'

We quickly began to advance on our original track, and found Bob after about 20 metres, then Dinger and Legs, all kneeling waiting for us. But that was where the line ended. There was no sign of Geordie, Mal or Vince.

'Where the fuck are the others?' Andy demanded immediately, directing the question at nobody in particular. 'I passed on to Geordie to wait up.'

The question didn't need answering, it was plain for everyone to see. A combination of fatigue, poor passage of information and the pitch-black desert night had all contributed to split our patrol. All we could hope for was that Geordie and the others were laid up somewhere just ahead, waiting for us to catch up.

Andy retrieved his TACBE once more, at the same time ordering us into extended line as we moved forward.

'Chris, Chris, this is Andy, over?' Silence.

We continued north in that fashion for half an hour before coming up against a small falaise, its silhouette stretching as far as the eye could see in both directions.

'Fuck!' Dinger cursed, 'they could have taken any route from here.'

Andy tried the TACBE one last time, but the result was the same. We were now well and truly separated from each other.

The five of us got together and took stock of the situation.

'We've two hours left till first light,' Andy began. 'I say we cut our losses here and head north at full speed. We haven't even crossed the MSR yet.'

Andy was right, although none of us wanted to admit it. We couldn't afford to keep dragging our heels this side of the MSR in the hope that we would meet up with the others again. Time was running short. I looked across at Dinger and could see that he was gutted, as we all were. A lot of things had gone wrong on this mission, but this was one that was definitely down to us, no excuses.

'Maybe we'll cross their path somewhere along the way,' he answered quietly. 'They should still be heading north.'

'That's right,' Andy finished, 'so let's get a fucking move on, then!'

Any elation we had felt at having contacted the aircraft was long gone, in fact I don't know if the news even made an impression on the others when they heard it. As we moved off once more, I couldn't help but think, 'Is there anything else that can go wrong now?' It wouldn't be long before I had my answer.

Not long after negotiating the falaise, we struck the MSR, its collection of rutted tracks only a couple of hundred metres across at this point. We were keen to strike out across it straightaway, but the high ground on the other side made us wary. The ground was not that much dissimilar to another piece of desert a little further east.

'Shit!' Andy suddenly cursed. 'Geordie's got the Kite sight.'

I had forgotten all about the night vision aid until now, and suddenly its importance, and the fact that we didn't possess one, struck home. That one piece of equipment could mean the difference between a good decision and a disastrous one, particularly with the limited ambient light about at night.

'Well, we can't hang about here all night,' Dinger whispered, eyeing the hill in front suspiciously as well. 'Just have to chance it.'

'Right, well, I'm not going to dawdle over there. The sooner we're on the other side, the better.'

The decision made, we raced across the series of tracks, bodies braced and weapons at the ready, almost convinced that a hail of bullets would be coming our way at any second. To our relief, this was not the case, and the MSR was negotiated without incident, enabling us to carry on past the small ridge and onto the plain beyond.

A couple of kilometres beyond the MSR we came across a two-metre deep dry concrete canal that ran generally east to west as far as the eye could see.

'What the hell is this doing here?' I asked in dismay, unable to fathom why there would be such a structure out in the middle of the desert.

'Maybe it's part of some grand scheme to irrigate the desert, you know, like the Israelis do,' Bob answered, but he didn't seem that convinced either.

Turning west, we walked parallel to the canal for a few hundred metres till a suitable crossing point presented itself: a small concrete bridge. A large, culvert-style pipe big enough to provide cover for the five of us supported the bridge.

'What do you reckon?' Andy asked. 'It might be the best thing available, and it's light in an hour.'

'It's bloody close to the MSR, mate,' Dinger replied. 'I don't think we should chance it.'

Tired as we were, Dinger was right. It was a sorely tempting option, especially this late in the night, but that close to the MSR, we would be asking for trouble.

'OK, then,' Andy continued, 'but we better find something before first light. I don't fancy being visible around here when the sun comes up.'

Trudging on ever northwards, the pace began to slow considerably. At the same time the eastern sky was becoming uncomfortably lighter; our ally was abandoning us as the early morning sun approached.

Desperately we scanned the ground ahead, urging the half-light to unveil a suitable hiding place that would keep us out of harm's way and hidden from prying eyes.

The night finally relinquished its grip and in doing so allowed the ground to unfold about us. To the west, no more than a kilometre distant, a group of small gravel knolls caught our attention, offering themselves up as prospective hosts. By the time we reached the outlying mounds, the dull morning sun was well and truly up, but thankfully, we were now amongst this strange collection of meandering hillocks, the largest of which was no more than 15 metres in height.

One offered what appeared to be some semblance of cover from view. Insignificant amongst its neighbours, it blended in nicely with the hills about it. More importantly, it had a partial rock wall no more than a third of a metre high on one side. We weren't in a position to be choosy; it was the best we were going to get.

A strong wind was beginning to blow as we climbed the gentle slope that led to the crest, our fatigued bodies screaming out for rest. I flopped down next to the small wall, Bob doing likewise next to me.

'I am knackered,' I said wearily. 'I feel like I could sleep for a year.'

'Me, too, mate. I think I'm going to have to retire after this lot.'

Andy sat himself on the other side of me. 'Can you get us a fix, Mike?'

'Yeah, sure, mate, give me a minute.'

The wind was really picking up now, and the already grey sky was beginning to look decidedly black. Bob said, 'You don't think it's going to rain, do you?'

I glanced up from the Magellan screen briefly, 'I don't know, mate. I would have thought it was unusual to have rain in the desert, but the way our luck is going, it wouldn't surprise me in the least.'

The latitude and longitude finally displayed on the LCD, allowing me to plot our position. 'Bloody hell, we covered some kilometres last night,' I said to no one in particular.

Pointing our position out to Andy, I continued, 'Reckon we tabbed about 75 clicks in total last night. It's amazing what you can do when someone is trying to put a 7.62 up your arse, isn't it?'

'That puts us 20-odd clicks north of the MSR. That's not too bad, I can live with that.'

'Close in, lads.' Andy briefed the remainder on our position then added the routine for our stay here. 'One-hour stags, all right? I'll start. Rest of you get some sleep. If we are lucky, that jet pilot will have reported in by now, and we could have a CSAR mission on the way today, so when you're on stag, listen out for any aircraft.'

From our perch on top of the knoll, we had a reasonable view of the surrounding desert, which would allow ample warning if anyone approached.

'What's that?' I nudged Dinger and pointed to the north-west.

Dinger regarded the thing with equal interest. 'Fucked if I know.'

Some 400 metres away we could see a large, rusty-brown metal object, cylindrical in shape on the desert floor, the top of its coned roof nearly five metres in height.

'Maybe it's a marker of some sort.'

'Don't worry about it, Kiwi, there aren't hordes of Iraqis in it and that is all that matters at the moment. Here, have a sip of this.'

Dinger had made a brew of sweet, hot tea on his mini cooker hexiblock. Between the five of us, the brew was polished off in no time and reality descended upon us once more.

Sitting down with my Minimi across my knees, I examined the underslung plastic container that had originally housed 200 rounds of linked 5.56 ammunition. The high cyclic rate of fire produced by the weapon was such that the short burst of fire I had returned in our contact had reduced that initial store of rounds by a third. The two other spare containers of ammunition were in my bergen, which, at this very moment, was probably being examined by Iraqi intelligence.

I had a quick vision of some intelligence officer sifting through my kit, expecting to find all sorts of secret equipment and codes and, to his surprise, coming across my stash of chocolate bars. I am a bit of a chocoholic and had packed 20 Yorkie bars for the mission. The thought of those bars of chocolate in somebody else's hands while I had none was most depressing.

Within half an hour of settling down in the LUP, I knew that sleep would be impossible. The frantic activity of the night before had hidden a menace that we all knew existed but had forgotten in our bid to escape the enemy forces. Now, as we tried to relax and our metabolisms calmed down, that threat emerged once more as icy cold penetrated our inadequate clothing and chilled us to the bone. My body was screaming for sleep but the uncontrollable fits of shivering that racked it prevented any chance of that occurring. I tried to wedge myself in against the low makeshift wall, something that had been built by a nomadic shepherd perhaps, but it was so small that a third of my body was left exposed, victim to the biting wind that swirled about.

All I had to protect me from the elements was my desert cams and a standard army-issue woollen jersey. My other kit was still packed away in the bergen. Sitting up, I stripped my jersey and shirt off, reversing their order so the wool of the jumper was next to my skin. It wasn't much better but it was a slight improvement. The shivering didn't decrease, however; if anything, it became progressively worse. I looked over towards Bob and saw that he was in much the same condition. In fact, everyone was.

'Fuck this,' I thought to myself. 'Time to stop acting hard and get some shared bodily warmth before we all go down with exposure.'

I jealously eyed Andy's thick duvet jacket. I hadn't noticed it before but I sure as hell did now. No one else had anything even remotely resembling it, but even that wasn't enough to cope with the freezing temperatures.

'Oi, Andy,' I whispered across, 'I think we should all lie together. In these conditions, it won't be long before somebody starts going down otherwise.'

I suspect that I had simply said aloud what everyone else had been thinking but were too embarrassed to say, for, without hesitation, we all grouped together and the benefits were noticeable immediately.

'Good idea,' Andy said. 'The guys on the ends are more exposed than the other three, so we'll rotate those on the outside each hour, combine it with the stag.'

Finally, fitful bouts of sleep were able to take effect, the odd twenty minutes here, five minutes there, not a lot, but it was a vast improvement on nothing.

The day dragged on endlessly, one of us always alert for any danger, the remainder trying to rest as much as possible, but nature still had another card up her sleeve, and just after midday she decided to play it.

The temperature had been plummeting all morning, just as the dark clouds above had hinted at rain almost since first light, but none of this prepared us for the driving storm that followed. It seemed to come out of nowhere, small specks at first that could have been mistaken for rain were soon followed by larger flakes that very quickly turned into a blizzard.

'I don't fucking believe this,' Legs groaned. 'Since when does it fucking snow in the desert?'

Within minutes the entire landscape was awash in a white torrent that obscured everything from view. The freshly fallen snow that settled on our clothing built up in such quantities that it had no chance to melt, simply covering our forms from head to toe in a frozen blanket.

We lay together like sardines packed in a can, trying as best we could to keep the weather off us. If it was your turn to be one of the unlucky ones on the outside of the pack, the minutes dragged like hours as the remorseless snow, wind and cold hacked at those parts of you that were exposed.

By four o'clock in the afternoon, the patrol had turned into one great shivering mass, the conditions exacting a horrendous toll.

Bob was the first to speak up. 'Listen up, Andy,' he began, 'I can't stay here like this. This fucking cold is killing me. I think we're better off to be on the move, try and get some blood circulating and warm ourselves up a bit. What do you think?'

I was on the outside at this stage and shivering like a pneumatic drill. 'Fucking A,' I said, agreeing with Bob. 'Someone is definitely going to get exposure if we carry on like this. Let's bugger off.'

The others mumbled their agreement, anything had to be better than this.

'OK, then,' Andy agreed, 'no one can see us in this shit anyway.'

I stood up and stumbled in the process, my frozen limbs refusing to co-operate. The others were in much the same state, staggering about like a bunch of drunks as they tried desperately to regain their co-ordination and balance.

'Get down!' Legs suddenly yelled. No sooner had we risen than we were on the deck again, crawling to the side of the rock wall in an attempt to conceal ourselves further. I could hear the roar of diesel engines now, closely followed by the clatter of tracks as two APCs came into view, each towing a small trailer.

'Jesus, they're coming straight for us,' Andy shouted. 'They must have clocked us.'

'Shit, I'm too fucking cold for a contact,' I said to no one in particular, as my numbed fingers struggled to set the Minimi in place, the others doing likewise either side of me.

The APCs were no more than 100 metres from us when the lead vehicle suddenly switched direction to the right and headed straight for the metal object to our east, closely followed by its number two.

Side on, the two vehicles passed no more than 50 metres from our position, hatches securely battened down, oblivious to our presence. On reaching the marker, once again they altered direction slightly, then carried on off towards the north-east, soon invisible as the snow closed in and hid them from our view.

'Well, if that thing isn't the strangest looking trig point I have ever seen,' Dinger said once they were out of sight, releasing the tension of the moment. 'I definitely think it is time we got the fuck out of here.'

Once again we struggled to our feet, now a lot keener to leave this place and distance ourselves from what appeared to be a route checkpoint for vehicles crossing the desert. Who knows what could have turned up on our doorstep.

Although it was still late afternoon, the driving snow provided almost as much cover as the night, allowing us to move freely towards the north. Slowly at first, we made our way through the incessant blizzard, ever towards the border that we estimated was now probably three nights' march away. Initially we set a good pace, the feeling of warmth generated by our activity taking the sting out of the worst of the conditions and giving our morale a much-needed boost. But the reprieve from the bitter cold was short-lived, the exertion of walking offering only an impression of warmth. The reality of the situation was that neither lying exposed on the hilltop nor walking headlong into this tempest was doing us any good.

Day soon passed into night, with no sign of any let-up in the weather. If anything, the setting sun only made the situation worse; whatever pathetic amount of heat it had been radiating on this godforsaken place was now lost completely, hidden beneath the horizon. To make matters worse, something that appeared almost impossible at this stage, the storm was coming from the north, forcing us to walk headlong into the teeth of it.

The longer the night went on, the more bedraggled and weary we became. Now no longer even looking like a patrol, the five of us were strung out over 50 or 60 metres, stumbling on hunched up against the elements, the snow having now turned to sleet. Oblivious to all about us, very soon we would lose someone again, or worse, succumb to the effects of exposure.

Up front, leading the way into the onslaught, Dinger stopped and turned his back to the weather. 'Andy, I think it's time we looked for some shelter, this is ridiculous.'

'Well, where the fuck are we going to find shelter from this shit?' Andy yelled back, trying to make himself heard over the howling wind.

The rest of us caught up, all now soaked to the skin, our meagre clothing no match for what was being thrown at us. This route had only one outcome: hypothermia, and I knew if we continued along it I would soon succumb. I was so cold my brain had virtually switched off, shutting down all but the most necessary of functions and almost turning me into an automaton.

'I don't know about the rest of you,' I said, 'but the wind chill is cutting right through me. At this rate, we'll all be shot by morning.'

'Mike's right, Andy,' Bob added. 'We haven't got the kit to stay out in weather like this, it would still be bad even if we did.'

'What about that small ditch we passed an hour or so ago?' Dinger continued. 'At the very least, we can get out of the wind.'

This was the crux of our problem. The terrain we were passing through was so open and exposed that it allowed the elements to batter us unhindered without chance of a respite. If we kept on moving north, we might not find a piece of cover for hours. At least we knew the ground that we had already covered and that there was some form of shelter, be it quite a way back, to be found.

Andy didn't take much convincing. Even his clothing wasn't coping too well with these conditions.

'C'mon, then, let's find that ditch.'

It was soul-destroying to have to turn back and retrace our steps: those few kilometres gained had been won at quite a cost. The only solace that we could take from our retreat was that the minute we turned our back, the storm became instantly more bearable. We relocated the trench, no more than a metre deep, within half an hour. The relief was almost instantaneous as the five of us gratefully took refuge inside its shallow walls and left the storm to blow itself out on the open desert above.

My 'non-Northern Hemisphere' physique was taking a pounding in these Arctic-like conditions, so Bob and Legs spent a couple of minutes briskly rubbing me down, trying to generate some heat through my sodden clothing. It didn't do much good, but everyone was well aware of the need to keep an eye on one another.

Dinger produced that magical little tin cooker once more, and within minutes had a steaming cup of sickly sweet black tea on the go. As the mug was passed about, the change in morale was obvious, the odd laugh escaping and quip exchanged; it was something we all needed.

'Come on, then, Andy, you good bloke,' Legs whispered, 'got superglue on your fingers or what?'

Andy passed the mug on to Legs. 'Yeah, and that goes for you as well!' the next in line added.

Feeling much improved, I pulled out a sachet of mixed fruit from my pouch. I had enough in my webbing to keep me going for a good week or so; it was the water that would be the problem.

'Bob, pass this around,' I said between chomps of peach and syrup.

'Regular picnic we've got now, isn't it?'

To this day I find it remarkable that, amidst this hardship and stress, the simple act of drinking a hot cup of tea could have such a profound effect on our emotions and thinking. For a few important minutes, all our problems were forgotten and the situation didn't appear so bad.

Bob brought us back to reality, though. 'I wonder how Geordie, Mal and Vince are getting on?'

'Yeah,' Legs added, 'I hope they got themselves out of this shit.'

It would be two months before we found out the answer to that question, an answer that none of us at the time would have liked to have contemplated.

Geordie, Mal and Vince were caught in the onslaught that day and night. During the evening, at the height of the blizzard, Vince became separated from the other two, and despite their efforts to find him, never reappeared. Vince's frozen body, dead from exposure, was found by the Iraqis some days later. Bravo Two Zero had lost its first member, and two more were soon to follow.

CHAPTER 7

IRAQ, DAY FOUR, JANUARY 1991

By four in the morning, the storm had finally blown itself out and we pressed on towards the north. Although the wind-chill factor was still present, the conditions were considerably more favourable than earlier, aided by the fact that the landscape finally began to change. The flat, exposed desert gave way to more diverse features, wadis and hills, all of which helped to break up the weather.

Just before dawn, we hit the main Baghdad-to-Syria trunk route and took a position in a shallow wadi approximately one kilometre away to both lie up and observe the road.

Two TACBEs remained between the five of us, and we alternated the calls on these to conserve their battery life for as long as possible, settling for an attempt every 12 hours. None was ever answered. This constant lack of communication with AWACS was something that none of us could get to grips with. If we hadn't made contact with the jet pilot the day before, we could have put it down to faulty handsets or something similar. But the fact that we had made contact proved that at least one of the radios worked, so why was there no reply from AWACS? It would be months before we had the answer to that question.

No sooner had the day begun than a steady stream of civilian traffic began to cruise up and down the highway, seemingly oblivious to all that was occurring elsewhere in the country.

'It seems like everyone out here owns a four-wheel-drive,' Andy said, watching the passing traffic. 'Could do with one of those right now. We'd be over the border in a couple of hours. Hoof it straight across the desert, no one would even spot us.'

'And how the fuck would we stop one without shooting the hell out of it?' Bob asked. 'They must be tanking along that road at about 80 to 100 miles an hour. You know what Arab drivers are like.'

'Yeah,' I butted in, 'that would look good on your headstone. Killed in an RTA 400 clicks behind enemy lines.'

'Well, don't forget, it's still about 150 clicks to the border. How many more nights like the last one do you think you can handle?'

Andy was right in that respect: another 24 hours even half as bad as the last and there probably wouldn't be many of us left standing. The seed had been planted now, and already Andy was formulating a plan. He had seen our ticket out of here; it was just a matter of working out how to get on board.

The day dragged on and on incessantly, the constant shivering of our frozen bodies prolonging its monotony. Ironically, though, we were in a catch-22 situation. We needed the night to arrive so the march could continue unseen, yet the thought of the unrelenting cold that would accompany the setting sun made the day all the more desirable. But there was no way we could afford to move in daylight; the risks were too great. We were losers either way. What little warmth the sun was providing did have one benefit, however: it gave our sodden clothing the opportunity to dry. That in itself could prove to be a life-saver against the biting night wind.

Towards late afternoon lady luck threw another spanner in the works, deciding that things were obviously a little too cushy for us at the moment. We were half-dozing, as much as the conditions would allow, when Legs kicked everyone awake.

'Get the fuck up!' he whispered vehemently. 'We've got another fucking goatherder coming this way!'

The moans were unanimous, 'You have got to be joking.' But unfortunately, that wasn't the case. Already the clink and jangle of bells could be easily heard. We pressed ourselves into the sides of the wadi, trying to make as small a profile as possible.

'Chances are he'll walk right by us,' Dinger began. 'This wadi twists and turns all over the place, we might get away with it.'

I looked around. We were hunted men now, and in the daylight it showed on all our faces. Three knives were drawn, mine included. If the shepherd was unfortunate enough to stumble upon us, I didn't think he would be long for this world.

There was a stretch of about ten straight metres along this particular part of the wadi that we were cached in, and the odds were pretty good that he would not see us, that was until four of his goats decided to join our gang.

Within minutes, a wizened old Bedouin, 80-odd if a day, draped in a thick, completely black dish-dash (Arab robe), was standing over us, not an ounce of emotion on his face. Suddenly a wide, toothless grin broke out and he began to babble in some completely foreign tongue that didn't even resemble Arabic. Almost guiltily, I sheathed my knife. I wasn't going to top the old boy, and I suspected no one else would either.

'This guy has got the whole of the Iraqi desert to use,' I started, 'and he has to walk straight to this ten-metre piece of wadi. The whole of the Republican Guard couldn't have done a better job of finding us!'

'Well, what are we going to do with him?' Bob asked. 'There's no point in killing him.'

'*Hadj*, where's the souk? Souk?' Andy babbled back at the old man, 'hadj' being a respectful Arab term for someone of advanced years.

Pointing to the south, the Bedouin rattled off some incomprehensible words at a hundred miles an hour, 'souk' appearing in the monologue every now and then.

'Fucking good one, Andy,' Dinger laughed. 'He's going to tell us where we can go and buy a couple of chickens and some sheep.'

The old boy was in no hurry to move on, quite content to stay there squatting at the edge of the wadi, chatting to his strange, newly found companions. Once again pointing to the south, he began making signs with his hands and noises that I can only assume were referring to warplanes and bombing raids, putting his hands to his ears at the same time and shaking his head. It would have looked quite bizarre to an onlooker, an Arab squatting at the side of a wadi having an animated conversation with either himself or his goats. But this is how we continued for about ten minutes, the five of us listening to his non-stop lecture before he at last stood up, raised his palms to the sky and said, '*Insha-Allah*' (if God wills it).

With that, he strode off to the north after his still-rambling goats that had moved on long since, well-bored with our company.

As we watched the hadj's tiny form disappear amongst the peaks and troughs of the desert, I felt a wave of relief that none of us had felt it necessary to kill him. Topping innocent civilians wasn't something I had equated with life in the SAS, and by the time that he had found someone willing enough to listen to his incredible story, without thinking that he had partaken of a little too much hashish, we would be long gone.

'What do we do now?' Bob asked, as the clinks of the goat bells were finally lost in the distance.

Andy glanced at his watch. 'Still an hour till last light. What do you reckon, chance it?'

Replying first, I answered, 'We have to assume that somewhere along the way the old boy will tell his tale, so getting any sort of distance between us and this position, even in daylight, has got to be a priority.'

'There's a reasonable amount of cover about as well,' Dinger added. 'So we can probably get away with it till sunset.'

'OK, then, I'll give the TACBE another try, then we'll move out. You take the front, Dinger, and keep us amongst these wadis.'

Dinger and the rest of us nodded our agreement as Andy set about trying the 12-hourly radio check on the TACBE, though by now our scepticism was such that we didn't even bother to listen to his calls.

'Hello any call sign, this is Bravo Two Zero transmitting on Turbo. Do you read, over?' Not only had we given up on trying to contact AWACS direct, but now we were opening our call up to any station that might be listening on the emergency frequency in the hope that someone, somewhere, would be able to assist us.

'Fucking useless.' Andy threw the TACBE back into his pouch, no longer even attempting to double up the call. 'Let's go.'

Taking a generally northern track, we headed off into the desert once more, feeling a little more comfortable and secure with our current surroundings. The undulating terrain about us provided good cover from view most of the time and allowed a freedom of movement we had not experienced thus far.

Twenty to thirty minutes out from the LUP, we received a shock that dispersed any illusions we may have been harbouring about our position. Bob, as tail-end charlie, noticed the vehicles first.

'Fucking hell! Oi, two four-tonners have just pulled off the road to the south, in the area of our LUP!'

It was about 1,500 metres from our current location to the point where we had rested up, and at that distance, the two drab olive green trucks were easily recognisable, along with their cargo.

Without panicking, the patrol went to ground. There was plenty of cover about.

'What do you reckon?' Andy asked, screwing his eyes in concentration as he tried to count the enemy forces disembarking from the vehicles.

'Thirty to forty, I would say,' Dinger replied. 'Not very good odds.'

'Well, that's nothing new on this job, is it?' Legs added. 'Somebody definitely doesn't like us.'

'It's strange,' I began, 'the trucks came from the south, but old Hadj went northwards off into the desert.'

'Yeah, well, he obviously went off and told some fucking soldiers straightaway, didn't he?' Andy replied, the frustration clearly showing in his voice. 'There's no way we can carry on. We'll have to wait till the sun buggers off.'

Watching the scores of diminutive figures jumping from the vehicles, I knew that this was severely bad news. In theory, the Iraqi troops should have thought that we were southbound, but this event put paid to that idea. The tension was back amongst us greater than ever before; we could almost feel the jaws of the trap closing in around us.

'That's it,' Andy suddenly said. 'We're going to hijack a vehicle.'

'Andy,' Dinger answered, 'we've already been through that. How are you going to stop one? If you go shooting up the road, that lot will be on us in a minute.'

'Listen, we do the wounded man routine. Two of us on the road, one looking really injured, wave down a vehicle. With our shamags on, at night, they won't notice till it's too late. Then the rest come out from hiding at the side of the road and Bob's your uncle, we've got a four-by-four. It's simple.'

'I don't like it,' Bob said. 'There are too many things that could go wrong. For a start, what if the vehicle doesn't stop and carries straight on to the nearest police or army checkpoint?'

'What if it doesn't stop and hits you?' I added.

'For fuck's sake, look at our situation, will you! We're all half done-in from the cold, we're running out of water and we've got 40 fucking ragheads searching for us less than a kilometre away! One of you lot come up with a better suggestion.'

Nobody spoke. When you put it like that, we certainly were up shit creek without a paddle.

'Good,' Andy carried on. 'It's sorted, then. Bob, you and I will do the stage act. We're the two smallest and pose the least likely threat. Dinger, you take Mike, Legs and yourself and set up an ambush position whereby you can react the minute the vehicle stops. All right?' Andy scanned all our faces intently. 'Come on, then, let's get going.'

I might not have been the most experienced member in the group, but even I knew that this route was fraught with danger. We were stepping outside the bounds of our training now, taking an almighty gamble in order to break out of the increasingly dire situation we were finding ourselves in. 'Desperate men seek desperate solutions' was a saying that came to mind. Funnily enough, I had not thought of our situation in those terms up until that moment, but when you took all the facts and evidence lined up against us, the odds were not good. Desperate was probably an apt description.

As soon as the light began to fade, the patrol made its way down towards the road, all the time keeping a wary eye on the area where we knew that the enemy was searching. Andy dropped back to walk beside me as we patrolled towards the road.

'Have you ever thought about dying?' he asked out of the blue. 'I mean, does it worry you?'

I looked at him for a minute, taken completely by surprise at this line of questioning. 'It's not something I have ever really considered, mate,' was all the response I could muster.

'I think about it. You know, I've got a little girl.' So the conversation continued for the next ten minutes, Andy telling me how he wanted to make sure if anything happened that his daughter was looked after right. I knew then that he wasn't convinced this course of action was the best, either.

Walking with Andy as he unloaded his story, it suddenly dawned on me what a huge strain the guys with families must be under, wives and children at home with no knowledge whatsoever of the danger that their husbands or daddies were in. I had only just started out with my girlfriend, Sue, and so didn't have the same level of commitment back home. It must have taken an enormous amount of courage just to get on the chopper and start the mission, not knowing whether you would see your loved ones again. I was fast learning the realities of war, and it most certainly wasn't a great big adventure.

* * *

It was dark by the time we reached the road, and, more worryingly, we hadn't seen a vehicle go by for quite some time.

'How the hell are we going to know what type of car we're stopping?' Dinger asked. 'All you will be able to see is a set of headlights screaming down the road.'

'Look, big round headlights, it's a truck and we ignore it. Small round headlights, it's a car or something and we stop it, OK?' Andy wanted to get on with it.

We found a suitable spot in no time and split ourselves into the respective groupings, then settled down to wait. Surprisingly, a set of headlights appeared from the north within minutes, visible for kilometres on the long straight stretch of road.

'This is it,' Andy said, wrapping his shamag about his face and head. 'Bob, you lean on me like you're hurt, and when the vehicle draws near, lie on the ground, OK? It will put the driver more at ease.'

Andy and Bob left their weapons behind in the small wadi that the remainder of us were cached in and made their way to the side of the highway. The vehicle was only a minute or so away now. With the beams starting to silhouette their shapes, Andy, with Bob hanging off him, walked out onto the road. The vehicle slowed, still indistinguishable due to the glare, and Andy let Bob fall to the ground. He waved his arms to signal the vehicle to stop, and, obligingly, it did. As soon as we heard the wheels grind to a halt, Dinger, Legs and I leapt from our hiding place and waylaid the vehicle, hoping the element of surprise would be enough to prevent the driver from taking off.

As I ran up to the car, I don't know who was more surprised: the fat, bearded driver, or me. We had just managed to hijack a huge bright yellow Dodge taxi, complete with five passengers.

'Get out of the car!' we all screamed at its occupants. 'Fucking move it!' The car's engine stalled as we raced up.

One by one the petrified passengers stumbled from the vehicle and were immediately shepherded off the road and into the wadi. The taxi driver himself was proving more of a problem. Obviously unwilling to abandon his pride and joy, he looked like he was going to try and make a run for it. I moved in as he reached for the key to restart the engine. Smashing the muzzle of the Minimi into the side of his head, I began to try dragging him out of the car, but he wouldn't move.

'Get the fuck out!' I yelled, prodding him again with the machine gun. He didn't need to understand English, the menacing threat of a soldier waving a weapon in your face is surely understood by everyone.

Sensing my patience was wearing thin, he started to manoeuvre himself clear of the vehicle and it became instantly apparent why I had not had any success doing it myself. He was so fat that the steering wheel was acting like an anchor wedging his obese stomach in place. When he finally freed himself, I herded him over to join the others.

'Now what do we do?' Bob asked. 'There's bloody six of them.'

One of the group was looking decidedly uneasy, and a closer inspection of him told me why.

'Hey, that bloke is wearing a uniform,' I pointed out. 'Looks like police or gendarme.'

Andy went rushing over and separated him from the rest, giving him a quick search at the same time. The policeman was absolutely terrified.

Pulling out a crucifix from around his neck, he began saying over and over 'Christian, Christian', obviously thinking that this would win him some Brownie points.

'We can use him as a guide. He can tell us where the troops are.'

'Andy,' Dinger said, 'he doesn't even speak English, he's shitting himself, how the fuck is that going to help us?'

'We're taking him, all right! Leave this lot,' he said, gesturing to the remaining Iraqis, then turned back to the vehicle. 'I'm driving, Mike and Bob, bring the copper.'

Bob, the copper and I jammed our way into the rear of the taxi while Andy, Legs and Dinger took the front. Starting the engine, Andy thrust the column change into first and threw the car into a U-turn. 'A hundred and twenty clicks to go. We'll be in Syria in an hour!' With that, Andy planted the accelerator and the taxi sped off northwards, leaving five dazed and bewildered former occupants by the side of the road.

AL JOUF, SAS FORWARD OPERATIONS BASE

The Operations Room was a hive of activity. Scores of signallers, intelligence reps and senior officers were moving about the confined space that was now the hub that directed the mission orders for over two squadrons of SAS soldiers.

'When was the last time you received a signal from Bravo Two Zero, then?' the Commanding Officer asked.

'About 48 hours ago,' OC B Squadron answered. 'It was broken but confirmed a compromise had occurred and asked for immediate exfil.'

'How in God's name were they able to deploy with the wrong frequencies?'

'We're looking into that, sir.'

'And what exactly did this message from the Americans say?'

The operations officer handed over a piece of message pad. 'The jet pilot forgot all about the radio message. He only remembered to file a report on it this afternoon.'

'But this report says he made contact with "Turbo" north of the MSR. Why are they heading north? All the regimental SOPs [standard operating procedures] we laid down for the squadrons specifically stated that any E & E was to be directed south towards the Saudi border. They are moving further away from the friendly forces.'

OC B cleared his throat uncomfortably. 'I told them to head for Syria, sir. It was much closer than the Saudi border.'

The CO eyed the officer coldly before continuing, 'This report states that the transmission occurred at 0215 hours, so that is still 40 hours ago approximately.' Turning to the ops officer he asked, 'Availability of Chinooks?'

'None of ours are free for another three days. D Squadron are the closest to that area and I have already informed them to be aware that Two Zero may be headed in their direction, but that appears to be unlikely now. As it is, both halves of D are over 150 clicks south-west of the original OP location. God knows how far away they are now. I could always try the Americans, see if they will send out a CSAR mission.'

'No, we'll clean up our own mess. Post Bravo Two Zero as MIA [missing in action]. Inform all ground call signs of the fact and also notify all our heli ops to monitor emergency frequencies when they are north of the Saudi border for any possible transmissions.'

'Next of kin?' the ops officer queried.

'No, we'll wait out on that one. I want to be 100 per cent sure that they are lost before informing the relatives. No point in worrying them unnecessarily.'

The CO turned to the huge operations map pinned to the wall, pins, tape, pen-lines indicating ongoing missions and group locations. Scanning the map, his eyes finally focused on Bravo Two Zero's marker, still in place next to the northern MSR, some 200-odd kilometres north-west of Baghdad.

'That's a hell of a walk to Syria, especially considering that there are no friendlies about to help. And what happens when and if they get there? We do not even know how the Syrians will react. They might just hand the patrol back to the Iraqis.'

Turning back to the two silent officers, he continued, 'Not an auspicious start to our campaign, is it? Let's hope they make it out in one piece.

'I had better go and inform the Colonel. I'm sure he will be extremely pleased. What a cock-up!'

With that, he departed, leaving his two sub-commanders to contemplate their next move.

It would be several days after the compromise message before a helicopter was able to be dispatched anywhere near the patrol's AO. But by then, the majority of the patrol was way beyond any help.

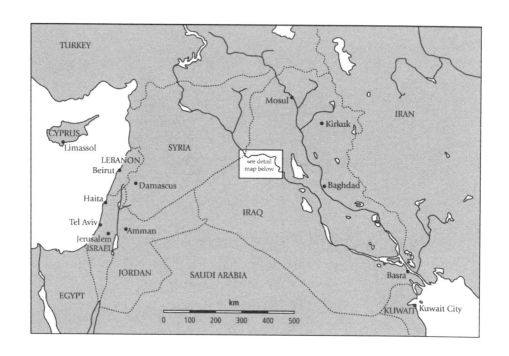

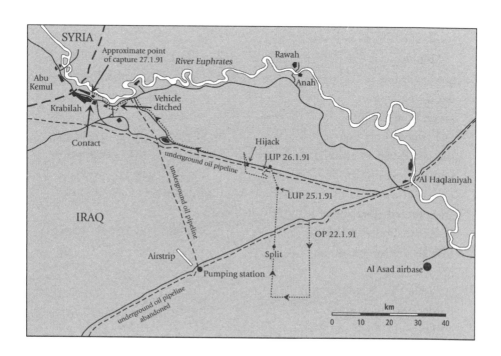

CHAPTER 8

IRAQ, EVENING DAY FOUR / DAY FIVE: THE LAST HOURS OF FREEDOM

The taxi had never been designed to carry six people, let alone five of them decked out in military paraphernalia, so consequently the space inside the vehicle was severely limited.

'This is more like it, isn't it, lads?' Andy was positively euphoric. 'Let's get the heater on.' He began to fiddle with a few of the buttons on the dash, and within no time a glorious blast of hot air was circulating around the cabin.

I removed my map and Magellan and began to sort out our position; the last thing we wanted to do was drive right up to the border post without realising it. Shining a torch beam along the highway route, I noticed the indicator for a track well to our north that left the main road and proceeded north-west towards the border.

'Andy, about 70 clicks from here there is a fork off to the left. We need to take that to get off this main road and take that track towards the border.'

'Yeah, OK, Kiwi,' he replied. 'Hey, ask our friend there what is at the border post, what kind of military.'

'How the fuck am I supposed to do that? He doesn't speak any English.'

'Just show him the map, make him understand.'

I turned to the Arab next to me, his eyes so huge that if they had increased in size any further I am sure they would literally have popped out of their sockets.

'This guy is shitting himself big style,' I said to Bob. 'We should have just left him with the others.'

'Yeah, well, it's too late now. He just had better behave himself and not do anything stupid.'

The policeman's head swivelled nervously between the two of us, understanding that he was the topic of conversation, but not knowing whether it was good or bad. Placing the map in front of him, I tried to show him what Andy wanted to know.

'Syria here.' I stabbed the map with my finger. 'Iraq here.' Repeating the gesture again. I traced my finger along the highway to the Iraqi–Syrian border. 'Soldiers, police, military?' I asked, my finger resting on the border.

He studied the map for a minute, then the realisation of what I was trying to say dawned on him, and he became very agitated. Babbling in Arabic, he broke in a couple of times with 'Soldiers, soldiers, many . . .' He then pretended to fire a rifle, all the while becoming more and more nervous. I think he could see himself going down in a hail of glory, a border shoot-out with a carload of crazy foreigners.

'It's OK,' I said, patting the guy on the arm, trying to calm him down a bit. The last thing we needed was this guy going berserk in the back of the car.

'Andy, I think he's trying to say that there are a shitload of troops on the border.' I would have expected nothing less.

'All right, all right. Got it.'

We had already done about ten clicks as I glanced down at the Magellan.

'I reckon in about 40 minutes you should start looking for that turning, mate.'

'Okay, Kiwi, don't worry.'

The heat inside the car was quite intense now, but after the last few days, that just made it all the more pleasurable. As the warmth relaxed our muscles, previously held rigid by the cold, we became increasingly sleepy. Within 20 minutes, heads were beginning to nod.

Although not asleep, I was definitely daydreaming when the car's change of direction brought me back to the land of the living. The road had finally broken its steady straight north-westerly track, veering 20 or so degrees to the right to head basically north.

Peering out the left-hand window, I was immediately alarmed to see the route that we needed to take flash past with no discernible decrease in the vehicle's speed.

'Andy,' I started, 'that's the track we need to take.'

'Don't worry about it,' he replied in a voice that would obviously not brook any argument. 'We're going to carry on up here, dump the car, then leg it the last couple of clicks to the border. You just keep your eye on the map.'

'How far is it to the border now?' Andy prompted, 'We can't have that far to go.'

Inspecting the map once again, I quickly estimated the distance. 'About 40 clicks. At this speed, we'll be there in less than half an hour.'

'Good. Give me a yell when we're a couple of clicks out.'

Keeping my own counsel, I looked at the map once more. I wanted to be well short of the border when we ditched the car. A couple of kilometres from the border put us in the middle of the sprawling frontier village that had grown up around the crossing point. Coupled with that, the Euphrates River ran practically alongside the village, which meant that there was probably a large agricultural workforce about also. Not a good place to try and abandon a vehicle, especially this early in the evening.

As it was, we had already reached the outskirts of the town. More and more frequently, the taxi's headlights illuminated ramshackle buildings and small crops next to the road. Everyone in the vehicle was wide awake and alert now, the increasing passage of farms and houses not going unnoticed.

'I think we had better ditch the car soon, Andy,' Dinger started. 'It's getting a bit busy around here.'

No sooner had the words left Dinger's mouth than a sign appeared on our right-hand side, written in both Arabic and English: 'Checkpoint'.

Andy slowed the car to a halt behind an abandoned wreck at the side of the road as the end of a vehicle queue came in sight. About 700 metres ahead we could see a dimly lit military roadblock, the soldiers inspecting the line of vehicles waiting to pass through.

'Shit!' Andy cursed. 'How far are we from the border?'

'About 16 clicks,' I answered immediately.

'Pop the hood,' Dinger said. 'Make it look like we've broken down.'

He jumped out and raised the bonnet. Although the soldiers had no chance of seeing us at that distance at night, it was better to be safe than sorry.

Andy turned in his seat and began speaking directly to the policeman. 'You drive to the other side,' he said, his hands making the movements associated with driving a vehicle. 'Pick us up.'

'You've got to be pissed,' Bob blurted out, 'there is no fucking way he will do that. He'll run straight to the checkpoint and dob us in!'

'C'mon,' Dinger hissed through the open door, stopping the debate dead in its tracks. 'Let's get a move on!'

I opened the door and made my way to the rear of the taxi, Bob following suit.

'You know we should top him,' Bob said quietly. 'He's going to head straight for that lot and we'll be in the shit again.'

As we deliberated, the policeman got out and stood by the car nervously wringing his hands, head swinging this way and that.

I think deep down, all of us knew we should have killed him, but being so close to the border we were confident that we could finish the few remaining kilometres under cover of darkness with time to spare. As it turned out, killing him would perhaps only have delayed our fate. Although we did not know it yet, we had already driven some way into a brigade position. There were hundreds of troops massed in barracks and dug into defensive positions for kilometres around.

We quickly took up a westerly track running perpendicular to the road before changing course and heading northwards once more. The ride in the taxi had definitely achieved one thing: my clothes were completely dry. For the first time in days, I felt well-rested and hardly noticed the cold.

We kept parallel to the road about a kilometre distant and soon bypassed the manned roadblock, which appeared to be operating as before.

Unfortunately, that was the end of the respite, for as we cleared the small rise in front of us, all hell broke loose.

Whap, whap, crack. The hail of automatic fire and red tracer came streaking in over our heads, causing the five of us to hit the ground. Immediately, we began to return fire, the tracer from our own machine guns arcing a deadly track towards the enemy lined out below.

'Break left, break left,' Andy screamed, jumping to his feet and heading toward a set of derelict buildings that were enticingly close, no more than 70 metres away.

The enemy below us were a substantial force, impossible to guess their numbers in the darkness, but the weight of fire heading in our direction told enough of a tale for us to know that we were heavily outnumbered. Fortunately, as is common with unseasoned marksmen, the majority of their rounds were way high, the soldiers not having made allowances for shooting at night. However, this was bound not to last – they would get the hang of it very shortly.

Two vehicles drove up behind the enemy position, briefly illuminating the scores of soldiers lying on the ground before they doused their headlights and discharged more troops.

'Time to get the fuck out of here,' Legs yelled, as one by one we followed Andy's lead and made our way safely into the collection of abandoned houses, with all the enemy fire still being directed at our old location.

'We must have been skylined when we crossed the crest,' Bob pushed out between pants of breath. 'They obviously lost sight of us again when we hit the deck.'

Running between the houses, we made a beeline for the border, passing within 100 metres of the enemy troops, who were still firing enthusiastically.

A stroke of luck finally came our way as the wail of an air-raid siren broke out, followed almost instantaneously by the resounding booms of AAA firing off into the night sky. Allied warplanes were on the prowl. The ground shook with the ferocity of the artillery bombardment, a great umbrella of red tracer reaching up into the Iraqi sky, searching desperately for the hated bombers.

Using this as a diversion, we cut east towards the Euphrates to reduce the distance to the border and to throw our confused pursuers off the scent. We hit the road again in no time, though we had to avoid some passing troop carriers that forced us to pause at the side of the highway. No doubt they were on their way to reinforce the troops already scouring the ground behind. Once the vehicles had passed, we sprinted across and immediately found ourselves in amongst a small warren of clay and stone houses. This was typical of many small villages that had sprung up near the frontier route; here people were able to take advantage of the volumes of traffic passing through and also the rich agricultural land that bordered the river.

Moving quickly and quietly down a bare clay path that separated the houses, we struck the river within minutes.

'Hold on a second,' I whispered urgently to Andy. 'Let's grab a water bottle each while we have the chance.'

All of us were running short of the precious liquid, and taking a minute to fill a bottle in the Euphrates might prove a life-saver later on. Sliding down to the water's edge, I got my first glimpse of the mighty and ancient river. It was massive, at least 600 metres across at this point, and the current was strong.

'Everyone done?' Andy asked, receiving a nod of heads in return. 'Off we go, then.'

Andy took the lead. I was next, followed by Bob, Legs and Dinger bringing up the rear. Initially we moved along a small track that ran alongside the waterway. Fortunately there was a three-metre bank above us to hide our progress. But the bank soon disappeared, and the path made its way back toward the village, forcing us to cut a new track north in order to maintain our bearing.

As we patrolled along, every fibre of every muscle in my body was tensed ready to explode into action. Once again the blood was pounding in my ears, my eyes boring into the night searching for a possible threat. The Minimi in my hands, safety off, was very light now, and I knew that one more burst of fire would see the last of my ammunition spent. After that I was down to a couple of M16 magazines that I still carried for emergencies (the Minimi had an interchangeable housing that could accommodate M16 magazines).

We came to the outskirts of another small village and Andy paused for a minute to get his bearings.

'How far to the border now, Mike?'

As I looked at the Magellan LCD, I could see the low-battery indicator flashing away. 'Don't do this to me, I just need you to hold out for another couple of hours,' I said, trying to coax the machine to work. Laboriously, it began to spew out the information.

'Just over six clicks to go.' On the map, a telecommunications mast was marked on the border between Syria and Iraq, and as we progressed stealthily northwards, its red hazard lights became visible, even at this distance. We were so close now.

Our bearing had now taken us into a field of crops. As we patrolled forward, we found ourselves once again in the peculiar situation of not being able to see anything more than a couple of metres away in any direction below head height, and yet all else above that was easily identifiable, bathed in iridescent moonlight. We felt completely exposed.

Twenty minutes further on saw the beginning of the end of our bid for freedom and the last time that the five of us were together as a patrol.

We had halted to take stock of a large re-entrant that now blocked our path, a small stream at its base trickle-feeding into the Euphrates 50 metres further east.

'You and I will climb down into the re-entrant and check out the other side,' Andy said to me. 'Pass it on to the others.'

I gave Andy a nod and stood up to make my way back to Bob, who was ten metres or so behind. As I did so, sporadic fire began to sound from the rear of the patrol, which was immediately followed by a long burst of automatic that could only have been from Dinger's Minimi.

Suddenly, tracer was coming in from every direction, including the other side of the re-entrant. We had managed to walk right into a dug-in Iraqi defensive position.

Swinging to the left, I dived to the ground, my left arm reaching forward to extend the collapsible stabilising legs that were housed underneath the machine gun's front stock. I heard the satisfying sound of the Minimi's working parts sliding forward and releasing a burst of fire towards the small red and white flashes that sparkled all around. Bob's Minimi did likewise.

Once again, most of the rounds were going way over my head but this time it was of little comfort – we were running out of options.

Clunk. My weapon ceased firing. 'Shit!' I yelled at no one in particular, and hauled back on the cocking handle. The DS (directing staff) stoppage drill went out the window. It would have taken too many precious seconds to complete the complicated clearing and reloading procedure that we had learnt in training. I knew I had just finished the last of my belted ammunition so I rolled onto my right-hand side and pulled a magazine from my pouch and slammed it home into the Minimi's second housing, releasing the working parts forward a millionth of a second later.

The enemy fire was starting to find its range now, and getting a little too close for comfort. Looking to my right I saw that Andy had already disappeared into the safety of the gully, a wise move considering the circumstances, and I looked back across to where Bob had been to relay to him to do likewise, but there was no sign of him.

I had to make a decision. If I stayed where I was, I would be a Swiss cheese in no time. Raising myself to one knee, I emptied the remainder of my magazine off in the direction from which the greatest concentration of fire appeared to be coming, then dashed the ten-odd metres to the re-entrant, throwing myself down its steep bank.

A cascade of stones and earth accompanied my slide to the bottom of the small ravine, where I found Andy waiting.

'Where the fuck are the others?' he demanded in a voice barely audible over the constant hammering of rifle and machine-gun fire.

'I haven't got a fucking clue!' I yelled back at him, my heart racing so fast it felt like it would explode. 'It's a fucking nightmare up there. One minute Bob was beside me, the next nothing. He must have withdrawn back towards the river with Dinger and Legs.'

'OK, let's bug out down here to the Euphrates and see if we can meet up with them.'

My heart rate was returning to some semblance of normality, probably operating at only 180 beats per minute as opposed to the 300 a few minutes earlier.

'Go on then, mate, let's get out of here anyway.'

As we moved on down the re-entrant, the fire about us began to die down until, finally, only the odd shot rang out.

'Sounds like they've run out of things to shoot at,' I said, removing the empty magazine from my weapon and replacing it in the pouch. But that was where my mag-change ended. 'Oh, shit!' I hissed.

Andy stopped and swung about, weapon at the ready. 'What's the matter?'

'I've lost my last magazine. It must have dropped out somewhere during the contact.'

'Christ, is that all? Don't worry about it, we'll be over the border in an hour and it won't matter then.'

Within minutes we hit an obstacle. The re-entrant had a large concrete weir across it that was too high to negotiate. This forced us to climb back out into the fields and then continue to the east and towards the river. A hundred metres further on we found ourselves at the bank of the Euphrates and began the search for any sign of Bob, Legs or Dinger, but there was none to be found.

'Shit!' Andy cursed. 'Well, now it's just me and you, Kiwi. At least you've got the Magellan.'

Gazing out across the dark waters, I was tempted for a moment to jump in and swim to the other side to escape the noose that was slowly but surely tightening round our necks. But I knew that trying to negotiate the freezing, fast-flowing current in our state would be courting disaster. That would have to remain the last option.

'We can't move up the river bank,' Andy began. 'Look, that bridge up there has sentries moving up and down it.'

Sure enough, 150 metres to the north a sentry-controlled road bridge spanned the river.

Turning back towards Andy, I said, 'They have obviously got some kind of skirmish line dug in around the area. The troops are sitting tight either waiting for us to bumble on into it or are waiting for first light. Either way, we have to make our way through. We've got precious few hours of darkness left.'

'What do you suggest?'

'I reckon we're going to have to leopard-crawl our way past. That way we will see them before they see us, and we can avoid confrontation. Chances are, once we're through, it will be a home run to the border. How much ammo have you got left?'

'I'm out,' Andy replied.

'Well, I'm not going to donate my Minimi to the Iraqi Army without a fight.'

I looked at the piece of black and blue metal that had become part of me over the last few days, now devoid of the teeth that gave it its bite. Moving to the side of the river, I submerged the weapon amongst the reeds that grew in the muddied waters along the riverbank's edge.

I then stripped off my belt-order and began rifling through the various pouches, switching items of use from the webbing to my pockets. A full water bottle, the Magellan, some freeze-dried food, my escape kit: everything else was consigned to the Euphrates. Andy didn't hesitate in following suit. We needed to be as unencumbered as possible for the crawl that lay ahead.

Within minutes we were ready. 'That's the lot, Kiwi!' Andy confirmed. 'Lead off.'

I led off westwards over the fields once more, feeling completely naked without a weapon but confident that I would recognise the point where we would need to go to ground and commence the crawl. After ten minutes or so I went down on one knee, just short of the point where our last contact had occurred, and turned to Andy, 'It's crawl time from here, mate.'

'Let's do it, then.'

Down on my stomach, I began the painfully slow process of crawling on knees and elbows across the flat cropland, only occasionally raising my body a few inches to cross one of the many berms that criss-crossed the area.

Our route took us past three enemy positions, one so close that I could see the silhouettes of the four soldiers in their foxhole, passing a cigarette amongst themselves and whispering in hushed Arabic tones. When that close, with every inch gained I would pause briefly to see if we'd been spotted, but the enemy seemed oblivious to our progress. It was one of the most nerve-racking things I have ever done.

Alternating the load between us, we continued like this for what seemed an age, but in fact it was only a matter of an hour – an hour to cover about 100 metres. With time running against us, it was a heavy price to pay for so little territory. Finally, it appeared that the line had been broken, that we had successfully made a passage through. I had not seen or heard anything to the contrary for a good 20 minutes, so, hesitantly at first, I slowly rose onto one knee. I remained still in that position for a couple of minutes, testing the water and assessing the situation.

'Looks OK, mate.' I passed back to Andy and began moving forward again in a half-crouch. 'Let's didi-mau.'

We continued on in this manner for some time, pausing every few minutes to scan the area and listen for the enemy. Soon, however, the ground began to work against us, a combination of a built-up area to the south and the re-entrant to the north channelling us in a direction that we didn't want to go. Eventually we could see that the ground was going to force us back to the main road, somewhere where we most definitely didn't want to be.

'We're going to have to cross the re-entrant, otherwise we'll be standing on the main road again in a minute,' I whispered.

'Fuck, there are tons of soldiers on the other side of that wadi. That's all we need!'

'Well, what do you suggest, then? They are bloody everywhere!'

Andy was silent for a minute. 'We'll have to chance it. Perhaps we are further west of them now anyway.'

With no more discussion we began to make our way north once again and descended into the depths of the wadi. I made the top of the opposite bank in a couple of minutes, the re-entrant itself a lot shallower there. Pausing at the top, I stayed motionless for about five minutes, desperately seeking some hint as to what lay beyond, but only silence and impenetrable blackness greeted my probing eyes and ears.

Half-crouched yet again, I began to slowly make my way forward, gaining confidence with every step. Perhaps it was as Andy suggested, and the troops were further to the east. I was 50-odd metres from the wadi, Andy just behind me, when it happened.

The cocking of the AK47 was what saved my life. The sharp scraping rasp of metal on metal gave me a split second to hit the ground before the shit hit the fan. I just had time to see Andy haring off back into the safety of the wadi before the hail of fire erupted around me from a series of foxholes that stretched east to west as far as I could see. Now I knew I was in serious trouble.

The Iraqis were about 20 metres to my front, spaced at about 10-

metre intervals, and fortunately they had chosen to dig their positions in fields of crops. Each field was marked out by small berms of compacted earth, one of which was at this very moment the recipient of all my affection. I pressed myself desperately into its meagre cover, using it as a stop bank to absorb those rounds that actually almost found their intended target.

The soldiers must have lost sight of me the minute I went to ground, and consequently their inaccurate and sporadic fire was now shooting off in every direction as they sought to shoot up any shadow or bush that moved or was perceived to be a threat. Ten minutes or so later, the shooting had died off once again to an occasional discharge.

Two of the braver soldiers then summoned up enough courage to move forward and inspect the 'killing ground' for any sign of what should have been a very riddled corpse. Chattering like a couple of monkeys, they made their way down to the edge of the re-entrant, walking past within two metres of where I lay. As they stood there looking over the bank, pointing their AKs into its depths, talking and laughing, I held my breath for fear they might see the steam as I exhaled.

'Come on, you bastards,' I thought to myself. 'Fuck off!'

My eyes bored into their backs, wishing that by sheer force of my will I could make them turn and leave without seeing me.

As it was, a vehicle drove up through the Iraqi line and the driver manoeuvred it so as to cast light down the length of the wadi. That escape route had just been neatly cut off.

The two soldiers then returned to their companions, not even glancing at my location, secure in the knowledge that no one would be using the wadi to attack them again that night.

My mind was racing now as it tried to work out a plan of action to extricate myself from this delicate position with my balls intact. Surprisingly, I felt very calm as I assessed the situation and my chances of surviving.

The first thing I had to do was get away from the vehicle's lights; it was definitely concentrating the attention of the soldiers just in front of me. With caterpillar-like movements, I began to inch my body away in the opposite direction, hugging the small wall of the berm for grim death. It took me over an hour just to move 20-odd metres and get out of the glare of the headlights.

From this point, I began to crawl a little faster along the berm until I hit my first obstacle: another berm perpendicular to the one I was following. To cross this would mean exposing my body to the soldiers above, a procedure I did not relish. Changing my position so that I was now lying alongside the new berm, I raised my right arm over its crest and used it as a lever to slowly manoeuvre the remainder onto the top. Once there, I quickly slid my foot across and then rolled myself onto the far side as silently as possible. The procedure completed, I held my breath, waiting to see if anyone had noticed. Fortunately, the Iraqis above were quite happy to wait till first light, which was now very rapidly approaching.

I allowed myself to glance at the illuminated dial on my diver's watch. 'Oh, shit!' I thought to myself, I had a little over 80 minutes before night would become day.

By crossing into a new field I had now lost the cover of a berm, and accordingly continued my crawl eastwards at a speed that I hoped would not attract attention. The field I was now in gave me an unrestricted view of the area, and I was able to see that the Iraqis had established their defensive line parallel to a small road, no doubt the one that led to the bridge nearby. A hundred or so metres further to the east of my present position two large military tents had been erected which, I assumed, must have constituted the command centre for these troops.

Moving south, west or east was definitely out of the question, and the option of trying to sneak my way through the staggered positions 20-odd metres to my north didn't appeal much either, but I needed to make a decision. I searched the area desperately, looking for some reprieve, some avenue of escape, and finally, my concentration was rewarded. A slight change in the contours of the ground 30 metres away told me that there was possibly a small ditch or berm running from north to south, one that split two of the Iraqi positions. It wasn't much, but there wasn't exactly a lot else on offer.

As fast as I dared, I made my way over to the undulation and to my surprise, and great relief, found that it was a drainage ditch, about half a metre deep – perfect. Not wasting any time, I slid into it and felt immediately more secure. There was no way they could possibly see me crawling in here. My only cause for concern was that the bottom of the ditch was lined with gravel, and I needed to be careful of the noise that my movements might cause.

To anyone else, this course of action might have appeared suicidal, impossible madness – actually crawling towards the enemy in an attempt to sneak by them. Under other circumstances I might have agreed, but I was now fast reaching the point of no longer caring. I needed to take action and this was my choice. With slow, controlled, caterpillar-like movements, I began to silently shuffle my way forward, keeping my face to the ground so as not to allow any hint of light reflection from its surface.

My whole being was concentrated on this single act, edging my way ever closer to the enemy positions and the relative freedom that I hoped existed on the other side. I had convinced myself of this fact: that once I had made it past this defensive line I would be home and hosed, just a couple of more kilometres to the border. It was the goal that kept me going.

I was perhaps five metres from the nearest of the Iraqis when my desperate bid for freedom was finally laid to rest, and the worst thing was, I felt totally helpless to prevent it.

An Iraqi soldier climbed out of one of the foxholes and wandered over to the ditch. He then jumped in and began walking down its length, chatting to all his mates in the process, probably so they didn't shoot him. The realisation of what was about to happen dawned on me the instant that he planted his first foot into the trench.

Lying there with nothing to defend myself with but a knife, I was certain that my time was up. We had all been briefed that the Iraqis would take no prisoners, and stories of the SAS soldiers who had had their heads paraded on spikes in the Dhofar campaign flashed through my racing mind. Almost in slow motion, I began to raise myself to my feet, my knife grasped tightly in my right hand, preparing to launch at the ever-nearing soldier, but it was a hopeless gesture.

He saw my movement from about two metres away and took a jump backwards in fright. Cocking the AK47 in his hands, he yelled frantically to his companions, at the same time emptying his weapon on full automatic in my direction. Two of his friends joined him in doing likewise seconds later. It was the end of the road.

PART II
CALL TO ARMS

CHAPTER 9

EARLY DAYS

I was born in Grey Lynn, Auckland, New Zealand, on 2 May 1964. Adopted at birth, I became the first child of a middle-class, expatriate British couple, both of whom were officers in the military.

After the Second World War, there had been a free flow of British immigrants to Australia and New Zealand, and both my parents found themselves part of this wave. My father, originally from West Ham in London, emigrated to New Zealand after he was demobbed. An ex-RAF bomber navigator, he had answered the call of the Royal New Zealand Air Force, which was desperately short of qualified navigators at that time. After visiting the New Zealand High Commission in London, filling out the appropriate forms and completing a rigorous medical, he simply had to wait for the vetting procedures to give him the all-clear. Within a few weeks he found himself on an all-expenses-paid flight (courtesy of the RNZAF) to New Zealand. The first his family in the UK knew of the emigration Down Under was a letter he sent to his brother some two years later. My father never had the chance to return to the UK again.

He was initially posted to Hobsonville Air Base, about a half-hour drive north-west of Auckland city centre, which at the time was the home of a flight of Sunderland flying boats.

My mother, born in Johnston, Scotland, was the elder of two children. Her English parents, both of whom were teachers, had decided to quit war-ravaged Britain for a better life in the dominions. Canada had been the original destination, but unable to find the Canadian Embassy in London, they stumbled across its New Zealand counterpart. The rest is history. My mother was 15 years old when she stepped off the SS *Captain Cook* in Wellington with her brother and parents.

At the age of 18, she began her formal nursing training at Wellington Hospital and on completion she joined the Army Nursing Corps as a lieutenant and was posted to Whenuapai, an air base just around the corner from Hobsonville. Thus my parents met through the military and were finally married in 1962.

As my mother had a successful career at the time, both she and my father decided that although they wanted children, at that stage they would prefer to adopt rather than for her to lose her job for a period. However, my adoption didn't go too smoothly. As my parents were living in Fiji at the time, my father serving with the Sunderland flying boat squadron stationed there, the authorities were reluctant to allow me to leave the country at such a young age.

Six weeks of fruitless negotiation with the health authority saw little movement on the issue. My mother had finally had enough and requested the help of a friend, who coincidentally happened to be the local MP. The situation was resolved very rapidly thereafter, and in no time I was winging my way over to Fiji, where I spent the next 18 months of my life.

On our return to New Zealand, my family moved to West Auckland, finally settling in Te Atatu South, which was a suburb particularly handy for downtown Auckland and Whenuapai. As an added bonus, it was centrally located for access to the beautiful east- and west-coast beaches of north Auckland and the awesome natural bush of the Waitakere Ranges. More importantly, Eden Park, the home of Auckland rugby, was but a half-hour drive away.

It has been said that living in New Zealand is like going back a decade in time compared with the UK, but in all honesty the differences are much more profound than that. The New Zealand lifestyle is something unique to the 'Land of the Long White Cloud', something not appreciated until one has lived overseas.

On our return to New Zealand, my father returned to Whenuapai, and my mother commenced a career in the civilian nursing sector. Somewhere between night shifts, housework and being a wife, she managed to raise three other children, all girls, and all of whom were less of a handful than me. Within a couple of years, my father also found himself stepping onto the civilian road as his service came to an end and he was discharged from the air force. With his pension, he was able to purchase a modest corner shop-cum-bookstore not far from our house in Te Atatu, which he ran for many years until his retirement.

By the time I had finished intermediate school, my parents had decided that I was to be groomed for greater things. My academic prowess had proved quite a surprise, not least of all to myself, and after much deliberation it was decided that I should attend an all-boys grammar school, the theory being that this environment would further nurture my academic ability.

Mount Albert Grammar School (MAGS) played a huge part in the formative years of my life, instilling in me a great sense of tradition, patriotism and loyalty, traits which stood me in good stead throughout my career in the military. It was here that the first stirrings of a young boy's romantic notions of serving and defending one's country heroically against some national or international threat began to germinate.

Every year, in the days leading up to Anzac Day, the main hall would be adorned with the photographs of MAGS old boys, ex-pupils who had given their lives in two world wars to defend our way of life. I would wander around the hall, a huge imposing building with a great vaulted ceiling, staring up at the fresh-faced young men, all of whom had made the ultimate sacrifice. Even at my young age, I found it very moving.

It was also at high school that I discovered a love and aptitude for history, especially that of Europe. With the aid of some very capable and enthusiastic teachers, I excelled in the subject, which fascinated me throughout my school years and culminated in my receiving honours as a top history student.

However, the best-laid plans of mice and men often never come to fruition and, as any parent can attest, those momentous and troubled teenage years through which children must pass before entering adulthood are littered with good intentions. Towards the final years of my schooling at MAGS, my parents separated and I went off the rails a bit. I got into boot boy territory – Doc Martens, skinhead and attitude – all of which coincided with a dramatic drop in my grades.

My mother and sisters moved to Wellington, which is where I was supposed to follow, but I did not want to move down there. My dad and I were not seeing eye to eye, as often happens at that age, so staying with him was not a good idea, either. The last and preferred option, in my opinion anyway, was to go and stay with friends of the family, Mike and Kaye Trubuhovich.

So, a 17-year-old boot boy entered the Trubuhovich household hellbent on blaming the world for everything that was wrong in his life. Through patience and more than a little perseverance, they managed to steer me down the right path, keep me on the straight and narrow, and ensure a reasonably sane and respectable young man emerged on the other side.

* * *

My education at MAGS continued to the seventh form, and as the end of 1981 approached, I found myself at one of the many crossroads in my life. I had failed my New Zealand scholarship exams abysmally, although I had qualified for the Higher School Certificate and entry to university. I was at a loss as to which way to turn. I finally decided to give myself some breathing space, and the following year I began a combined BA/LLB degree at Auckland University.

I spent the next few months kidding myself that this was what I wanted to do, attending lectures on political science, Shakespearean English and other equally riveting subjects, but deep down I always knew that this was simply a way of marking time. The only problem was, for what?

In April 1982, the Argentine armed forces invaded an obscure and little-known group of British-held islands in the South Atlantic, claiming that they were the sovereign territories of Argentina. I followed events during the Falklands War and became fascinated with the heroics associated with such names as Goose Green and Wireless Ridge. This was the stuff that legends were made of, and it was perhaps Britain's finest hour, the last great colonial war. I felt extremely privileged that, years later, I served alongside men who could lay claim to having been there and 'done the business'.

By the time June came around and the Falklands had been successfully restored to British hands, the idea of joining the army had been firmly planted in my head. I turned up at the forces recruiting office in Queen Street, Auckland, and because of my current status as a university student, was pointed towards the Regular Officer Selection Board. Within weeks I was flown down to Burnham, Christchurch, along with scores of other applicants to attend the officer board test week, designed to earmark potential officer candidates for further training and a career with the army.

Although I enjoyed the course thoroughly, I was unsuccessful and had my hopes dashed. However, I had been given a small taste of military life, and it appealed to me.

* * *

At the beginning of the 1980s, the 1st New Zealand Special Air Service Squadron was in the grip of a manning crisis. The strict and difficult regime laid down to select soldiers wishing to join the SAS was proving too great an obstacle for the limited number of applicants who turned up to attempt it. The then commanding officer of the day, and his advisors, came up with a plan to broaden the recruitment base for potential candidates by recruiting directly from Civvy Street.

This was not a new concept. Indeed, when the New Zealand SAS was initially formed back in 1955 for the Malayan campaign, a great recruiting drive was undertaken across the country to find suitable personnel. It had worked successfully back then, why should it not be as successful now? So, a full-scale advertising campaign was put into effect, encouraging anyone between the ages of 20 and 35 to apply to join the Special Air Service.

About 320 people applied. By September they had whittled that number down to a dozen, who then went on a three-month pre-selection training camp. Five turned up to join the regular SAS selection course of 1984; I was one of those five, and at nineteen years of age, I was the youngest-ever candidate to attempt selection. I had been given an age dispensation because I would be aged 20 by the 'badging' ceremony, if successful.

I found the three-week NZSAS selection one of the most gruelling experiences of my life, certainly more so than the 22 SAS course.

Whereas the emphasis on the UK selection was placed on long arduous walks (tabs), the NZ course of that time (the format of which is now run on more similar lines to its UK counterpart) introduced the elements of sleep and food deprivation, along with physical and psychological harassment.

Yet, despite all this, I found the course quite exciting, and most certainly adventurous, and at the end of the three weeks, I was among those candidates still standing (in fact, all the civilian applicants had managed to survive).

Over the ensuing three months, those of us who had managed to stay the distance were given specialist training in various areas that were pivotal to the basic make-up of an SAS trooper. Signals, medical, SAS tactics and escape and evasion were skills taught as part of phase one of the training cycle. At the end of this phase the candidates were badged, binned, or, if they weren't quite up to scratch but had potential, given the option to take a TOD (tour of duty) with the infantry. The latter was my reward.

I vividly remember being marched in front of the training officer. A Vietnam veteran and soldier of some 20-odd years' standing, Captain Bill was the man that any aspiring young SAS trooper wanted to emulate. He commanded such respect that, to this day, I still regard him as one of the principal influences in my army career. To be stood in front of him and told that I was to be sent away to improve my basic infantry skills was completely demoralising.

Leaving the unit was a huge blow to me at the time, but in retrospect, Captain Bill and the training staff did me an immense favour. I certainly did not have either the maturity or sufficient infantry grounding to achieve the required standards, and the SAS did not have the time, or the men to spare, to help me catch up.

Of the five original civilian applicants, one was thrown out for fighting before completing the cycle, two decided to join the territorial

SAS unit, one, big Ken, remained, and went on to join 22 SAS some three years later, where he enjoyed a very successful career. Last but not least, I was packed off to the infantry for a year TOD.

I said my goodbyes enviously to those who had been deservedly badged, boarded a plane for Christchurch and prepared to join the 1st Battalion Royal New Zealand Infantry Regiment.

* * *

New Zealand's army is nowhere near being one of the largest, best-equipped or well-paid military organisations in the world, but it is without doubt one of the most professionally trained and highly motivated. The Royal New Zealand Infantry Regiment in particular, which consists of only two regular battalions, has a proud, honourable history, and its soldiers are well-respected all over the world.

Situated amidst the vast expanse of the Canterbury Plains, in the South Island of New Zealand, Burnham was the home of the infantry's Operational Battalion, its sister unit stationed in Singapore being designated as the Training Battalion. On my arrival there, I was posted into Depot Company, where all newcomers to the infantry found themselves, and was immediately thrust into the rigours of the basic infantryman.

The 'green army' was a complete shock to my system after the intense and demanding training regime of the SAS. I also proved somewhat of a quandary for my infantry instructors, section commanders and platoon sergeants, many of whom had attempted SAS selection in the past, often unsuccessfully. Here they had a soldier who had an excellent grounding in small-team, close-quarter battle tactics, who was weapons, signals and medically trained to a high level, yet who had a woefully inadequate understanding of infantry tactics and formations, and couldn't march or perform parade drill to save himself. It was quite a bizarre situation.

I have to say that my instructors coped with the situation admirably and, without any malice or ill will, integrated me into my company, platoon and section so well that within a matter of weeks one would never have known that I had been anywhere else. Three months later, I passed out with the November intake, and took my place amongst the rest of the infantrymen in 2/1 RNZIR.

About six months after joining the battalion, I found myself facing a rather large dilemma. Everyone knew that I was expected to return to the SAS in a few months' time, but the OC of my company had given me the option of taking a two-year tour in Singapore. I resolved the question by placing a call to Captain Bill, as I was concerned that by taking the tour I would forfeit my right to return to the SAS without doing another selection. His answer was all the incentive I needed: 'Get your arse over there, and we'll see you in two years' time.' Three weeks later, I was on the plane to Singapore.

SINGAPORE, 1985

The absolute oppressiveness of the humidity almost knocked me over when I got off the plane at Changi International Airport. Within minutes of arriving and walking to the terminal, I was soaked to the skin in sweat; my sharp dress greens were reduced to a soggy mess.

As this was my first time abroad since the age of two, I found the whole experience an exciting adventure, as did most of the debutants.

After the formalities of customs and immigration were completed, we were guided to a waiting area outside the terminal, obviously reserved for large group arrivals and the like, then shepherded aboard the famous and affectionately named 'white elephants' – white-painted buses – which would take us to our destination.

Dieppe Barracks at the northern end of the island was the home of the 1st Battalion Royal New Zealand Infantry Regiment, the only foreign force left in Singapore since the British pulled out in 1971. The battalion had come to prominence in the region first of all during the Malayan and Borneo emergencies, then later on during the Vietnam War; in fact, most of the SNCOs (senior non-commissioned officers) serving with the battalion wore Vietnam ribbons on their chests.

Singapore itself was a young soldier's dream, an exotic, well-paid posting where working hard and playing hard definitely held sway. It was the New Zealand Army's foremost training establishment and showpiece, and it held pride of place amongst New Zealand's military establishments.

The first week in Singapore was spent preparing us for our theatre indoctrination course, fondly called the TIC course. Everyone arriving at the battalion, whether for the first time or the tenth, had to endure the training. The course itself was designed to familiarise and acclimatise those recent arrivals in Singapore and Malaysia to the wonders of the South-east Asian jungle.

We left Dieppe five days later and headed for Johor State in southern Malaysia. The crossing between Singapore and Malaysia is most frequently made via the causeway, a long bridge that joins the island state with the Malay peninsula. One of the first welcome signs we saw near the customs toll area was a huge depiction of a hanging skeleton, with the inscriptions 'drug trafficking' and 'death' written in Malay and English. Nothing more needed to be said.

Immediately upon crossing the causeway, you knew that you had entered another country. The contrast between the clinical opulence of Singapore and the sprawling poverty of Johor Bahru could hardly have been starker.

The TIC course was a unique experience in its own right and most definitely achieved all its objectives. Over 23 days, we were subjected to an intense training package which ranged from jungle navigation and patrolling to hygiene and water sterilisation. No stone was left unturned, nor an hour in the day wasted, in the bid to pump out a capable jungle soldier. Your initial apprehension and fear of all the creepy crawlies that could do you harm in the J (jungle) soon vanished as the workload increased.

There was a story recounted many times over. Your first couple of nights out in the J, you would clear an area as big as a heli pad for a basher, but a few days' TIC training always cured that, and eventually you simply slept where you stopped, totally exhausted with no thought for what might be underneath you.

So, 23 days later we emerged from the trees a good deal thinner, stinking to high heaven and certainly a lot wiser in the ways of our chosen profession. On returning to Dieppe, we dispersed to our allotted companies and settled down to battalion life once more.

* * *

As a young single soldier living in Singapore, I had a life that I could never before have imagined, and one that was certainly enviable. The mixture of diverse Asian cultures, moulded together in a semi-Western style, was intoxicating and addictive. An awesome nightlife, with all-night bars and clubs (something completely unknown in New Zealand at that time), the ability to visit foreign countries almost at will, coupled with unparalleled camaraderie, made a two-year Singapore posting fly by.

I managed tours in both HQ Coy and A Coy whilst serving with 1 RNZIR, and was fortunate enough to participate in a variety of representative tasks such as the Hong Kong Mortar Concentration, Brunei Shooting Competition and the Malaysian rugby sevens tournament. It was not until I was due to return to New Zealand and to the SAS that I fully realised how much more competent and confident I had become.

Two days before my departure to New Zealand, I came down to earth with a bang. Asleep in the transit barracks with the rest of my platoon, I was awoken by the camp guard commander.

'Mike, Mike,' he said, at the same time shaking me awake. I stared at him with sleep-blurred eyes, and glanced at my watch. It was 3.30 a.m.

'What?' was about all I could manage at that ungodly hour.

'I've had a call from Land Forces in Auckland. I'm sorry, your father has just died.' It was that blunt, but then I suppose there isn't an easy way of passing on tragic news. I know I certainly wouldn't want to do it.

I was on the Air New Zealand flight back home five hours later, still not really believing it could have happened. I hadn't seen nor spoken to my father since leaving for Singapore, the only communication between us having been a couple of letters, and to have him die two days before my return was a cruel blow.

I don't think that it really sunk in until after the funeral. Until you see the body lying there in a coffin, it all seems a bit surreal. My father had always been a very reserved person, living alone since his divorce, never confiding much in anyone, and certainly never wanting to rely on anyone else's help. On the day of his death, he walked to the local ambulance station some 15 minutes away and said, 'I think I may have just had a heart attack.' Six hours later, in hospital, he had a massive coronary and died.

One week after returning to New Zealand, I recommenced my SAS training. My father never had the chance to see me serve.

CHAPTER 10

1 NZSAS GP, PAPAKURA MILITARY BASE, 1985

The intense regime of the SAS cycle was probably the best elixir for me at that time. Being able to thrust myself into the training took my mind off the death of my father. I was fortunate that several of my good friends from Singapore were also on the course at the same time: Pete, Ex, Dave and big Hoki, all of whom rallied round and supported me through this difficult period, mainly through good sessions on the pop.

As I was basically out of date with my signals and medical skills, I retook these courses along with my fellow prospective troopers. The crunch course for me was small tactics, otherwise known as 'patrol procedures', which had been the stumbling block on my first attempt. This course taught the bread-and-butter skills of the four-man SAS patrol, the mainstay of a sabre squadron.

The patrol procedures course was both mentally and physically demanding, and more often than not it proved to be the most telling factor in the student failure rate, after selection itself. The training package covered a wide range of subjects, including patrolling techniques, observation position construction and routine, contact drills, ambushing, booby traps, close target recces and much more. All this culminated in a final exercise that endeavoured to test both the individual and patrol in all the newly acquired skills.

This time around I was determined not to slip up, and armed with my Singaporean experience, I felt confident and sure that there would be no repeat disappointment. This proved to be the case, and at the end of the package I received a glowing report which dispelled the last few remaining doubts that plagued me. Not only had I vindicated myself, but also the system had shown faith in my ability by allowing me to return, and I had fully lived up to that decision.

Patrol procedures was also a course that really cemented the students on the cycle together, forcing people to rely on, trust and believe in one another. An almost invincible feeling of camaraderie developed over these weeks; friendships were made that would last a lifetime. Four of us from this intake would go on to successfully join 22 SAS regiment.

Following the patrol course, we commenced the dreaded 'combat survival'. I had already completed this course on my first cycle, losing over a stone in weight in the process, so the pressure was off me to some extent. I would carry on with the course for the first two instructional weeks, but when it came to the final exercise, I was to be spared (thank God).

Combat survival was exactly what its name implied. As an SAS patrol more often than not is required to operate a considerable distance behind enemy lines, the chances of capture if compromised are extremely high. The aim of this course was to teach SAS soldiers the art of surviving in a hostile environment, assuming the worst scenario: that they have lost all their equipment, are on the run from the enemy and are living off the land.

To that end, various techniques are taught to maximise the chances of survival: astral navigation, fauna and flora recognition, hunting and trapping, use of agent rendezvous, improvised clothing and shelters, dog and man evasion, and, last but not least, resistance to interrogation. The latter is an extremely interesting week where former prisoners of war are brought in to recount their experiences, and actual interrogators come and give lectures on the methodology of their profession.

The course as a whole is quite enjoyable, and certainly informative, right up until the final exercise, which is an absolute ball-breaker. The scenario for the exercise takes on a tried and tested format. The candidates are rounded up, blindfolded and driven off in trucks to a pre-determined location: normally the desolate wasteland of the Waiouru Army Training Area. On arrival, already in their patrols, they are dropped off in the dead of night, given an improvised escape map, told their first agent rendezvous location and timing, and then told to bugger off. The patrol now takes on the identity of four escapees from a POW camp trying to evade capture through living off the land and moving through a series of agent rendezvous. At the same time there is a 'hunter force' with considerable assets at their disposal, both on land and in the air, trying to recapture the runners.

Always run in midwinter, the course guarantees that you will be cold, wet, hungry and miserable the whole way through. It is particularly demoralising when, at an agent RV, a lucky dip bag is thrust into your cold, numbed hands containing the patrol's 'rations' for the next 24 hours. On later examination, it holds a couple of slices of bread each, two or three potatoes and a piece of raw tripe – mouth-wateringly delicious.

Providing you are not caught earlier, students move from agent to agent over the period of about a week, before being deliberately recaptured and then taken in for a gruelling interrogation phase. Name, rank, number and date of birth is the sum total of the information you are allowed to divulge; any more and you are given your marching orders.

Some 30-odd hours later, whilst seated in the interrogation room, your blindfold is suddenly removed and there standing before you is the training officer, umpire's armband affixed, saying 'End Ex'. It is one of the most memorable moments of your life. A steaming hot cup of ridiculously sweet tea is gratefully received, and you are led to a room where there is enough food to feed an army. Finally you can dare to think, 'Thank God that's over!' One by one, the other students file through, all with that stunned but relieved look on their face. Then, all at once you begin to talk, and suddenly it didn't seem all that bad.

The following afternoon, the course assembles in the bar with the rest of the group. Without any pretence or ceremony, the commanding officer calls each one of the successful candidates forward to receive his famous beige beret, winged dagger attached. Suffice to say, the beer flows until the wee small hours. Looking back on the evening when I received my beret, I would never have guessed that within five years, four of these proud, recently badged troopers would terminate their NZSAS service and do it all over again in a country 20,000 kilometres away.

Your 'badging' is not the end of the cycle in New Zealand, however. Unlike its more famous British counterpart, the SAS training continues to incorporate other skills such as demolitions, mountaineering, amphibious insertion, specialist warfare (otherwise known as counter-terrorist training) and the parachute course, for those not already para-trained.

It was on our mountaineering course that I had my inaugural taste of 'living on the edge' with the SAS. The initial rock-climbing phase of the course was run at Leigh, an idyllic spot a few hours' drive north of Auckland. At first, I found it quite daunting. The idea of climbing up a sheer rock face with a rope attached to little wire wedges as the only means of safety was not initially my idea of fun. However, as the days progressed, and my confidence increased, I began to enjoy it more.

'Bouldering' on huge pieces of broken rock strewn about the foot of the rock faces, practising holds and techniques necessary to successfully negotiate the cliffs themselves, was our introduction. Climbs soon followed, increasing progressively in difficulty and duration. However, as with all things in the SAS, just when you think you have got yourself onto a good thing, they go and introduce the military element. Suddenly, I found myself attached to a rope, in the pitch black of night, climbing up a 50-metre cliff lugging a bergen and rifle. This is the real world.

Still, I managed to survive this phase intact and reasonably unscathed. Next we were to move on to mountaineering and arctic survival, the basic training for which was also run at Leigh. You need a mountain to train mountaineers, obviously, so the course headed south. Situated on the high central plateau of the North Island, the 2,797-metre, occasionally active volcano Mount Ruapehu dominates the region, holding sway over its smaller and less illustrious volcano sisters, Tongariro and Ngauruhoe.

At the mountain's ski resort, we looked a sorry bunch of individuals, dressed in a mish-mash of camouflaged whites and greens, carrying bergens as we trekked our way up towards the summit, past the hordes of trendy ski bums with all their Gucci kit. It was on this phase of the course that the adage 'Don't fuck with the mountain' sprung into our vocabulary. Anyone who has spent time on a mountain, be it for skiing or climbing, knows how changeable, dangerous and unpredictable alpine weather can be.

We were about two-thirds the distance to the hut when the storm hit. There appeared to be no warning, one minute clear blue sky, and the next, white out. Within minutes, 100-kilometre per hour winds carrying whipped-up snow and ice were bombarding us. You were fortunate if you could see more than a metre ahead. The ferocity of the storm was such that the only way to bear it was to turn your back into the maelstrom and crouch down; a standing figure would have no chance of withstanding the onslaught.

Our instructors realised very quickly that this was a dire situation. There were only three of them looking after fourteen novice mountaineers, most of whom had never been on a mountain before, let alone encountered these conditions. Although we were only a few hundred metres short of the summit and the safety of the mountain lodge, there was no way of accurately finding it in this weather, just as there was no way of finding our way safely back down the mountain with the amount of daylight remaining. The instructors had a quick conflab and decided that the only option left was to stay where we were and try to ride the storm out.

By now we were being hit with bullets of ice that were increasing in size. Phil, one of the instructors, made his way over to Pete, Bomber and me, yelling at us over the roar of the wind. 'We're staying put. Get your shovels out and dig a snow cave.'

We had received a lesson on snow cave construction a few days earlier, in the safe and snug confines of a classroom, but to have to put it into effect in such conditions was taking the practical application of a lesson to the extreme. I began to wrestle with the clips on my bergen. Lesson one, keep the shovel on the outside of your pack: the clips were frozen solid with compacted ice. Bomber had managed to get his shovel out, so

I borrowed it, beat my bergen until the ice broke away, then retrieved my own.

The first job was to dig our packs in, because by now the winds were so strong that they were starting to blow the unattended bergens back down the mountain. That done, we began to dig, starting with the trench, which needed to be about two metres deep and a metre and a half long, at right angles to the prevailing wind. Channelling the trench took forever, and we were not helped by the fact that, after about ten minutes of shovelling, our hands began to lose all sensation, thus necessitating the removal of our gloves in order to thrust our frozen digits under our armpits to re-warm them. Once the warmth was restored, and sensation returned, the pain was excruciating, but the only alternative to this was a cold injury such as frostbite, or worse.

Bomber, an ex-gunner and body-building freak who stood almost 5 ft 6 in. tall in platforms if he was lucky, was shovelling like a berserker. So much so, in fact, that in his haste he lost grip of his shovel, and that was the last we ever saw of it, tumbling through the wind-blown snow into the night.

We rotated the work between the three of us, two digging and one trying to build a snow wall against the incoming onslaught, without much success. Once the trench was completed, the task of actually excavating the cave began. Under normal conditions this is difficult enough, let alone in conditions such as these. We had to burrow an entrance at a right angle to the trench, before digging the actual cave itself. Working now, minus the battering of wind, snow and ice, proved a lot easier.

Throughout, the instructors were constantly moving from group to group, making sure the design was correct and that we were taking sufficient precautions against frostbite, hypothermia and the like. 'Keep an eye on each other at all times,' was always their parting advice.

By three in the morning, every group had safely buried themselves underground, and the respite from the storm was heavenly. However, now more than ever, we had to be on our guard. It is easy for carbon monoxide to build up in a snow cave unless you maintain a vent for it to escape. Pushing a ski pole through the roof afforded such a vent, but you had to make sure it remained clear; hence, one person stayed awake at all times to keep it so.

Despite the reprieve from the incessant wind, it was still desperately cold inside; our bodies were now resorting to violent shivering fits in an attempt to get warm again. None of us had the arctic equipment necessary to sustain a long vigil in these conditions; we were kitted out for a leisurely stay in a mountain lodge. The concept had been to work out in the snow and ice during the day and return to the relative luxury of the hut at the first sign of adverse weather.

Although we had made enough room for the three of us to lie down, it was still necessary to take turns at sleeping, not that you could really sleep in these conditions. We took two-hour turns on watch, with a brew on the boil, maintaining the roof vent and access tunnel, but most importantly of all, keeping an eye on the other two trying to sleep.

By nine in the morning, the blizzard had still not abated, and another crucial decision had to be made. Did we stay put until the storm blew over, or did we chance heading back down the mountain in relative daylight for fear of it, or our own physical condition, becoming worse? Our instructors chose the latter, and within the hour, we were on our way back. With the benefit of hindsight, this was undoubtedly a life-saving decision. It was better to make the attempt while everyone was still reasonably strong, than to sit and wait.

Stepping back out into the full force of that storm was a nightmare, to say the least. Having been out of its fury for a few hours, voluntarily putting myself back into its clutches made the situation seem even worse.

We began our slow march back down the mountain, still able to see only a few metres ahead. We were in single file, always keeping an eye on the man to the front and rear. Slowly but surely we lost altitude, descending ever so gradually out of the clutches of the blizzard, until finally, like an oasis in the desert, we reached the deserted sanctuary of the ski field and our base camp.

Out of all the dangerous activities in which I have been involved, this in particular has remained indelibly etched in my mind, for many reasons. Firstly, we were raw and untrained, and through faith in our instructors, our own abilities and our mates, we survived an ordeal that could have had far more serious consequences. Lessons learned through harsh experience are never forgotten, and I learnt many lessons on that mountain. Most poignant of all, however, was the fate of another expedition on the same mountain a couple of years later.

A group of nine soldiers, two of whom were instructors, had ventured on a hike up to the summit lodge for adventure training, only to be caught out in a blizzard. One instructor managed to find his way back to the mountain rescue centre and raised the alarm. The group was not located for three days due to the terrible conditions, and when the rescuers got to them, they found two of their number dead and the remaining survivors suffering from hypothermia and frostbite. To this day, I know that we were lucky not to suffer a similar fate.

* * *

Christmas leave came and went, and I was posted to B Squadron, Air Troop. The NZSAS only has two squadrons, and they operate a rotation of one year on the 'Green Role', referring to the more conventional spheres of SAS infiltration and patrolling, and one year on the 'Black Role', which encompasses the counter-terrorist team (CTT). B Squadron was in the process of taking over the CTT responsibility, and those of us recently joined slotted straight in with the training programme.

I had topped the sniper course on the specialist warfare phase, just edging out Pete in the process. This was a feat I would repeat four years later on the 22 SAS sniper course, much to Pete's annoyance – and naturally, I never remind him of the fact.

Wicky, a former MAGS old boy like myself, was the number one sniper with whom I was partnered, and it was to be under his tutelage that I would learn many of the sniper's tricks of the trade. Snipers enjoy the best of both worlds when it comes to the CTT. They get to train in both their primary role and also in their secondary role as 'assaulters'.

There was always a lot of slagging and rivalry between the two groups; the snipers were nicknamed Julies, a reference to the sniper group call sign 'Juliet' and also because of their seemingly easier task. The assaulters, on the other hand, had the honour of being known as 'nut nuts' because it took a brain the size of a peanut to swing through a window and engage a target a few metres away. However, underlying all this was a mutual professional respect which made the squadron almost akin to a large family.

The two group commanders at the time were completely contrasting characters. Brozzo, the assault group commander, had been one of my instructors on the cycle and had been recently posted back to B Squadron after completion of his tour with the training wing. About 5 ft 10 in. tall, and 13-odd st., Brozzo was a physical fitness freak, meticulously professional, a born leader who inspired those around him. Aggressive and highly competitive, he also assumed the mantle of the unarmed combat instructor, a role that he particularly enjoyed, usually to the detriment of the rest of us. Be it work, rugby or drinking, you could guarantee that he would be in the thick of things.

Phil, the sniper team commander, was so laid back he was nearly asleep. Wiry and tall, he had just returned to the group after a voluntary absence of some few years spent fighting for the South African-backed Namibian armed forces against Angolan terrorist insurgents. Armed with this experience, and a lot of new ideas, he transformed the training of the sniper team during his stewardship, introducing many techniques acquired through his years of active service. Hardened through his years spent hunting terrorists in the African bush, about the only thing that could raise his blood pressure was the thought of having to do some PT, or the fact that the bar was going to close before he had a chance to order another beer. One of his favourite tricks was to hold a 'hun's head' target at arm's length, then radio his snipers to check zero on it at 100 metres.

The first three months of our tour in the CTT were intense, ensuring that every aspect of the skills required were practised, rehearsed and implemented until they became second nature. For the sniper team, three days out of a normal five-day week were generally spent sniper training, usually at moving targets out to 600 metres. The remaining two days would be allocated to assault training and all the associated skills: fast roping, abseiling, close-quarter battle, explosive method of entry and much more. On top of this, at least once a month (invariably commencing on a Friday afternoon) the team as a whole would be 'exercised' in a hostage scenario, introducing as many elements and twists as possible, testing every trooper, group and commander to the max.

As a young trooper, with an insatiable appetite to learn, these were exciting times. Although I had enjoyed my time in the infantry, it could not compare to the realistic and unique training that one undertook in the SAS. This was what had inspired me to join.

CHAPTER 11

1 NZSAS GP, 1989

Thanks to a reshuffling of the operational running of the unit, B Squadron's tour on the counter-terrorist team was extended from one to almost two years. This, on the face of things, didn't appear to be a problem, but with the limitations that are placed on the CTT, even the best of commanders run out of ideas on how to avoid repetitive training. So it was with a huge sigh of relief that I finally handed back the sniper and assaulter equipment to the storeman, without incurring any costs for lost equipment, ready for my opposite number in A Squadron to sign out. The most satisfying moment, though, was getting rid of the bane of my life, the bloody pager. Spending 22 months on 30 minutes' notice to move starts to become somewhat tiresome.

At that first squadron parade in late October, the order of the day was to get those men not already qualified in their troop infiltration skills, of which there were quite a few, up to speed. The older hands either broke down into their respective troops for continuation training, or moved on to further course packages such as advanced demolitions, medical, signals – the options were endless.

Along with five others, including Pete and Marsh, I began the military freefall course run by the PTSU (Parachute Training School

Unit) out at Whenuapai Air Base. The course was scheduled to last six weeks, weather and planes permitting, by which point a student was supposedly competent enough to execute stable freefall, both HAHO (high altitude, high opening) and HALO (high altitude, low opening) navigation and formations under canopy, by night, with full equipment (i.e. bergen, belt-order and weapon).

The first couple of days on the course were spent in the classroom learning meteorological theory and calculations for determining your drop and impact points; or inside the huge parachute training hangar practising freefall positions, canopy control and emergency procedures.

Emergency procedures, not only in freefall but in any type of parachuting, tend to take on a lot more significance than in other subjects. This, I believe, is due to the fact that you are already in a severely heightened state of awareness. Knowledge can be counterproductive, especially when you are about to disembark from a perfectly good aircraft at x thousands of metres for the first time. The idea of plummeting to the earth at over 160 kilometres per hour can seem a trifle unappealing. Your only solace is those two pre-packed pieces of flimsy silk, attached by numerous small nylon ropes to your back – the sure thing between you and an untimely demise.

Well, those were some of the thoughts going through my mind as I sat on the Hercules C130 at 3,000 metres, heading into the wind over Waitemata Harbour, minutes before I was due to take my initial dive into the unknown. It was made all the worse by the fact that the day before I had got to this stage, on the tail ramp, psyched-up ready to go, and at the last minute the jump had been cancelled as cloud moved in and obscured the DZ (drop zone) for the whole day. Now, 24 hours later, I watched Ben and Charlie on the lowered tail ramp, wind whistling around us all, one instructor holding onto each of them, another lying on the floor looking for the visual release point. Then, with a hand signal and a slap on the back, they were gone.

Rock and I were next. We stood on that tailgate, staring out into the abyss, the incessant drones of the engines and the sucking vortex whipping about my legs compounding the drum beating in my ears.

'Two minutes.' The call was passed along with a corresponding hand signal, and the PTI (Parachute Training Instructor) pushed us to within a metre of the abyss. Although I was conscious of everything around me, I felt like an automaton, going through the motions whether I liked them or not.

'Stand-by.' The 30-second warning rang in my ear, closely followed by the screamed 'Go' and a slap on my shoulder.

I dived out the plane and was surprised for a millisecond at the calmness of the air about me, but this was short-lived as I exited the vacuum of air that sits immediately behind an aircraft and hit the full force of the slipstream. I arched my back, pulling my shoulders back at the same time, feeling for the 'frog' position that would stabilise my flight. Although unsteady, I was stable and finally able to take a breath, though not confident enough to enjoy the view.

Suddenly, my instructor appeared in front of me, grinning from ear to ear and giving me the thumbs-up signal. He then proceeded to take the piss by flying around me, putting my legs in the proper position, before moving off and preparing to watch me dump (pull the ripcord).

The height finder controlled our first two parachute deployments; it was an automatic parachute release (APR), which was pre-calibrated and set before each jump. The device worked on barometric pressure and would automatically deploy either the main, as in this case, or the reserve parachute, whichever it had been placed on at the designated altitude.

Despite the height finder, we were still practising the pre-dumping drills. I checked my altimeter, 100 feet short of the deployment height, 3,000 feet. Crossing my arms in front of me several times to indicate that I was about to deploy my chute, I was very conscious of the fact that even this slight movement was destabilising my flight. With a pop the APR kicked in and in the space of a few seconds I went from 160 kilometres per hour plus to about 25.

The force of the opening was horrendous. It felt as though my back had split in two and the pain in my sinuses and eardrums after the rapid deceleration and depressurisation was excruciating. Worst of all, however, was the thought that I had just provided myself with the ultimate contraceptive and would be requiring a major surgical procedure to remove what was left of my manhood from my abdominal cavity.

I checked the canopy, released the steering toggles, then quickly pinched my nose and cleared my ears. Orientating myself to the DZ, I adjusted the harness to return my vocal chords to their correct pitch, then took time out to enjoy the ride and admire the spectacular view.

There is a saying at the jump school among those fortunate to take the basic static-line parachute course, 'You don't land, you arrive!' Such is the force of the bone-jarring impact when body meets terra firma – the standard army issue T10 is not the most forgiving of parachutes.

Now, even though the MT1X square is a drivable chute, with all the properties of a normal sports parachute but slightly larger to accommodate heavy loads, until you have actually landed a freefall chute, you don't know how hard the impact will be. Thus, it was with the natural cynicism of a paratrooper that I approached the DZ marker.

The PTI on the DZ held hand panels, very much like those that guide aircraft, and over the final 50 feet he motioned them so as to give me an indication on when to 'flare' the chute. I was already tucked up for a 'front right' landing just in case, and as I flared, the chute responded accordingly, collapsing at the last moment to give me a reasonably gentle landing. Like an idiot, because I was so tensed up in the 'para position', I ended up on my arse anyway and tried to execute a para roll to hide my embarrassment. I hauled in the parachute, stuffed it away, then grabbed my second chute and headed off towards the now taxiing C130. I couldn't wait to do it all over again – it was the most exhilarating thing that I had ever done.

* * *

The minimum number of freefall jumps required to qualify on the course was set at 40, of which a certain number had to be descents by day, night, with equipment and long transit under canopy. Halfway through the course a huge spanner was thrown in the works, which made the likelihood of completing the required amount of jumps in the available time almost impossible.

The principal aircraft that we were using was the Andover, the C130s being too few and far between to be at our constant beck and call for six or so weeks. One of the Andovers had been going through its x-thousand-hours overhaul, and the inspection had found a large number of fuselage rivets either missing or barely attached. Within the hour every Andover in the country had been grounded indefinitely, pending a detailed inspection. Our jumping schedule went from two a day to about two a week. Luckily, help was at hand from a totally unexpected quarter.

B Squadron 22 SAS had arrived for a two-month exchange/training trip that would encompass both New Zealand and Australia. In particular, B Squadron Air Troop would be co-located with us at Whenuapai on their 'Fast Glide' exercise, which basically meant that they would be jumping every day, for up to six times a day, using their own C130. It took barely a day to receive the clearance to use their aircraft and, naturally, the offer was reciprocated. Within no time at all we were back on track, heading for, and finally overtaking, the magical 40-jump mark well within time.

It was the first time that I had worked with another special forces unit, and it became a milestone in my military career. By the end of our course, the 22 SAS operation had left a huge impression on both Pete and myself.

* * *

The culmination of the British trip was a rugby match between the two SAS units, and B Squadron 22 SAS certainly fancied their chances against the less illustrious opposition.

Big Ken had been with B Squadron 22 SAS for two years now. He had left 1 NZSAS the year I returned from Singapore and had successfully completed the 22 SAS selection course of that same year. As a rugby utility back, I was a useful player who could put together a decent performance, but rarely a great one. Ken, on the other hand, was an outstanding rugby player, a former New Zealand Schoolboy representative who stood 6 ft tall and weighed about 16 st. He was characteristic of his troop at this time, B Squadron Boat being affectionately known throughout the regiment as 'sumo' troop. Nearly all of the Brits' forward pack was made up of sumo troop members, and most were much of a muchness size-wise.

Every time we met up on the pop, Ken would go on about how they were the regimental rugby champions and how much he was going to enjoy kicking our arses, especially mine. The conversation would always swing onto the topic. 'Yeah, Big Nose, what are you going to do when I come crashing through that maul and hammer you in a devastating tackle?' was usually his favourite line.

'Get a life, Jaw-Head, you would have to lose at least three stone to get anywhere near catching me. The only thing you are going to see is the colour of my studs as I scream past you for that try line,' and so it would go on.

The day of the big game arrived. The occasion warranted such attention that the Papakura camp commander had given all personnel not on essential duty the afternoon off to watch. The home team, myself included, had been practising a haka for the last couple of days to give the game some atmosphere and issue the time-honoured challenge. Unfortunately, half the team were Pakeha, and our pathetic efforts to do the war challenge justice proved so embarrassing that as many of us as possible were banished to the rear rank, where we most definitely belonged. Needless to say, on the day, the white boys looked a mess, but our mates in pole position did the unit proud, and the haka had the desired effect on all of us: we were ready for the kill.

What a lot of rugby-playing people around the world do not realise is that rugby is not just a game to New Zealanders; it is a religion, a way of life, and something that we all take very seriously. Be it for competition or just a friendly, you can be mates on opposing sides before and after the match, but while the match is being played, no prisoners are taken and no quarter given.

The camp RSM (Regimental Sergeant Major), who refereed in the local Counties Senior rugby championship, took charge of the game, and from the first blast on his whistle, he knew he had his hands full. The opening 20 minutes were basically a mass brawl, as the two opposing packs and half-backs tried to gain the ascendancy. Very little rugby was being played. The halves had been shortened to 30 minutes to give the home side less of an advantage, but by the end of the first half, the score indicated that this hadn't been necessary. At 13 points to nil in our favour, the Brits were more than holding their own. But the second half was a different story.

We started the second half determined not to let B Squadron's spoiling tactics dictate the game, and began to release quick ball out to the backs, with immediate results. By the final whistle we had amassed a total of 48 points, the only blemish being an intercept try of dubious quality (I'm sure the RSM was feeling sorry for them) scored by bloody Dinger of all people. When he scored, you would have thought that they had just won the World Cup, such was the celebration and self-congratulation.

I managed to score myself, but the most memorable moment of all was when I waltzed around Ken showing him a clean pair of heels. I even took the liberty of looking over my shoulder as I neared the try line, just in time to see him giving up the chase and wave a two-fingered salute. It is a moment I always like to bring up when he gets out of hand, and he and I both know that there is irrefutable proof of the event: it was video recorded, and I am the proud owner of a copy of the tape. Ken has yet to find it.

* * *

This cross-training between the Kiwi and British Special Forces proved to be the catalyst that both Pete and I were looking for. The two of us had considered resigning from the New Zealand Army and journeying overseas to try our fortunes on the 22 SAS selection course, but the visit of B Squadron provided the final impetus.

We felt like rugby players on the substitutes' bench, week in, week out, itching to get a game, to prove our worth, yet never getting the opportunity. As soldiers in the New Zealand Army, we didn't get the chance to test ourselves; so it was necessary to look further afield.

This wasn't a transition that was unique to our generation of soldiers – the path to 22 SAS had been well trodden before myself, Pete or Ken had even left primary school. Since the Vietnam War, there had been a steady trickle of Kiwis from what was then known as 1 Ranger Squadron SAS to the mother unit. Ambitious, confident and determined enough to travel 20,000 kilometres to risk all and start from scratch, most had succeeded. It was a flow of men that 22 didn't actively encourage but, by the same token, did nothing to discourage.

At B Squadron's departure function, I pulled Ken to one side and told him of our decision. Even in his inebriated condition, support for the resolution forced its way to the surface, 'Good one, Big Nose, I'll get a chance to beast your arse over the Fan.'

Pete and I had decided to aim for the August 1990 selection nine months hence and therefore laid down plans to coincide with that date. The first order of the day was to give notice to the unit, put in our 717s – request for voluntary discharge. The two of us, individually, were interviewed by both our squadron OC, and then commanding officer, but once the reason for our departure became apparent, they refrained from trying to dissuade us and wished us the best of luck.

B Squadron's Malaysian trip in January of the following year proved to be the last exercise we would participate in with the Kiwi unit. The squadron boarded a C130 Hercules at Whenuapai Air Base for the two-day flight to Malacca, Malaysia.

Within days we were into the routine: acclimatisation, recces, patrol administration and preparation for the ensuing three weeks. Initially, the squadron participated in an exchange with elements of the Malaysian Army, running small courses for them on subjects ranging from ambushing to tracking. In return, the Malaysians provided a short jungle survival course, run by some of the Ibans amongst them.

The exercise was my first chance to return to Malaysia since leaving the battalion, and the change within the country over the intervening three years was stark. Training areas that I knew quite well, previously lush primary jungle, had been cleared to make way for plantation development, new road systems and motorways. This was never more evident than on the final exercise. Recces had been carried out for the areas in question the year previously. The patrols infiltrated to their respective AOs, only to find huge areas of recently cleared jungle now replanted with oil palms, and numerous small villages housing locals scattered about providing an abundance of manpower. It took a lot of the impetus out of the squadron's training.

Our final week of the Malaysian trip allowed the squadron five days R & R, at which point a few of us decided to make the most of the opportunity and take a nostalgic journey south of the border to check out Singapore.

The Labour Government of David Lange had sealed the fate of the

New Zealand deployment in Singapore early in 1987, declaring that New Zealand forces would begin running down their operations in the country and finally depart the region for good by 1989.

Sitting at the customs/immigration point on the Malaysian side, waiting to be cleared to enter Singapore, evoked fond memories. Returning to Singapore via this route was commonplace after jungle training in the north, and once at the border, you knew that you were at most only a half-hour's drive from a good wash, meal and more than a few hard-earned, serious beers.

Our week in Singapore proved somewhat of an anti-climax. All of us were looking to try and recreate the atmosphere and ambience of a bygone era. We frequented a few of the old haunts, but without the raucous banter of 20 or so Kiwi grunts, or the twang of 'Ten Guitars', it just wasn't the same.

Within a few days of arriving in 'Singas', I made a pilgrimage to Dieppe Barracks, looking to see if there was any reminder of what had been. Driving my hire car off Sembawang Road and onto the small slipway that gives access to the camp, straightaway I could see that things had changed.

The high mesh and barbed-wire topped fence that surrounded the garrison prevented my access, but not my scrutiny. Staring through at the overgrown lawns, drab barrack blocks and leaf-covered roads, the garrison was hardly recognisable. A great wave of sadness passed over me, for it now struck home that the Dieppe I knew and had loved was no longer.

In that instant I was able to draw an analogy between the vision before me and my own path that was soon to commence. All things must come to an end sometime; Dieppe's time was over, just as mine in the New Zealand Army was soon to be. It was time to move on.

The week passed quickly, and soon we found ourselves back on the C130 headed for New Zealand. For Pete and I, the two-day trek gave us time to focus our thoughts and work out a plan of attack for the next couple of months leading up to our departure for the UK.

May 1990 was the month of discharge from the New Zealand Army that both Pete and myself had chosen, and it came along with astonishing speed. Once the administrative and logistical accounts had been settled with the NZSAS, all that was left was the group and squadron send-offs, both of which entailed copious amounts of alcohol consumption. At the official group 'piss-up', speeches were made and plaques presented. The hopes, expectations and best wishes of the Kiwi SAS were passed on to the two of us.

I don't think that until that moment it really struck home how much faith the members of the unit had in us, or how much we carried the pride and honour of our Kiwi squadron on our shoulders. A lot was expected of us, on both sides of the world. The Kiwis wanted us to show that they produced 'good fighting stock', able to mix it with the best. At the same time, however, the Brits expected the ex-Kiwi SAS candidates to do well and achieve an above average standard, and rightly so.

The squadron farewell 'do' was a much more relaxed affair but also emotionally more draining. The family atmosphere of B Squadron, the genuine warmth and respect that the guys had for each other, was definitely something unique, and I knew that it would be sorely missed. To this day, friendships forged in B Squadron 1 NZSAS Group have remained solid and can be picked up again at a moment's notice even after years without contact.

CHAPTER 12

22 SAS SELECTION, 1990

The weight of expectation bore heavily on our shoulders as Pete and I boarded the plane bound for Singapore, the first leg of our outward journey to the UK. A couple of mates turned up to see us off, but goodbyes are not either Pete's or my own forte, and we kept them as brief as possible.

As the plane departed Auckland International Airport, banking to the north-west to begin its long journey toward Australia and beyond, we were given a final glimpse of our home. Pete reached across and grasped my hand in a firm shake.

'This is it, mate,' he said, grinning broadly from cheek to cheek. 'Good luck.'

'Yeah, and to you, mate,' I replied, but at the same time, I could not help but wonder, 'Will I be back again?'

* * *

It was a warm summer's day when we finally landed at Lyneham, and there to meet us was Blue, a serving sergeant major in 22 SAS. He had long been a point of contact for Kiwis making the trip from NZSAS to Hereford, a trip he himself had made many years previously after completing his service in Vietnam.

SOLDIER FIVE

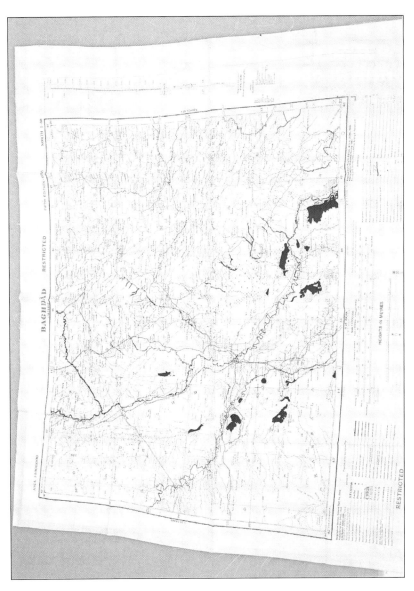

Escape map issued to the SAS troops.

NZ SAS continuation training Mount Ruapehu – white out.

SAS jungle training.

SOLDIER FIVE

B Squadron patrol, 1 NZSAS GP Malaysian exercise, 1990.

SOLDIER FIVE

Mike and Bomber take time out during snow
cave construction on Mount Ruapehu.

Mortar training, UAE.

SOLDIER FIVE

Author 'under canopy' – AFF (advanced free fall) course, NZSAS.

SOLDIER FIVE

4 Troop, A Squadron 22 SAS, Camp Manama, UAE, January 1991.

SOLDIER FIVE

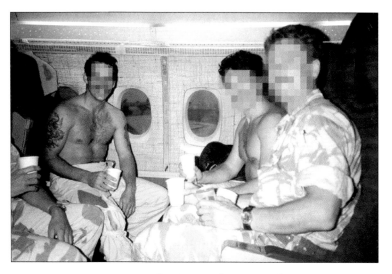

Happy campers a few hours after release from Iraq
– RAF shuttle from Saudi to Cyprus.

'Not rice again!' – first wholesome meal in weeks.

SOLDIER FIVE

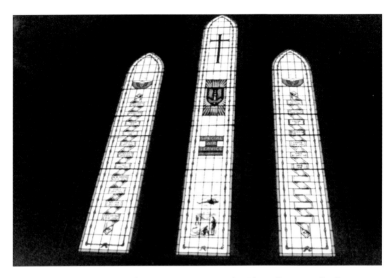

SAS Regimental corner, St Martin's Church, Hereford.
Stained glass dedication with SAS battle honours.

Mike and Pete training on the Brecons,
summer 1990.

SOLDIER FIVE

Final resting places for Vince Phillips (left) and Bob Consiglio (right).
Steve Lane has a plaque on an adjacent wall.

SOLDIER FIVE

Author's POW jacket, issued by the Iraqis on the day
of his handover to the International Red Cross.

SOLDIER FIVE

The famous beige beret and blue stable belt
worn by the Special Air Service.

SOLDIER FIVE

SOLDIER FIVE

من ، لفتنـــانت جنـــرال بيـــتر دي لا بيلـــير
From : Lieutenant General Sir Peter de la Billiere KCB CBE DSO MC

British Forces Commander Middle East
Headquarters
British Forces Middle East
Riyadh
BFPO 646
Tel. : 4766960

القوات البريطانية بالشرق الاوسط
قيـــادة
القوات البريطانية بالشرق الاوسط
الرياض
بي أف بي او ٦٤٦
تليفون ٤٧٦٦٩٦.

CDR/600/BFME

Trooper M J Coburn
c/o Commanding Officer
22 Special Air Service
Stirling Lines
Hereford

21 March 1991

I was delighted to hear of your release from Iraqi custody on
6 March 1991. I am aware that the period of internment must
have been a tense and stressful time and one that may take
some time to overcome. Please be assured that you were never
far from our thoughts during that period and any assistance I,
or my welfare staffs can give to ease any difficulties you may
encounter is most freely available.

I would like to thank you for the significant contribution you
made to the war effort. As you are aware, your mission was
one of the series vital to our plan and I know you pursued
your task with great diligence and endeavour. You will by now
be enjoying a well earned rest with your family and I am sure
this will be a happy and I hope a relaxed time. I hope that
after this period of leave you return refreshed to your duties
and I wish you well for the future.

*I hope we may meet later in
the year at Hereford*

*Yours
Sincerely
Peter de la Billiere*

Letter from Lieutenant General Sir Peter de la Billiere
following the author's release.

The two-hour drive to Hereford passed quickly, as Blue quietly detailed the events that would take place over the ensuing days, interspersed with little anecdotes relating to villages or points of interest along the way. Although I had been to England before, that visit had really only constituted a glorified drinking binge in London for a week, and I had most certainly never seen countryside or houses like those that passed by me. It was one thing learning Elizabethan or Victorian history in a New Zealand classroom, but actually seeing examples of architecture from this period – thatched cottages, 'black and whites', houses with walls that bowed out at angles that defied gravity – was fascinating.

As the ten-mile indicator for Hereford approached, Blue changed direction and skirted off to the north, explaining that we would be staying in one of many small satellite villages that were located around the city. We drove through a picturesque little village that reeked of the 'Old World' and pulled into the entrance of an old cottage.

'Well, this is your home for the next couple of months. Come on in and we'll get a brew on.'

Blue's cottage was an old sheriff's residence that dated back to the 1600s. He had lovingly restored and modernised it over the years so that it now gave the dweller the best of both worlds, old-world charm coupled with modern conveniences. The family was all there to greet us, now long-used to the nomadic visitors who habitually invaded their lives for a few short months.

After a quick guided tour, we settled down with Blue in the kitchen and mapped out the plan of action for the weeks leading up to the selection start date in August.

'The other boys have left an old Chevette for the two of you to use, but it needs to be re-taxed and tested. You will also need to change your New Zealand licences over to UK ones and then get insurance to cover the vehicle.'

'It will cost you about 200 pounds to insure if you have got proof of no claims from NZ, otherwise it will be a lot more,' Gail, Blue's wife added. 'I will take you into Hereford tomorrow and show you where to get it all sorted out.'

We had only been in the country a couple of hours, but already the expense of running a vehicle here was taking its toll on our budget. It would prove to be a costly necessity in the weeks ahead.

It had all seemed so easy in New Zealand – get out of the army, buy a ticket and get on a plane to the UK, do some training, start selection. What could be simpler?

The mountain of administration that our arrival had precipitated was truly a sight to behold. We not only had to contend with our own personal needs, such as opening bank accounts, car documentation, insurance and medical cover, but also the military's requirements, which were twice as comprehensive.

Normally a soldier had to have had four years' service in the British forces before being allowed to volunteer for SAS selection. Thus, he was already a documented and known quantity to the system. In our case, there was no history to fall back on, we didn't even have a parent unit to sponsor us for selection. Thus, to a large extent we had to 'bluff the system'. Joining R Squadron 22 SAS, the territorial arm of the regular regiment, became our route of admission.

We would be able to join in on their selection-training course run by 22 and supervised with both regular and ex-regular members. This proved to have many beneficial side effects, not least of which included gaining a valuable insight into the expectations of 22 SAS and having the opportunity to earn some much-needed cash in the process.

The deluge of forms and questionnaires that preceded this process took most of an afternoon to complete, and we needed Blue's assistance to help us decipher some of it.

The day was interrupted occasionally by various people turning up to say hello and wish us well, including Big Ken, who fronted up in the late afternoon.

'Hey there, Big Nose,' his usual greeting boomed across the house. 'So you've turned up to get your beasting after all!'

Ken shook hands with Pete and me and then continued, 'Right, I will be taking you up Brecon to visit the Fan on Saturday morning. Be ready to go at eight o'clock, OK.' Ken had obviously got all the pleasantries out of the way.

Penn-y-Fan, and its associated march known as the Fan Dance on selection, was one of the initial ball-busting walks which had to be completed in under an undisclosed time (set by the Training Wing DS according to the conditions of the day). Aspirants had to carry bergen and rifle. It was an extremely arduous and infamous walk that was designed to weed out the weaker members on selection, setting a minimum standard for the remainder of the course.

* * *

Saturday came, and along with it the first sight of what was to be our second home in the months to come, the Brecon Beacons. As we proceeded through the idyllic Welsh countryside, glimpses of what lay ahead came into view more and more frequently until we found ourselves winding our way amongst huge hills devoid of any vegetation apart from grass and the odd outcrop of trees. Ancient dry-stone walls separated pasture blocks upon which windblown sheep grazed, oblivious to the endless stream of vehicles that passed them by.

The traffic congestion that existed throughout the country took some getting used to. Being from Auckland, I was used to large volumes of vehicles, but whereas in New Zealand when you left the cities you could expect a relatively free and open road, here in the UK there was no such luck. The enormous constant flow of traffic everywhere was both mind-boggling and frustrating.

Deeper into the mountainous country we drove until Ken finally pointed out our objective, looming large and ominous amongst the surrounding hills, the highest amongst them.

'Over there, to your left.' We craned our necks to identify the peak.

'You can see Penn-y-Fan's escarpment now.'

The Fan stood proud atop the Brecons, joined on one side by a narrow ridge to a lesser cousin, its western approach a sheer cliff face, as if cleaved by an almighty axe stroke millions of years ago.

We parked at the Storey Arms car park at the base of the hills and unloaded a couple of day sacks that were packed with warm clothing, food and a hot flask. Although the weather appeared good, as I had found out to my detriment all those years before, you could never trust mountain climates to do the expected. Every year the Brecons exact some kind of toll on intrepid hikers who venture up their rugged slopes. The Mountain Rescue Team based in the Beacons are kept constantly busy thanks to those foolish enough to climb without taking the proper precautions.

Ken acted as guide, taking us along a public path that gradually wound its way amongst the lower reaches of Penn-y-Fan. From its base I couldn't really ascertain its size, as a continuous series of false crests kept the summit hidden for most of the time.

What began as a gentle stroll soon turned into a full-on hike, the incline increasing rapidly as we left the lower reaches. Now the true nature of the beast could be seen. Its stark barren features, with shale and slate boulders of all sizes haphazardly scattered around, were testament to the upheavals time had wrought here long ago. Although foreboding, it was at the same time majestic.

It took over an hour and a half to finally reach the summit, all of us bathed in a light sheen of sweat and slightly breathless from our exertions.

'You can see the full extent of the Fan Dance from here,' Ken said once his breathing had returned to normal.

It certainly was a spectacular scene, one that gave the observer an awesome view of the surrounding countryside, picture-postcard stuff.

'You two better make the most of this, because once you're on selection you'll never get the time to appreciate it.'

Ken described the route that the candidates had to follow, which entailed climbing the Fan twice, and then indicated points of note which were also relevant on other selection test walks. Pete and I listened intently, trying to absorb as much information as possible. Standing there on the precipice, one could easily have become severely intimidated by the scale of the task ahead. The terrain was daunting enough to navigate without the added encumbrances of weight and time handicaps.

'We'll move back down at the pace you need to be looking at to complete the march. It works out at about six kilometres per hour.'

Off we went, descending at what appeared to me to be reckless break-neck speed, although later on I would consider this the norm. It was a blistering pace to move at, considering that we had yet to be carrying any significant weight, or a weapon for that matter. Passers-by, those not quite so deranged as we, looked on with complete confusion as we barrelled on down, half-running, half-skipping down the steep slopes.

We managed to reach the bottom and the safety of the car park in one piece, although considerably more out of breath than before.

'What a fucking stupid way to get down a mountain,' I moaned between gasps. 'That's asking for torn ligaments and tendons at the very least!'

'Well, everyone goes through the same thing, Big Nose, so it is obviously possible.'

I could sense the prod coming out again. 'Just a matter of conditioning, I suppose,' I responded as my breathing normalised. 'Just hate to think of coming all this way and blowing it on an injury.'

Both Pete and I were fully aware of the devastating effects that an early injury would have on our selection chances. The very nature of the selection process, the way it was designed to build up your stamina at the same time as increasing the pressure on you to perform harder and more demanding tasks, left no room for the body to recover. If you picked up an injury early on, your chances of completing selection successfully were negligible. The thought of failing selection never entered our minds, but the mortal fear of incurring a debilitating injury was ever-present. We had neither the luxury of income or a home base to fall back on if an injury occurred.

The drive back to Hereford gave me a chance to ponder the challenge ahead. Standing there on top of the Fan had finally brought home the reality of the situation. Failure was not an option; pride alone meant that I would would not allow myself to be overcome by the rigours and demands of selection. I knew that if I could master the Fan Dance, all else would fall into place.

On our return to Blue's cottage, Pete and I held a serious conference, both realising the necessity of training that would condition us well enough to achieve the required standards, but not allow us to peak too soon.

We agreed that the Fan Dance would be our benchmark and that, as we had eight weeks till the beginning of selection, it would be good to aim for the four-week point as the date to test ourselves on this route. To gauge our progress in this manner gave us the option to alter our training, if need be, to suit the result. Getting out a calendar, we planned our assault accordingly. It was decided that four days a week up on the hills should be ample to start with, the remaining three days being used for alternative training, such as running, cycling, swimming and non-loadbearing walks. The most balanced programme worked out as two days' hill work with bergens, one day alternative training, two days with bergens again, followed by two days of alternative training or rest. This also allowed us the flexibility to increase the intensity if required.

So, charged full of enthusiasm and vigour, we dived headfirst into our self-imposed training regime. Early each morning, as the programme dictated, we would load up the 'Blue Streak' with our gear and head off on the hour-plus journey to Brecon.

At first the body rejected such a continuous hammering, leaving the two of us sore and exhausted, both physically and mentally. But this was simply a question of breaking through the pain barrier, which is something we had done before on many different projects.

Although on a totally different plane, both Pete and I had been into triathlon training at one stage, which presented the participant with a similar kind of challenge and a not-so-dissimilar barrier to cross.

The days of hill- and road-work very rapidly turned into weeks, and the body stubbornly responded, finally acceding to the demands being made upon it. Although neither of us was fat, the amount of calories our metabolisms consumed in the course of a day ensured that even the last vestiges of excess weight were soon lost: lean, hard muscle appearing in its stead. What at first had proved hard and laborious, even with little weight on our backs to contend with, now proved to be hardly a challenge at all, our legs seemingly capable of eating up the steep Welsh slopes with inordinate ease.

But a slightly worrying factor still remained. Without actually knowing the routes or timings, it was extremely difficult to judge if our progress was sufficiently advanced to pass the selection pace that would be set. We could make all the assumptions in the world, but only a known test over a known route would allay any nagging doubts that might exist. It was time for our own Fan Dance.

The Beacons presented us with a stunningly beautiful summer's morning to mount our charge on the Fan. As I thought of the 26 kilometres of rugged, mountainous Welsh countryside that lay in wait for us, I knew that if we blitzed the route it would give us both a huge psychological boost. Of course, the opposite would occur if we blew it, but that was not going to happen.

Loading the 45-lb bergen onto my back, the slightly modified and well-worn padded straps creaking as the weight distributed itself through them and onto my now-acclimatised shoulders, I glanced at Pete. 'Time to put our money where our mouths are, mate. Let's blow this mother away!'

Pete stood stony-faced and squinting as he regarded the distant summit. I could almost see him visualising the route and climb in his mind, a picture of concentration. Always a deep thinker, he was never as impulsive as me, but then he was about 50 years older, or looked that way at least.

Consulting his watch, he replied, 'Twenty-six Ks in under four hours. That's six and a half Ks an hour minimum. No problem, let's do it!'

Stopwatches running, we hit the track at half-pace to start with, giving the body time to kick into gear, blood to circulate through all the muscles and joints to limber up. Within ten minutes we were in full stride, somewhere between a half-run and a power walk, alternating between the two to fit the ground. The trick was to keep a good steady pace throughout the march. As fast as possible on the ascent, which would obviously slow somewhat as the gradient increased, a slight jog on the plateaux and a full-on run downhill. This was the only way to maintain the required average speed over the whole route.

Within the hour we reached the first major hurdle en route, known as 'Jacob's Ladder', a name that aptly described the method needed to conquer the obstacle. Although only a short stretch of hill, about 50 metres or so, it was a near-vertical climb over huge scattered boulders that provided no easy path to the summit, which lay just a few more metres beyond.

We attacked Jacob's Ladder with gusto, but soon slowed to a crawl, the fierceness of the ascent exacting vicious physical retribution on the body, which converted into a loss of average speed. To make matters worse, the time penalty was not one that could be reversed on the return route, for caution, not speed, would be the order of the day descending.

Clearing the Ladder first, I carried on to the summit, eager to reach it first and needing to ease the strain off my screaming quads and calves.

Pausing at the crest, I turned expecting to see Pete right beside me, but he was still someway back. Normally either I would be on Pete's shoulder or he on mine, the two of us competitively pushing each other on, so to see him lagging behind was extremely unusual.

Marking time to keep myself warm, I yelled some encouragement in his direction. 'Come on then, you old scrote, we haven't got all day.' No sooner were the words out of my mouth than I noticed that he wasn't walking too freely. Joviality immediately turned to concern. 'What have you done, mate?'

'I slipped and twisted my knee. I can feel it starting to swell already.'

We were silent for a minute, not wishing to acknowledge the implications of that occurrence. I took note of the time before dropping my bergen and retrieving the small medical pack.

'Roll your trouser leg up; I'll strap the knee up. At least that will reduce the swelling.'

As with all soft-tissue injuries, RICE (Rest, Ice, Compression and Elevation) treatment was the best solution to control the injury and aid recovery. The Rest, Ice and Elevation elements were out of the question at this stage, but at least applying a compression bandage went some way towards sorting the problem out.

Pete dropped his bergen, sat on it and did as I ordered. Taking the crepe bandage from its package, I strapped the knee tightly, trying to restrict the blood flow to that area to as little as possible.

'It doesn't hurt that much,' he said, 'but it's not worth risking. I'm going to bin it here and take a leisurely walk back down to the car.'

Although he didn't say it, I could tell he was severely pissed off with himself.

'You've only stopped for a couple of minutes, so crack on and I'll see you at the other end.'

I regarded him for a minute before answering. 'All right, then. Just make sure you don't push it. We've plenty of time before selection, so there's no panic.'

With that, I hoisted my bergen once again and set off along the ridge towards Storey Arms at full stretch, both aiming to make up for lost time and trying not to think of the implications of Pete's injury.

I made the halfway point in good time, the ten-minute halt on the summit not having any effect thus far, but this was no real indication of my progress as the 60-degree hike back up to the summit was the real test of character. The next hour seemed like a lifetime, my chest heaving and legs screaming under the constant strain of the climb, but I reached the Fan's peak still on target, which left the downhill stretch to the vehicle.

Upon my return, Pete was lying next to the car, shirt stripped off, bronzing himself – 'becoming one with nature', no doubt. We all knew there was a repressed hippie inside of him waiting to burst out of the closet.

Freeing my aching back of its load, I threw the bergen beside the vehicle, checking my stopwatch at the same time. 'Three hours, 25 minutes. That's including the short stop at the top. All right, kicked arse,' I said to no one in particular. It didn't matter to anyone but myself that the psychological barrier had been successfully crossed. I felt strong, confident and elated. The last lagging doubts had been quashed, and I knew I was ready.

Pete's injury proved to be serious enough to keep him from hill training for a week, but an intensive regime of physiotherapy complemented with plenty of swimming saw him in action again very quickly. It was, however, enough of a scare to emphasise to both of us the importance of concentrating on the task at hand, especially when carrying heavy loads.

We decided that the remaining weeks leading up to selection did not require such an intensive programme, and concluded that by simply keeping the training ticking over, we could maintain our current levels without peaking too soon or burning out. There would be more than enough hills to climb in the weeks preceding 'Test Week'.

STIRLING LINES, 2 AUGUST 1990

Pete and I stood out like sore thumbs as the first parade of selection 2/90 assembled in the quadrangle at Stirling Lines. Standing there in our combat DPMs (camouflage uniforms), devoid of any regimental embellishment with which to show our affiliation, we received more than a few curious stares.

It appeared as though the whole of the British Army was represented here in one form or another. Some of the array of cap badges on display were, to our uninformed and ignorant eyes, bizarre to say the least, and to this day I still have no idea what regiment they were associated with. There was, as one would expect, a good proportion of paras scattered about, congregating in their little groups. The paras alone probably supplied nearly 40-odd per cent of the manpower that 22 SAS had on call.

The roll was called. We were organised into our various syndicates and allocated barrack rooms. The barracks were sectioned off into ten-man rooms, and as I unpacked my equipment I wondered how many of these bed spaces would still be occupied in four weeks' time.

I have always been a firm believer in first impressions. As soon as I entered my room, I assessed the blokes around me and immediately rated their chances, something that I am sure was reciprocated. As it was, our syndicate proved to be very strong, and most of the ten beds were still occupied by the close of test week. The same could not be said of Pete's room, however; by the end of play, he was the last left.

Selection started in earnest the next day and began with the military's standard fitness tests: a short pack and weapon march to be completed in under two hours and a two-mile run to be completed in under nine minutes. Surprisingly, some failed these benchmarks and were immediately shown the door.

Day four was the big day for the candidates and one that all the course talked about. Lots of the blokes were on their second or third selection and knew the routine off by heart, but still the Fan Dance was the make-or-break point.

At 0600, the candidates were packed into row upon row of green canvassed trucks and driven the now-familiar two-hour route to Brecon. I had been feeling very confident the evening before but now felt a little uneasy, a mood that revealed itself in a feeling of travel sickness as we drove on to the Beacons.

Due to the numbers involved, the course was separated into two groups, each starting from either end of the march. Once again, the candidates were split into small groups, separated at five-minute intervals, and each had its own DS who would set the pace for the march.

'If you stick with the DS, you will finish in under the time,' were the words of advice from the chief instructor.

* * *

As soon as the march commenced, I knew that something was not right; the feeling of nausea had not disappeared. My legs felt like lead weights, even at the beginning of the route, and I was struggling to keep up with the leaders. The mind was willing but the body wouldn't respond.

At the summit I was a minute or so behind the DS, at the halfway point a couple of minutes, and on the return, on top of Penn-y-Fan again, a good five minutes distant.

All the while I kept an eye on my watch, judging the pace that the DS was setting and comparing it to my own. At this rate, I would come in about ten minutes behind him. I would be cutting it fine.

I finally completed the march in three hours fifty minutes, some twelve minutes after the DS had finished, and was completely shattered. Somewhere, somehow, the plan had gone horribly wrong. As it turned out, my time was good enough to avoid the compulsory cut-off mark that had originally been set at four hours.

The Fan Dance had achieved its aim, helped in no small measure by the scorching temperatures that blasted the candidates during the day, several of whom had to be treated for heat injuries both on the tab and afterwards. This reduction in numbers to an amount that was workable was a necessary evil for the selection staff. The idea was to have about 40 or so candidates left after the completion of test week to carry on the process for the jungle phase in Brunei later on.

I wasn't able to talk to Pete till later on that evening, but then found that he also was feeling under the weather. Our speculation was confirmed later that evening when the two of us came down with severe bouts of vomiting and diarrhoea – what a time to pick up a bug. Fortunately the next few days were not too intense and we had time to recover from the illness. Soon I felt my strength return to normal and I was able to attack the ensuing tests full of enthusiasm.

* * *

The final and most difficult challenge facing the candidates on selection was 'Endurance'. This was an arduous march that encompassed 100 kilometres of mountainous Brecon countryside. We had to carry 60 lb of weight and complete it in under 18 hours.

By the time Endurance comes along, the course has just about sorted itself out. Those who have made it this far are not the type to pack it in so close to the end, so, barring injury, you would expect more than 90 per cent to finish in time.

A pitch black and chilly 0330 kick-off was what awaited us when we finally arrived in Brecon. The now-not-so-numerous candidates wound their way up the steep slopes single file, trudging on one after the other at the five-minute intervals dictated by the DS.

The early morning light revealed a line of soldiers that stretched intermittently for kilometres, the small orange draped bergens visible at great distances.

I reached the halfway stage in seven hours and then, a couple of hours into the return leg, I paused on top of a ridgeline for a quick brew and something to eat. I had just settled down to my fare when two camouflaged men rudely interrupted me.

'Hello, there,' one of the men said in a very posh-sounding voice. 'Do you think you've got time to spare for that?'

I regarded the two of them cautiously over my mug of steaming coffee. Neither was carrying a bergen of any sort; in fact, both looked as if they were out for a quiet country stroll.

'I'm well ahead on my time so I'm allowing myself a 15-minute break before continuing.'

'You're not British. Where are you from, Australia?'

If only I had a dollar for every time someone had asked me that question since I had arrived in the UK. You would think that my country didn't exist.

'New Zealand,' I replied carefully, aware that I was obviously talking to an officer of some sort.

The man turned to his companion. 'I didn't know we had any foreigners on selection.'

'Yes, sir,' he replied. 'There are a couple of Kiwis on this one.'

He turned back towards me. 'Well, I wouldn't stay here too long. You still have a considerable distance to go.'

With that, the two of them moved off down the ridge and were out of my sight within minutes. I didn't know it at the time, but that was my first introduction to the CO and RSM of 22 SAS.

Pete and I met up at various stages on Endurance, each of us keeping the other's spirits up, pushing and cajoling one another on. As the kilometres increased, however, the pace slowed considerably, the weeks of constant walking without respite beginning to take their toll.

The last few hours were some of the most painful I had ever walked. My feet were swollen and blistered inside what felt like leaden, glass-filled combat boots. It was this type of barrier, one of both body and mind, that had to be conquered in order to claim the prize, one that was now so close.

Standing atop that last peak, staring down the beautiful pine-forested ridge that plummeted straight into a reservoir of crystal-clear water bathed in early evening light, the thought briefly registered that people part with hard-earned cash to see sights such as these. But at that moment, the only vista that mattered to me was the line of small green trucks parked abreast a picnic area some five short kilometres distant. These trucks constituted the end of my current ordeal.

By the time I was able to pass my name to the DS standing by the waiting wagons, nearly 17 hours had elapsed since first stepping out on Endurance's opening leg.

CHAPTER 13

CONTINUATION TRAINING, 1990

The days immediately following the end of test week were given over to leave and recuperation, a chance at last for the body to recover from the non-stop barrage of the past 24 days. It also was the first time that we had come to grips with what had happened in the world over the last three weeks. News of Iraq's invasion of Kuwait, although interesting, didn't seem to have much bearing on our immediate situation.

Pete and I were invited to a hangi that B Squadron was putting on in one of the lad's backyards. The Kiwi presence on show – Big Ken, Pete, myself and George, one of the NZSAS guys over on exchange – were expected to do the honours, but we were about as much use as tits on a bull. Our expertise lay in eating hangis, not cooking them. Still, we managed to bluff our way through and a good night was had by all, the copious amounts of beer consumed going some way towards alleviating the pain our bodies still felt.

The next phase of selection took place in the deep primary jungles of South-east Asia, courtesy of the independent state of Brunei. We flew out to Hong Kong with British Airways, this in itself a novelty for me, as I had never travelled anywhere with the New Zealand Army on anything other than military aircraft. From Hong Kong we were supposed to catch an RAF Tristar to Brunei, but the massive build-up in the Gulf that was unexpectedly under way meant that no aircraft was available to fly us there. So we ended up being stranded in Hong Kong for five days, much to our disappointment (not), before being whisked away by Air Brunei.

Over 40 candidates arrived in Brunei to start the jungle selection, and by the end of the 5 weeks, 13 would emerge unscathed and ready to carry on the challenge in the UK.

The first week in Brunei was spent acclimatising to the heat, humidity and the new time zone, as well as patrol allocation and preparation. Jungle selection appeared to cause more apprehension with the candidates than test week did, which, considering the fact that the majority of the soldiers had never seen the J, let alone had to live in it for weeks on end, was not all that surprising.

Pete and myself, while not over-confident, were relaxed about this phase. After all, most of our military experience had been gained in this type of theatre, but there was still no room for complacency.

Within the first week of entering the jungle, the number of VWs (voluntary withdrawals) had reduced our number by a third. The 'green wall' was too much for some of them.

My patrol went through a number of personnel changes; only Quinny, a stocky Yorkshireman nicknamed 'The Cube', and I survived from our original group.

The first Navex (navigation exercise) patrol we embarked upon nearly resulted in a shouting match between Quinny and myself. Because of our accents, neither of us was able to understand what the other was saying. However, we gained a mutual respect for each other over the ensuing weeks and became friends.

Jungle selection was one of the most intense courses I had ever experienced, one that demanded every spare minute of the day, and then some. The patrols were worked from dawn till dusk, virtually without respite, incorporating lessons on subject matter ranging from simple navigation to complex ambushing techniques.

Live firing exercises were staged to bring on both confidence and skill levels, the margins for error so tight that the slightest doubt in an instructor's mind over the competence of a soldier resulted in his dismissal. In conditions such as these, where rounds were quite literally being fired over your head, you had to be able to trust your companions implicitly.

The persistent rain, heat and oppressive humidity combined to do their utmost to increase the stress that all were placed under. It was an environment specifically selected to do just that.

At various stages, exercises were thrown in to both test and confirm the skills taught and under conditions designed to produce results that were the next best thing to those of combat.

Of the weight-diminished, filthy and unshaven candidates who emerged after four weeks, many were to be deemed not up to the required standard. The remainder who were successful could look forward to a couple of days off before attempting the next hurdle: combat survival.

* * *

On our return from Brunei, it became evident to me very quickly that the crisis in the Gulf was not something that was just going to blow over. I was amazed at the speed with which the United States and Britain had mobilised forces in such great numbers to send to the region. However, I still couldn't bring myself to believe that Saddam Hussein would continue to defy the United Nations Security Council and the majority of world opinion by opting to keep Iraqi occupying forces in Kuwait.

I recalled a conversation I had with Blue after dinner on our first evening.

'Mark my words,' he had said, 'it will all kick off in the Gulf within the next six to twelve months. I guarantee it.' I had not pressed him further on the comment at the time but, looking back, it was either a very good guess, or Blue had an extremely astute grasp of events and the political manoeuvrings that forever grip that troubled region.

* * *

I was not looking forward to combat survival at all. Memories of my New Zealand course and the stone and a half in weight I had lost were still vividly clear, even six years on.

The course was actually open to all elements of the British armed forces, and invited guests from other foreign forces were also allowed to participate. Run over a three-week period, it covered a variety of subjects ranging from resistance to interrogation and escape and evasion techniques, to traps, snares and living off the land. This all culminated in the final exercise when the participants, in their separate syndicates, were let loose in the remote northern Welsh countryside to fend for themselves and navigate through a network of agents, at the same time trying to avoid capture by a sizeable hunter force.

Freezing my backside off in the middle of the Welsh winter, wishing the days to pass quickly so the course would be over, the thought never once occurred to me that I could be conducting the same routine, only for real, in a few months' time. The irony of the situation was not lost on me come January the following year.

The course ended with all the syndicates being 'captured' and then subjected to interrogation of one kind or another, the prospective SAS candidates singled out for special treatment as befitted their lofty aspirations.

Thus, providing the candidates emerged from the final exercise without having 'cracked' under interrogation, the coveted beige beret and blue belt, both adorned with the famous winged dagger, were there for the taking.

* * *

Four months on from the commencement of selection, 13 of us sat in the conference room in Training Wing as the CI (Chief Instructor) came in with a large, brown cardboard box. Walking to the middle of the room, he simply dipped his hand in and began throwing out the berets to each of us.

'We don't stand on ceremony here, and this doesn't mean your selection has finished,' he said. 'You have continuation training, para training for those of you who haven't already jumped, and then you are on probation for a year. So, it's still easy to fuck up!'

Even so, he couldn't suppress the pride we all felt at having achieved our goal. Pete and I were particularly chuffed, for we had put it all on the line to be here at this point, to be successful.

The CI then read out the list of who was going to what squadron, and both Pete and I were rewarded with A Squadron. We treated this news with excitement, for the whole regiment knew that A Squadron was definitely being deployed to the Gulf and the others would have to fight it out.

The remaining weeks leading up to Christmas were spent on the counter-terrorist team training course.

I had found the counter-terrorist training fascinating on my New Zealand selection, but having spent two solid years on stand-by with the NZ CTT, the novelty had worn off. My thoughts now were concentrated towards events in the Gulf and my imminent deployment there with A Squadron. Although the tactics of room combat and hostage rescue remained basically the same, there were subtle differences in techniques that Pete and I had to master, much the same as we did in the jungle with the different contact drills. We were here to assimilate, so being able to adapt our previous training and knowledge was essential to avoid conflict.

The course ended a week into December and we were posted to our relevant squadrons soon after, the various troops eager to get their hands on the much-needed new manpower.

Pete and I, along with the other crows (new squadron members), had barely time to assemble in the A Squadron interest room, let alone meet the other 50-odd guys who made up our complement, before the details of our departure for the Gulf were announced.

'Twenty-fourth, 2200 hours on a Galaxy out of Brize. The armoury will be open from 1800 to draw personal weapons, transport departs at 1830,' the Squadron Sergeant Major announced to the group.

'Parade on the 23rd to load the trucks with your kit. The rest of the time is your own. If you miss that plane, then you better get straight down the travel agent and buy yourself a ticket out there, because we won't be waiting!

'That's it: all the troop staff sergeants and the new lads stay behind. The rest of you bugger off and enjoy the Bun Fight.'

At this point we found out to what troops we had been assigned; mine was Boat Troop. I heaved a sigh of relief at this news, having had no desire to be in Air Troop again – I wanted something different.

After being introduced to the squadron head-shed, I was welcomed by the Four Troop boss and staff sergeant.

'I know you haven't got much time to meet everyone, let alone sort your kit out, but you'll have plenty of time when we get to the UAE and start the build-up package,' the boss explained. 'Till then, make the most of your leave, it will probably be the last for a while.'

* * *

The Bun Fight is an annual event at which the regiment lets its hair down for an afternoon and evening. Normally, the Bun Fight commences with the Inter-Squadron rugby final and is followed close after by the consumption of vast quantities of alcohol.

Christmas is one of the few times of the year that sees the regiment in Hereford as a whole. For the most part, you are lucky if there are two squadrons in town at any one time, hence the Bun Fight is an opportunity for everyone to catch up on past months and have a few beers in the process.

The rugby final this year was between the combined teams of B Squadron/Headquarters Squadron and G Squadron/Signals. Ken had already approached me to play for B/HQ Squadron while I was still with Training Wing, and because A Squadron was not represented, there was no conflict of interest. So I agreed.

I took to the field in a completely borrowed strip, boots included, and then proceeded to play one of the worst games of my life, as a first-five eighth. Playing amongst some of the guys whom I had helped demolish in New Zealand the year earlier was an interesting experience, as was their total lack of team co-ordination. However, the combined B/HQ team managed to prevail on the day and won by a comfortable margin, their opponents proving slightly more disorganised.

The evening's festivities provided the opportunity for all and sundry to let their hair down, en masse, for one night of the year. I awoke the next morning with a hangover from hell, but that was somewhat alleviated by the news that our flight had been delayed by 48 hours. We would be spending Christmas in the UK after all.

* * *

The 27th of December was our eventual deployment date, a cold and miserable winter's day across the country. On arriving at Brize Norton, we were directed to a huge aircraft that dwarfed the rows of Hercules

C130s near it. On entering the Galaxy, I could see row upon row of Landrovers, motorcycles, palletised kit, stores and munitions. It was like a vast long warehouse. No seats were visible, so I assumed that we were to find a space amongst all the freight.

Much to my surprise, a ladder was lowered from the ceiling, and this took us to a level within the aircraft that was decked out 747-style, with rows of comfortable seats stretching its length and breadth. An American master sergeant, complete with .44 Magnum pistol slung shoulder-holster fashion, was allocating seats and distributing food cartons for the journey.

An American military base in Germany was our initial stop. It was my first experience of an American military establishment and quite an eye-opener. The base had been designated as a transit stop for traffic headed to the Gulf, and therefore had set up facilities to cater for this. The marquee that had been raised to cater for the influx of troops could only be described as colossal and its interior was something else to behold.

Inside, various entertainment facilities had been set up that could best be described as a combined amusement arcade-cum-video centre. There was everything from pinball machines to space invader games, along with banks of televisions and video recorders. Stretched the length of the tent, a distance of probably a hundred metres or more, were rows of tables housing goods and small gifts that the American public had sent to their 'boys' overseas.

Last but by no means least, the walls of the marquee were adorned with hundreds of letters from schoolchildren, mothers, fathers, Americans from all walks of life, all wishing the soldiers that passed through well and reassuring them that God and country were behind them 100 per cent.

It was quite a bizarre experience for someone from such a small and conservative country as New Zealand to see this outpouring of emotion from complete strangers. The Americans sure had a different way of doing things.

Our brief sojourn in Germany lasted only a couple of hours, and before long we were aboard the Galaxy once more, outward bound for the United Arab Emirates.

* * *

The first thing that struck me about the UAE was the searing dry heat that caught the back of my throat, completely different to the heat combined with 100 per cent humidity you experienced in South-east Asia. Although it was winter, the daytime temperatures still regularly exceeded 30 degrees centigrade, dropping to a pleasant and more manageable 18 degrees at night.

We arrived at a large military base in Abu Dhabi and were then transported by C130 to our training area in the desert, near a town called Manama. The training camp we took over had only recently been vacated by G Squadron, who, much to their disgust, having finished their three-month tour in the Gulf, were forced to return to Hereford and begin the process of taking over the CTT role from B Squadron.

Things were heating up between the UN and Iraq, and the deadline of 15 January 1991 that Saddam had been given by the Security Council to withdraw all forces from Kuwait was drawing ever closer.

The squadron set about methodically training in as many aspects of desert warfare as possible, the emphasis being placed on vehicle-mounted operations with accompanied heavy support weapon systems. I had never even seen the desert, let alone trained for war in it, and so I dived into the package full of enthusiasm, eager to learn as much as possible in the short time available.

The squadron would be deploying as two half-squadron entities, each half a mixture of youth, skills and experience, though maintaining troop integrity as much as possible.

All manner of desert warfare was practised, from the mundane such as digging out sand-trapped vehicles, to the full-on action of night assaults with combined mortar and vehicle-mounted heavy weapon fire support. There weren't enough hours in the day to accomplish all that needed to be revised and taught, but the basics were covered and what was left was put down to 'on the job training'.

New Year's Eve rolled on in and the squadron celebrated with plenty of cases of beer and the umpteenth re-run of *Zulu*, a favourite with the boys. A ten o'clock start the next day was all the reprieve that could be afforded for those with a hangover, and to make matters worse the first order of the day was the parade in front of the RMO (Regimental Medical Officer) to receive every jab and inoculation known to mankind.

Many were concerned about the effects such a large dose of drugs would have in one shot, but with the January deadline drawing ever nearer, such reservations soon faded into the background.

The 13th of January saw the squadron placed on 24 hours' notice to move forward to the Special Forces Group Forward Mounting Base in Saudi Arabia. Everyone knew that something was up – until now we had been training in the hope that some sort of mission would be passed our way in the event of full-on hostilities. Perhaps this heightening of our alert status boded well for that wish.

The training over the previous three weeks had brought me up to scratch with all the SOPs and weapons systems that I would be dealing with in a desert campaign, and had taught me how to settle into a comfortable routine living out of a pinkie. Hence, when the order to move arrived less than a day and a half later, it was with boyish enthusiasm that I boarded the C130 bound for Saudi and whatever lay beyond.

By mid-January 1991, two massive armies, both consisting of over half a million men, stood on opposite sides of the Saudi–Kuwait border, each convinced of the righteousness of their cause. The scale of men and machinery assembled had not been seen anywhere since the Second World War, and the two combatants looked set for confrontation, no matter what diplomatic manoeuvring was attempted.

At 0300, 17 January 1991, the American-led coalition forces launched air attacks against Iraqi military and industrial targets, signalling the end of Operation Desert Shield and the commencement of Operation Desert Storm. The Persian Gulf War had just begun.

PART III
GUEST OF SADDAM

CHAPTER 14

KRABILAH, NORTHERN IRAQ

There was no pain, only shock, as if someone had taken a sledgehammer to my ankle and smashed it into a million little pieces. I was certain I had just lost my right foot. A brief, intense wave of nausea swept through me. And then the pain hit, totally possessing my mind, body and soul.

I fell to the ground, all thoughts of using the knife dispelled. Instinctively I tried to protect my head with my arms, an old habit used to ward off errant rugby boots whilst underneath a ruck. However, the futility of this gesture was exposed immediately as a second round cleaved my right tricep, missing my head by centimetres. Fear finally had a chance to truly manifest itself as the bullets continued to dance all around. All pretence at bravado long gone, I was shitting myself. Screaming like a banshee as the pain, frustration and fear overtook all my thoughts, I had time to wonder, 'What the fuck have I done to deserve this?' And, to my surprise, in a moment of absolute clarity I found myself reciting the Lord's Prayer, utterly convinced that my own death was but a few seconds away.

All this took a minute at most, but in my demented state it appeared never-ending. I almost wished that a final bullet would bring it to an end.

The firing stopped abruptly, the Iraqis realising that the pathetic figure prostrate before them was no longer a threat, or they had run out of ammunition. Either way, it made little difference to me as I lay writhing in agony on the ground, desperately clutching at my injured leg.

Within seconds I was surrounded by dozens of screaming Iraqis ecstatic at their success in capturing one of the hated enemy. Suddenly they were all over me, hands thrusting into any conceivable pocket that might reward the searcher with a trophy or something of value. My diver's watch was gone in seconds, a small scuffle ensuing over who should actually be the proud new owner. At the same time, they were firing off their AKs into the air in all directions and yelling that ear-piercing yell that only Arabs can make, to celebrate their success.

For a minute I thought they had forgotten all about me, such was the intensity of their joy, but all too soon their carnival air vanished and the boots and rifle butts began raining in. The pain that had only seconds previously been centred in my lower right leg was once again dispersed throughout my body. What the bullets hadn't managed to do, the beating would surely finish off successfully.

I was on the verge of unconsciousness when the pounding finally stopped. Somebody realised that their victim was no longer responding to their affections. An SNCO, who had instigated much of the bombardment, exerted a modicum of restraint and control over what was fast becoming a lynch mob, obviously realising that things were getting out of control. He ordered two of the nearest soldiers to grab my arms and I was unceremoniously dragged the remaining 15 metres to the road where a Toyota pick-up was parked.

Fear now held full sway. I was completely at the mercy of these people and it looked as if it would take very little for one of them to simply give me a coup de grâce at any moment. The fact that I had survived this far was nothing short of a miracle.

A new group of soldiers waiting by the vehicle were now able to get their hands on me. The whole cycle started over again. Thankfully an officer arrived on the scene and called a halt to the soldiers' enthusiastic sport, only allowing the new boys a minute or so of fun. More important people were now aware of my capture and eagerly awaited their chance.

A rapid burst of Arabic scattered the massed ranks, allowing the officer to get his first good look at me. In the half-light of early morning I could see little but the outline of his dark-green military jacket and black beret, but his smiling and nodding head gave me the impression that he was well-pleased with his work. Careful not to get too close, he ordered a couple of soldiers to search me, which they did with surprising reluctance. I was patted-down with such timidity that an onlooker would have thought there was a possibility that I was going to suddenly leap up and slit all their throats.

The next major drama was the removal of the Magellan from my possession. The group of assembled Iraqis, who must have numbered over 40 by now, all took a few paces back, fearing that they had just discovered a bomb that was in imminent danger of exploding. I braced myself for the barrage of kicks and rifle butts that I was sure would accompany that discovery, but, to my surprise, once they realised that the small machine was inert, they returned and continued with the search in the same vein. Aching all over, I tried to present myself as no threat whatsoever to my captors, allowing myself to be searched, moved, pushed and prodded at will, trying not to provoke another attack.

The cursory search finished, another order was barked and I was manhandled onto the waiting Toyota. Three soldiers leapt into the back to keep me company, two maintaining guard while the third proceeded to tie my arms, spread-eagle fashion, to the sides of the vehicle. The breaking dawn gave me a last taunting view of my surroundings before a blindfold was slipped over my eyes. The communications mast that marked the border was clear on the skyline, no more than a couple of kilometres away. It was so close that I had to forcibly hold back the tears of frustration and failure. It may as well have been 200 kilometres away.

Within minutes of the vehicle starting to move, I had lost all sense of direction. I was having enough trouble maintaining my sanity, let alone trying to remember which way the pick-up was travelling. The dull ache throughout my body was a constant companion, but one that was regularly overridden as the jolting Toyota bounced my injured leg about the rear of the pick-up. As the vehicle moved about, the muzzle of an AK constantly bashed into the side of my temple; one of the guards was either trying to steady himself, or simply reminding me that I was being closely watched.

At one point we slowed almost to a crawl, the massed voices of scores of Arabs coupled with incoming stones informing me that I was being paraded through the village for all to see and gloat over. This source of amusement quickly faded, however, as the indignant guards realised that they were probably on the receiving end of as many, if not more, missile hits. A particularly loud yelp followed by a rush of Arabic had us moving once more toward the intended destination.

The sudden halt and burst of automatic gunfire into the air announced our arrival. I could feel tens of pairs of hands trying to pull me from the truck, even before my bonds had been released. A scream of pain ripped from my throat as they tried to use my injured leg as a fulcrum with which to lever me from the vehicle. This only heightened the level of raucous Arabic and ill-humoured laughter that battered my senses from all directions; the air of malicious intent was palpable.

Still blindfolded, I was dragged away once more, across grass and tarmac until a building was reached. By that time, I was shaking violently from a combination of cold, shock, pain, exhaustion, blood loss and plain fear – fear of what I knew was about to happen. All were exacting a toll.

The blast of warm air told me that we had arrived at our destination, and for a moment I was instantly transported three months back in time to the interrogation centre at Hereford. The blast of warm air reminded me exactly of how I felt when I entered the interrogation room for the first time, blindfolded and cold.

My eyes fought to refocus as the blindfold was torn from my face, and immediately I knew that this was where the similarities ended. The cold, unsmiling faces of three Iraqi officers presented themselves before me. The most senior, and apparent owner of the plush office, was seated behind a huge polished wooden desk. He had obviously been recently awoken, as he was wearing a dressing gown over a military shirt. A cigarette burned slowly in his right hand, the acrid smoke spiralling towards the ceiling in a wispy cloud. The other two more junior officers were fully attired, and both wore the rank of what I assumed was captain. They both stood deferentially on the right flank of the commander's desk, waiting for their cue.

Numerous armed soldiers loitered about the rear of the room, out of my view but no doubt within easy reach of me. One of these soldiers, the SNCO who had been there at my capture, stood behind me, pinning my arms to the sides of the chair as if his life depended upon it. Not a word was said, they all just stared at me, the commander in particular. His eyes bored into mine with such venom that even at a distance of three-odd metres I could feel the cold hatred that lay behind them.

I tried not to let my gaze fall on any one person; rather I kept my eyes averted toward the floor and the huge Persian rug under my chair. This also allowed me to see my shot ankle for the first time. I could see that I still had a foot, which was a massive relief, but I could also make out that the foot was grotesquely deformed within the confines of my blood-stained canvas desert boot.

A commotion in the corridor broke the eerie silence in the room and a soldier rushed in, bringing himself rigidly to attention before the officers. A short conversation ensued between the soldier and one of the captains before the soldier spun around and moved quickly toward me, at the same time removing a pair of old steel handcuffs from his pocket. The SNCO took great pleasure in wrenching my arms further around the back of the chair to facilitate the fixing of the manacles, never once relinquishing his iron grip upon my arms. Satisfied that I was now adequately restrained, one of the captains made his way over, stopping just out of arm's reach.

'What is your name?' he began in accented English.

According to the Geneva Convention there are only four questions that you are required to answer under interrogation; in the British Army these are known as the Big Four. They are: name, rank, serial number and date of birth. The combat survival course that is run in both New Zealand and the UK places a huge amount of emphasis on adherence to the Big Four – no matter what is asked, nothing else is permitted to be revealed. Of course, I had the utmost faith that these men questioning me would uphold the principles of the convention.

'Coburn, Michael,' I answered in a neutral, quiet voice.

'And what is your rank?' he continued.

I was way ahead of him on that one, and there was no way that I was going to tell him that I was a trooper, a rank synonymous with armoured units, of which I was most definitely not a member, and the SAS.

'Private,' I answered. So far so good.

'And so Private Coburn, what is your unit?'

This was the crunch question; we had skipped the last two of the Big Four, this guy was after real facts.

'I'm sorry, sir,' I began the DS-scripted answer, 'I am not allowed to answer that question.' I tried to keep my voice non-confrontational, respectful and timid. My face was impassive, but my racing heartbeat told a different story. He would not accept that answer, I knew it, and he knew that I knew it. I just didn't know what his reaction would be.

'What is your unit?' a little more forcefully this time.

'I'm sorry, sir . . .' I never finished the sentence, as with a slight nod he cut me short. I never saw the rifle butt that came smashing down on my injured leg, making the shock and fright almost an exact re-enactment of the initial wounding.

The chair fell over as I tried to roll with the pain. A scream tore from my throat at the same time, tears of pain streaming down my face as the agony rolled over me. They left me like that, pathetically trying to move myself on the floor, for a minute or so before I was hauled upright once more to continue the questioning.

'Private Coburn,' he continued once more, still no trace of emotion in his voice. 'Take a look at your situation. You are badly wounded. You have lost a lot of blood and need urgent medical attention. Unless you co-operate with us, you will not receive any. How much blood do you think that you can lose?' He left the question open and purposely unanswered, knowing full well that these thoughts were already racing through my mind.

In the condition I was in, I had no idea how long I could last, how much more abuse my rapidly deteriorating body could take. The slowly congealing pool of blood under my foot finally determined my decision. I knew that the cover story was the only avenue left open to me, and that it was fraught with danger, especially as I was not in any sort of condition to enter a war of minds and words with these men.

Special Forces units recognise that the likelihood of capture on deep penetration operations behind enemy lines in time of war is a very real prospect and that while the Big Four are still the standard practice, to try and survive using these answers only is totally unrealistic. To that end, depending on your mission, a form of cover story is often sanctioned to try and buy time for both yourself, and for any other members. The danger of this tactic is that if other members from the same patrol are caught, it is easy to find fault in the story, for the cover will only bear cursory scrutiny. Therefore, the best course of action is to try and base the story loosely on the operation, just altering the facts accordingly. The real problem would be trying to explain away the bergens with comms, explosive and OP kit that was now undoubtedly in the Iraqis' possession. These were not the tools of a pilot rescue team.

These thoughts were bouncing about my brain as he repeated his question: 'What is your unit?' The question was repeated once more, and I felt my arms being gripped even more tightly. Allowing a few seconds to pass, I answered quietly, 'I am with the Parachute regiment.' I then made myself appear even more dejected than before.

'Now that wasn't so hard, was it?' he replied. 'It is much better this way. We can have you in a medical facility in no time. All you need to do is co-operate.'

I let the shivering and shaking of my body commence once again, which wasn't difficult. I needed to look weak and miserable, which also wasn't far from the truth, incapable of any form of resistance. It was essential if I was to have any chance at all of bullshitting my way out of this mess.

'But the Parachute regiment does not operate 300 kilometres behind enemy lines, do they? How do you explain that?' Now the walk across thin ice began.

'I am attached to the pilot rescue team as a medic,' I answered.

A brief discussion ensued between the captain and his superior. 'Where are the rest of your team? We know that there are eight of you.'

My thought processes were working at the speed of light now, trying to anticipate his line of questioning and formulate answers. This change of track was easy to accommodate, however; a slight bending of the truth would provide all the answers that he needed.

'I don't know. We became separated by the road and I have been by myself ever since.'

Once again, this precipitated a brief discussion, and whether it included a translation of my answer I'll never know. But I strongly suspected that the commander could understand every word I said. His eyes never left my face throughout the interrogation.

'What are the names of the rest of your team members?' the captain resumed.

'Shit, how am I going to bluff this one?' I thought, as I desperately sought a solution. The seconds ticked by and the obvious answer came to my rescue. 'Dickhead!' I berated myself, 'just use their nicknames.'

'Mac, Geordie, Aus, Legs, Dinger –' I never had the chance to finish.

'Stop! What kind of names are these? They are not real names!'

Once again a bit of truth combined with a lie served as a reply. 'I was only attached to the team at the last minute; I am new to the job, just a private. I do not know the proper names of the men, only their nicknames.'

This line of questioning was to my benefit. My rank and poor responses were already leading them towards dismissing me as a waste of time, or so I hoped. It would be inconceivable in the Iraqi armed forces that a mere private would have any responsibility or vital knowledge in an operation. It was to my advantage to encourage such assumptions.

'What was your mission?'

I played for time, 'I am sorry, I don't understand the question.'

'In your British orders the mission statement is repeated twice, is that not so?'

That comment threw me completely. Although the orders format is not secret, the last thing I expected was an Iraqi captain stationed on the Syrian border to have a working knowledge of such procedures. This did not bode well.

'To aid the recovery of downed coalition pilots,' I replied carefully, trying to conceal my shock at his statement.

'Where our troops first found you, were you looking for a pilot there?' There was an edge of excitement in his voice as he asked this question, obviously thinking that there was the possibility of another more important prisoner, a prized pilot waiting to be picked up.

However, I had to be careful now. I was getting onto severely dodgy ground. I would have to make up a story and run with it, and not contradict myself.

'No, sir.' It was time for some respect.

'Then what were you doing there?' he continued, a slight edge of frustration now creeping into his voice.

'Waiting for orders,' I replied quietly.

'Orders for what?' he shot back straightaway.

In the same timid and respectful voice, I continued, 'I don't know, sir. I am only a private, I get told very little.'

He was very close now, and the smack of the back of his hand against my face caught me by surprise. 'Do you think we are stupid?' he spat back at me. 'You must know what your orders were. You are not helping us!'

The slap hadn't hurt that much compared with the way the rest of my body felt. I was just a little stunned by it. But it wouldn't be long before he resorted to more serious measures. I was making this guy angry and that wasn't in the plan. I let my head hang limply to one side and allowed the shaking to begin again. It was essential that I appeared submissive to show the interrogator that he was the boss and on top of me.

'I am sorry, sir,' I began, 'but I am only a private, I am only told things on a need-to-know basis. I just do as I'm told.'

He turned his back on me and walked to the centre of the room. Still facing away, he continued, 'You were by the river when we captured you. The others are hiding nearby, perhaps?'

This constant switching of questioning was a deliberate ploy to catch me out. So far I was coherent enough to keep up with it, but for how long? I needed to persuade these men that I was genuine.

'I can't say. I have been on my own for hours, I didn't even know where I was. They could be anywhere.'

He turned to me once more. 'They left you on your own? These compatriots of yours are not very thoughtful, are they?'

I remained silent, staring dejectedly at the floor.

'I can't see why you should have any loyalty toward people who ran away and left you to die. I wouldn't.'

He was trying every trick in the book, and I needed to give him something to make him feel that he was succeeding. 'It was dark, lots of shooting. I was very confused, I'm only a medic.'

The sounds of several vehicles pulling up outside the office, closely followed by the opening and slamming of doors and scores of excited yelling voices interrupted the questioning. Moving to the window, the captain glanced out then moved over to his superior and spoke quietly in his ear. For the first time since I had entered the room, the commander stopped looking at me, turning his head to the captain to listen. A brief exchange followed, and the result was a terse command from the captain in Arabic directed at the guards in the room.

Two soldiers hurried over. They replaced the blindfold across my eyes before manhandling me off the chair and out of the room. I was dragged through a series of corridors and rooms, my loose limbs banging off various walls and doorways in the process. Although I had no knowledge of the fact at the time, another captured member of our patrol had just arrived, and by mid-morning all bar one would be in Iraqi hands.

The smell of fresh air and the slight warmth of the morning sun told me I was outside again. More soldiers came to the aid of my two struggling guards. I felt several pairs of hands lifting my legs and body, immediately increasing the speed of my progress. Within minutes the hollow echo of an empty room warned me that I was inside a building once again. When the blindfold was removed, my suspicions were confirmed.

The room was windowless and quite small, three metres by three metres at most. It looked as if it had been hastily converted from an old storeroom into a makeshift medical bay, the peeling and fading light-blue paint that adorned the walls the only form of decoration. I had been placed on a medical examination trolley, the propped-up back allowing me to observe the whole of my new surroundings rather than just the ceiling.

Besides myself, there were three others in the room, all soldiers and all armed. As I expected, the SNCO was one of them. He had taken a particular shine to me now; I was his prisoner, his charge. He was chatting animatedly with the other two guards, which gave me the opportunity to get my first good look at him in the clear light of day. Sporting the trademark Saddam look-a-like moustache, his podgy frame shook as he waved his arms about violently to emphasise a point, his body language an important means of expression, as with most Arabs.

Suddenly he turned to me and thrust his face right next to mine. His animosity had always been apparent, but now it was positively malevolent. He raised his right hand and then slowly drew his forefinger in a cutting motion across his neck, at the same time nodding his head and grinning to bare his teeth. His intentions were crystal clear. Still grinning, he punched the side of my head, nearly sending me sprawling off the trolley. He then walked over to his two companions, laughing and repeating the slitting motion.

At all times I made an effort to avoid his gaze, steadfastly staring at my boots whenever possible. This particular Iraqi scared the living daylights out of me, and I didn't think that he was too stable. I actually found myself wishing for another interrogator to arrive, someone to keep this lunatic in check.

It was hours before my wish was finally realised. In the meantime, the soldiers in the room made the most of their unsupervised freedom. Whether it was out of anger, frustration or just plain simple malice, they entertained themselves by punching me, bashing me with rifle butts and threatening me with decapitation. The only consoling thought was that I had been shot in the lower leg. My medical training told me that the poor blood supply down there would work in my favour initially – at least it was unlikely that I would bleed to death.

I knew that this was all part of the 'conditioning' or softening-up process, but being aware of what was likely to happen didn't make the experience all that much easier to handle. The longer I was able to ponder my fate, the worse my situation appeared. To be forced to surrender your independence, to be totally at the mercy of your enemies, to feel so absolutely and completely helpless, was an utterly demeaning and frightening experience.

Voices in the corridor announced the arrival of the new interrogation team, and one look at the two suited men who entered told me that they were a totally different kettle of fish. The beatings from the soldiers were mindless and seldom intense, no thought or motive behind them. But the new men who now stood before me looked as though inflicting human suffering was their way of life. I knew I was looking at a couple of secret policemen.

A tall officer, large by Arab standards, accompanied the two policemen into the room, his green uniform partially covered by a dirty white doctor's coat. The three of them made their way to the foot of the trolley, positioning themselves so that they had my full attention. The two policemen could have been twins: the same build, height, slicked-back hair and regulation Saddam moustache. Even their drab grey suits and dark ties were a match; perhaps they were bad-arse issue for the Iraqi Gestapo. Whatever, they definitely looked a double act.

One of the policemen moved forward and nonchalantly inspected my injured leg, moving the foot to see what reaction it provoked. Trying not to leap off the trolley at the instant lancing pain which shot up my leg, I thrust hard against my manacled wrists in an attempt to divert some of the distress my body was suffering, tears of pain welling up in my eyes. Satisfied with this result, the policeman stepped back and mumbled something in Arabic, prompting the doctor to start questioning me.

'I am Doctor Al-Bayeth,' he began in absolutely flawless English. 'What is your name?'

'Michael Coburn,' I answered once again.

'Well, Mr Coburn, these two gentlemen are policemen and they would like you to answer their questions. I am to inform you that you will not be entitled to any medical treatment until you have satisfied this request. Do you understand?'

I nodded my head accordingly, my heart racing away once more.

'Good. You are aware that failure to comply will result in severe consequences. I can do nothing to help you without your co-operation.'

Once again I remained silent and simply nodded my head.

'What is your unit?'

'Parachute Regiment,' I replied.

'What part of the Parachute Regiment?'

'I am attached to the pilot rescue team.'

He paused and looked at me for a minute. 'You are not British; you do not have a British accent. You are an Australian?'

'New Zealander.' My response was automatic, the same question had been asked of me so many times that it was out of my mouth before I had even consciously formed the answer.

The doctor relayed this information to the two policemen and a new more sinister line of questioning ensued, one that I could never have anticipated.

'So, you are a mercenary. Working for the Israelis, no doubt.'

The shock must have registered in my face. This unexpected tack was one I most definitely wanted to avoid. 'No, I am a British soldier; I hold a British passport. I was born in New Zealand and only moved to the UK a couple of years ago.' This came out with such a rush that I hoped it would be convincing enough for them.

'Why would someone leave New Zealand to join the British Army? You do not look British, in fact you look like a Jew.'

My eyes switched alternatively between the policemen and the doctor as I desperately tried to gauge where this was leading. Surely they wanted to know about my equipment, who my commanders in Saudi were, how many other pilot rescue teams were operating in Iraq. These were important questions that I had formulated answers to. I wasn't expecting questions about my ethnic origins or whether I was a mercenary!

'I am not an Israeli, nor do I work for them,' I emphasised quickly. 'I am a private, a medic in the British Army.'

'We know that the Israelis have sent commandos into northern Iraq, which is where you have been, isn't it?'

I remained silent, this line of questioning was getting seriously out of hand. The Arab paranoia about Israel was very evident. To be able to prove a link between Israeli commandos mounting operations in Iraq and the British or Americans would give the Iraqis further ammunition to try and destabilise the support of the Arab nations amongst the coalition.

'No, you've got it all wrong,' I answered.

'But we captured you, by yourself, near the Syrian border. You are in Krabilah. This is northern Iraq. These are facts you cannot deny.' His voice took on a disgusted tone. 'You do not speak English properly. I worked in Harley Street for eight years, I know English people. You are an Israeli spy!'

I didn't know if this was an act, a wind-up or if they genuinely believed that I was an Israeli agent. But I knew that I was in even more desperate trouble, if such a thing was possible, if they considered this the truth.

'Look at my dog tags, they confirm that what I am saying is the truth.' My dog tags were still suspended around my neck, so poor had the search of my person been. In fact, I still had many items of equipment concealed in my clothing, not that they were of any use to me at the time.

'Where are your dog tags, then?'

'They are around my neck.'

The doctor turned to the policemen and relayed all this information in Arabic. A command was barked at the SNCO and he rushed forward obsequiously. Relieving me of the dog tags, he handed them over to the police, who in turn gave them to the doctor for translation. The identity tags themselves were attached by a length of para-cord and covered with black electrician's tape to prevent the chink of metal on metal. More of interest to the doctor, however, were the two morphine syrettes also taped to the cord.

'Why are you carrying morphine sulphate around your neck?' he asked.

This was a golden opportunity to elaborate on my cover story, to strengthen my case simply by bending the truth a little. 'In case of emergency, I can help the casualty straightaway, relieve his pain. It saves time, not having to rummage through my medical kit.'

The doctor seemed to like this answer, and he took the time to explain to his companions in great detail what the syrettes were and their use. Finally, he turned back to me, continuing where he left off. 'The eight men in your team are all medics, then?'

I had been waiting for this question for some time and decided that a play on words would be the best answer, allowing further elaboration once the link between the bergens in the desert, with all the associated non-medical equipment, and myself was established. 'We are all medically trained.'

'Are you concerned about your injuries?'

Once again, the change in the line of questioning; did everyone in this country do a course of interrogation or what?

'Yes,' I answered meekly.

'I will do something about that now. But you must realise that our brave soldiers and the helpless civilians you have been murdering have priority.'

I nodded my head once again, not wishing to get involved in this rhetoric.

'We will talk again.' And with that statement, he and the two policemen left the room.

I didn't doubt that they would be back very soon. The longer I could drag out my interrogation, the more chance the others had of escaping across the border. In a sudden moment of selfish self-pity, I cursed inwardly at the bad luck that had allowed me to be the one to be captured – it wasn't fair.

A new entrant broke this train of thought. He was a slight midget of a man sporting a filthy white coat which, I assumed, was supposed to certify he had medical credentials. Bobbing his head up and down, grinning from ear to ear, he produced two dressings from a soiled pocket and proceeded to wrap them around the blood-stained shirt on my right arm and, more unbelievably, around the outside of my right boot. On finishing, he stood back and surveyed his handiwork, grinning even more and giving me the thumbs-up. Smiling back at him, I thought to myself, 'Yeah, right, mate, great job, you dickhead.'

He continued to stand beside me, curiously looking me up and down.

'Water, water.' I took the opportunity to try and get a drink out of him, poking my tongue out and making swallowing motions at the same time to emphasise the request. He cottoned on straightaway and disappeared, returning moments later with a cup of ice-cold water.

He slowly poured the liquid into my mouth. It tasted like nectar. I hadn't realised how dehydrated I had become; so much had gone on that my body's warning mechanism had been overridden by a multitude of other demands. The last drop gone, I motioned for a second cup and he willingly moved to oblige. But my old mate the SNCO was still in the room and, in his opinion, one cup was perfectly enough for me. He kicked the orderly out of the room, yelling abuse at him as he left.

Alone with my guards once more, I prepared myself for the beatings that I thought would now recommence. Surprisingly, however, they kept their distance, sitting in a corner of the room chatting quietly amongst themselves. I was now the property of the Ministry of Internal Affairs, and the secret police didn't like people messing with their goods.

* * *

The remainder of the day dragged interminably, made worse by the fact that I was left to my own devices and able to dwell uninterrupted on my current situation and possible fate. I had no idea that the only reason they let up on me was the fact that the Iraqis now had Andy, Dinger and Mal to play with, all of whom were currently on the receiving end of Iraqi hospitality. As yet the system didn't have the resources available to run four interrogations at once, but that would change.

The circumstances of my capture and present condition made it extremely hard for me to maintain a positive mental attitude. Accusations raced through my head: Why the fuck hadn't the chopper turned up? How had we become separated? What happened to the comms? Where was the AWACS? Since the jet pilot heard us, why wasn't there a chopper then? Where are all the others? Why am I the only dickhead who got caught? I also kept mulling over these questions: Why didn't I crawl further east before trying to sneak through the Iraqi lines? Why the fuck didn't Andy turn off the road where I said? What if I get gangrene in my leg? Will it need to be amputated?

I was fast becoming my own worst enemy, dissecting every move, action and decision I had made. The burden of failure bore heavily upon my shoulders. Over the ensuing weeks the above questions, and many others, would be my constant companions. I became my own judge and jury.

It was early evening before I was visited again, and this time the trio were accompanied by an unexpected guest, the policeman from the taxi.

'You recognise this man?' the doctor asked aggressively, as the policeman smiled and nodded his head up and down at me.

'No, I don't think so,' I tried hopefully. But the copper was now holding my shoulder and talking excitedly in Arabic to the others, and he was sounding a lot more confident than me.

'You were in the taxi with this man,' the doctor continued. 'One of the men from that car has now died. You killed him!'

My expression was impassive as I tried not to convey any hint that I was sweating and alarmed. What the fuck is he on about? They were all right when we left. Maybe the fat bloke had a coronary after I dragged him out of the vehicle. I tried to think how any of the passengers could have been killed, but nothing came to mind. He's got to be bluffing, another ploy to get me to open up.

This war of words was wearing me down, but one thing was certain: the policeman had identified me, bang to rights.

'Where are the rest of your criminal accomplices?' he continued once the policeman had left the room. 'You must help us, if you wish to survive.'

'I swear to you, I do not know,' I pleaded, once again taking on a submissive attitude, trying desperately to get him to believe me. 'When we left the taxi there was lots of shooting, it was so dark, I was very frightened.' I looked at the other two interrogators. 'I'm only a medic. I became separated and I haven't seen them since.'

This line of questioning was at the same time both encouraging and depressing. It led me to believe (falsely, as it turned out) that the Iraqis still hadn't captured anybody else. But on the other hand, it made me feel worse about my own predicament, more alone.

Without warning, one of the secret policemen thrust the clipboard he was carrying at his companion and charged over to me, his furious intent obvious.

Whack. The back of his hand hammered into the side of my head, closely followed by a tirade of Arabic spat in my face. If this was the good cop–bad cop routine, they certainly had it off-pat.

'Mr Michael,' a soft reasonable voice interrupted from the doorway behind me, 'you are not helping us. You are not helping yourself. Why do you continue to lie to us? We know that you are part of an Israeli commando team, sneaking into Iraq like terrorists to injure and kill innocent Iraqi people, women, children, old men. Why do you not just admit it and we can then see to your wounds?'

Unable to see this new interrogator, I answered, 'I keep telling you all, I am not an Israeli. I'm no commando, I treat people, I am a medic. I am not in Iraq to kill anybody.'

They were starting to confuse me now, and I was struggling to keep up with them. There appeared to be no part of my body that didn't ache, and I was aching mentally. I felt so, so tired. I had no idea how much blood I had lost, but the lethargy in my body told me that the system was struggling to cope with the demands placed upon it.

The new inquisitor walked around to stand before me, another suited Arab, holding a smouldering cigarette between the third and fourth fingers of his right hand. Small and stocky in stature, sporting a non-regulation Saddam moustache for a change, there was no doubt that he had graduated from the same school as the two other policemen in the room, and also that he was most definitely the boss.

'We have got as long as it takes. You will be our guest here for a very long time, so why do you not start to co-operate, to tell us what we want to know?'

The beatings were not so frequent, there was no need; my condition was such that to continue doing so would only hinder their efforts to gain coherent responses.

'How many mercenaries like yourself are now operating in Iraq? When do the Israelis intend to invade? You are not helping us. You are lying, why are you in Iraq? Why are you bombing our women and children? You Jews can never beat the Iraqi people.' On and on the questioning continued, with only slight variations on the same theme, but you could always count on Israel entering the equation.

I lost track of the passage of time, there seemed no end to the constant bombardment and no acceptance of my repetitive denials. I couldn't fathom why their interrogation was so obscure. There seemed no logical reason for maintaining the line of questioning, although it made it easier for me to disguise my actual profession.

There was no let-up in their desire to prove that Israel was the real reason behind my presence in Iraq, as if any other tactical or operational knowledge that I might possess was of no consequence. Perhaps the possibility that a mere private could hold information of any value was beyond them, and the next best course of action was to implicate me in an American–Israeli conspiracy to invade their country.

The fact that other Arab nations – Saudi Arabia and Kuwait, for example – were lined up against Iraq never entered into their thinking. Such an acknowledgment could not be made, it was impossible. Everything was geared toward anti-American–Israeli rhetoric.

Within minutes of the policemen's departure the friendly orderly returned and wheeled my trolley out into the corridor, leaving me with two of the guards. The SNCO, much to my relief, had either decided that he was surplus to requirement, or was in need of sleep, for he disappeared and I never saw him again.

The decor of the corridor wasn't that different from the room I had just vacated; the main difference was that the peeling paint was magnolia rather than pale blue. I was parked next to the main entrance doors that gave ample opportunity for those who had not already done so to come and have a good look at the enemy.

Before long I was wheeled off once again, into an adjoining room that served as the field hospital. A single light was suspended from the centre of the room under which a long black operating table, still covered in dried blood, was positioned. A single stainless-steel trolley strewn with various surgical instruments was next to the table; the floor was awash with numerous discarded dressings, suturing needles and bloody bandages. It didn't inspire confidence, but by this stage, I no longer gave a shit. I just wanted my leg sorted out.

The two guards manoeuvred me onto the operating table, happily chatting amongst themselves in the process. I think they finally realised that the likelihood of my attempting to escape or causing trouble was remote. After 16-odd hours of continual use, the handcuffs were at last released and I gratefully massaged my hands and wrists, swollen from their constricting grip.

A young female nurse, no more than 18 years old, entered the room wearing a green surgical smock and the traditional white headdress favoured by Muslim women. She began busying herself about the table, obviously curious about the foreigner who lay before her.

The pain from my over-extended bladder was becoming more acute than that from my leg. All day is a long time even when you are dehydrated. I tried, hoping that she understood English, to explain my discomfort. 'Excuse me,' I began, 'I need to use the toilet.'

'I will find you a bucket,' she replied in excellent English, and then disappeared out of the room, returning seconds later with a large white plastic paint pot. Passing it to me, she excused herself and left the room, not that my embarrassment would have prevented nature taking its much-needed course.

Five minutes later she was back, simply taking the bucket from me and slipping it under the bench. 'I hope to study nursing in England,' she began out of the blue, 'London is a wonderful city, I know I will like it. Are you from London?'

'No, sorry, I am not,' I replied, conscious that this could be a set-up.

'I was preparing to travel to London when the war started. As soon as it is over, I will go there,' she continued simply, as if the huge forces of war that now opposed and sparred with each other were just an unfortunate and insignificant hiccup in her plans.

The door burst open and in strode Dr Al-Bayeth, now free of his police shadows. 'How are you feeling, Michael?' he asked amiably, with no trace of the animosity that had accompanied his earlier questions.

'Very tired,' I answered truthfully.

'You have lost a considerable amount of blood, and I am afraid that you will lose some more before I am through with excising your wound.'

I listened intently; at least he sounded like a genuine surgeon.

'We can afford to let you have two units of whole blood, but I am afraid that that is it. Your own body will have to supply the deficit.'

He took my right arm, examining the wound in my tricep at the same time. 'You are an extremely lucky young man. The bullet has made a clean entry and exit just below the surface. Not a problem.'

I was glad he thought so. I didn't feel lucky at the moment.

As he unwound the dressing on my foot, his expression changed; concentration was etched on his face. Even this simple process caused me to wince in pain and he shook his head, mumbling in Arabic to himself. We hadn't even got round to removing the boot yet.

'Will I be able to walk again?' I asked fearfully, a question that had been preying on my mind for hours.

'We shall see,' he replied, still eyeing the offending limb.

Turning away, he picked a green cannula off the trolley. He grasped my right arm firmly, at the same time explaining, 'I am going to insert this into your arm so that I can administer the general anaesthetic and fluids.'

The sharp prick and pressure pop told me he had found the vein. I felt the gritty resistance as the plastic sheath advanced till it was flush against my skin. The doctor removed the metal guide and it was discarded on the floor as he turned once more to the trolley. This time he returned with a syringe, its clear plastic vial filled with a white murky liquid. A slight squeeze of the plunger allowed a small spurt of the substance to escape, clearing any trapped air that may have been residing in the top of the vial. Once again the needle was thrown to the floor and the end of the syringe placed into the cannula receiving port. As he forced the liquid into my vein, he said, 'Do not try to fight this. Try and relax.'

I turned to find the young nurse holding my free hand and the last thing I remembered was her pale white face smiling benevolently as I slipped into unconsciousness.

CHAPTER 15

BAGHDAD

I came to with a start, completely disorientated and lying in total darkness. My woozy brain tried to make sense of my present circumstances. Where was I? Why didn't this feel like a hospital bed? Realisation dawned on me slowly; the banter of Arabic coming from behind my head immediately brought the depressing reality home. I tried to sit up but I was tightly restrained to a narrow surgical trolley. As the minutes passed and my senses returned, I suddenly realised that I was moving; in fact, I was in the rear of a small Hi-Ace.

My eyes slowly accustomed themselves to the surroundings of the makeshift ambulance: the three soldiers in the front, the small windows on each side of the vehicle, a drip stand with a nearly empty 500 ml bag of blood hanging from it, the line snaking down into my right arm. I shifted my gaze hesitantly down towards my feet, the conflicting emotions of dread and hope fighting for supremacy. I still had my desert-cam trousers on; the doctor had simply cut up the material to gain access to the limb, and the whole of the lower right leg was a mass of white bandage. As I focused on the end of my leg and saw that my foot was still attached and in place, the feeling of relief was almost euphoric. A slight attempt at articulating the ankle joint, however, brought me back to reality very rapidly. Intense pain shot from the affected area and up my leg, and it hadn't even taken a great deal of movement. The healing process would take a considerable amount of time.

I was not in a position to peer out the windows, not that I would have had a clue which way we were heading. The piercing twang of Arab music began to circulate about the vehicle, along with the voice of one of the guards desperately trying to keep in tune. Neither was pleasing to the ear.

My mind wasn't thinking too clearly, I couldn't work out why I was being moved; it seemed very ominous. As if reading my thoughts, the vehicle suddenly pulled off the road, dousing its headlights in the process. My heart started racing once more. This was it. I was about to be pulled out of the van, shot in the head and left to rot in the middle of the desert somewhere, another casualty of the war. I had served my purpose.

The van came to a halt and the Iraqis remained seated, the incessant music still screeching away. They lit up cigarettes and continued to chat, not taking the slightest bit of interest in me in the rear. The real reason for our sudden departure from the highway became apparent within minutes. Crump! Deep, resounding booms could be heard not too far away, as great shock waves ripped across the desert. Allied warplanes were releasing 1,000-lb bombs on unsuspecting Iraqi targets.

It took me a while to work out how they knew to pull off the road, but the memory of anti-aircraft artillery shells arcing their way skywards surfaced from my confused and exhausted mind. My escorts had obviously seen this before them and decided that caution was the better part of valour. That suited me fine, the last thing I needed was a bored fighter jock cruising about the skies, itching to mallet a target but having to wait while his flock of bombers reeked havoc on the Iraqis below.

Half an hour passed in this manner before the noise of the bombing ceased and my guards felt secure enough to venture out onto the open road once more. Now fully awake, I was able to assess my situation. My initial fears of a summary execution in the desert had been dispelled but that didn't alter the fact that I didn't have a clue why or where I was being moved.

The vehicle continued slowly on through the night, probably travelling at no more than 30 kilometres per hour. Not long after the initial stop, the sound of a renewed bombing offensive echoed about, prompting the driver to pull off the main road once more. This time, however, we did not simply pull off to the side of the road, we continued into the desert. It appeared that we were travelling along some kind of track.

As I tried to see out of the windows from my prone position, a huge grey mass loomed large, its façade constructed like the top of a hexagon. Two perfectly angled concrete stanchions supported a roof three to four metres thick, constructed of the same material. It looked bombproof. The structure was no more than five metres in height, but the sheer size of it dwarfed the Hi-Ace. I had no doubt that it was some type of military facility, but exactly what type I had no idea.

Two Iraqi soldiers came wandering over to the vehicle as it came to a halt at the main entrance. After they and my escorts greeted one another, there then ensued an excited conversation in Arabic, followed by much finger pointing and gesticulation in my general direction. Before I had a chance to realise what was happening, the rear doors of the van were torn open and I was hauled out of the back, surrounded by what seemed to be hundreds of screaming Iraqi soldiers.

Slaps, punches and kicks began raining in once more, only this time I was fastened to the trolley in such a way that I could not protect myself. To their credit, my guards jumped in and tried to push the mob away, obviously realising the situation was getting out of control. What had initially started as an opportunity to show off a captured enemy soldier was deteriorating at a rapid rate.

Suddenly a large, fat Iraqi face appeared above my own, the man's piercing black eyes almost popping from their sockets in anger. He stabbed his finger into my face and spat out in broken English, 'To us you are not a man; you are woman!' He moved away, laughing maniacally, and it took a couple of seconds for his words to sink in. When they did, I forgot all about the beatings. I could be facing something unbelievably worse.

I was rapidly wheeled through a set of huge sliding metal doors, above which was a large portrait of Saddam Hussein, into the interior of the complex, and its secrets slowly began to unfold. The structure's low profile concealed an underground labyrinth of corridors, offices and small roads. This was an underground military base, a bunker hidden from the view of the roving allied bombers, its size unfathomable.

My trolley came to rest in one of a series of obscure corridors. Thankfully, most of the baying mob were left behind. Iraqi officers began to emerge from the nearby doors and soon a large group had gathered around, discussing my battered miserable state, joking and laughing. I wasn't much of an enemy to fear.

One of the officers spoke to me in reasonable English, perhaps keen to show his expertise in front of his peers. 'I have been to London. It is a wonderful city.'

I looked up at his genial smiling face; this man was not in the least bit interested in an interrogation.

'You will soon be in Baghdad, my capital. It is also a wondrous city full of great history and sights. You will enjoy your stay there.'

My eyes darted around the assembled faces, seeing varying expressions ranging from curiosity to outright disgust and hatred. Somehow I sensed that his comments would prove to be slightly optimistic.

The bombing raid must have finished quite quickly, as we didn't stay long and I was wheeled back to the waiting Hi-Ace, this time largely ignored by the passing soldiers. To my immense relief, the vehicle set off once more, with no further allusions having been made in respect of my sexual status, continuing on its south-easterly track toward the capital.

The journey was indeed harrowing. On two more occasions the vehicle was forced to quit the road and hide from the bombers. While the guards sought refuge inside bunkers, I was left locked up in the Hi-Ace. Although this prevented inquisitive Iraqis giving me another beating, it also left me vulnerable to a friendly, wayward heat-seeking missile, something that could quite easily lock on to the warm engine of the van. I couldn't win either way.

* * *

The sun was well and truly up by the time we entered the outskirts of Baghdad. The sprawling apartment blocks, with clothing hanging from every balcony, towered above as we drove through myriad streets. It wasn't long before our final destination was reached and, for the first time since entering the city, the vehicle was forced to grind to a halt. Our objective was a large multi-storeyed complex surrounded by a high barbed-wire topped fence which was guarded by numerous soldiers sporting red berets – the infamous Iraqi Republican Guard.

The sheer volume of people that were congregating at the entrance to the complex had halted the vehicle, and once one of them realised that it was a foreigner inside the van, all hell broke loose. For the umpteenth time since my capture, the spectre of mob rule reared its ugly head. The crowd overwhelmed the small vehicle, banging on its sides, rocking it to and fro in an attempt to get at the occupant inside, all the while screaming hysterically. I think my guards were as terrified as I was at this point, for if the crowd managed to get at me, they too would have fallen victims to the frenzied attack.

As it was, the Republican Guard soldiers on the gate reacted instantly to the danger, opening the gates and forcing a path through the mêlée, allowing the van to proceed to the relative safety of the compound within.

The makeshift ambulance pulled up in front of a reasonably new-looking entranceway, built to accept casualties by the look of it. I had been moved to a military hospital.

A misleading air of calm prevailed inside the protective enclosure of the hospital now that the hundreds of distraught civilians had been locked outside. Without haste or ceremony, I was removed from the rear of the vehicle and wheeled into the main reception foyer of the building, where complete chaos met my eyes.

No matter where I looked, the floor was littered with injured Iraqis, 90 per cent of whom were wearing a uniform of some description. Orderlies, nurses and doctors rushed about from casualty to casualty, assessing the injured and rushing away those in need of urgent, life-saving medical attention.

My own injuries paled into insignificance in comparison to some of the horrific cases surrounding me. I felt the first pinch of guilt and embarrassment. I was part of the force that had put these young men in this condition, maimed, burnt and dismembered on the floor of a hospital. It might not have been the fault of the Allied forces that the

210

war had commenced, but the simple soldiers about me had no choice in the matter either.

A doctor suddenly appeared before me, flustered and tired, sick of what he had to witness.

'We have been expecting you,' he began. 'You are Michael Coburn?'

'Yes,' I answered meekly.

He avoided looking at me directly and proceeded to examine my injured leg, unwrapping the new bandages that now covered the wound. With every slight movement, I flinched in pain. He ignored my protest and removed the last of the bandages, exposing the foot itself, now horribly deformed. It was the first opportunity I had been given to see my injury, and the sight of the black, blue and yellow foot, swollen to over twice its normal size, shocked me to the core. It was not the leg of someone who would be able to walk again.

The doctor moved to the head of my trolley and began scribbling furiously on a medical board, suddenly stopping to yell, 'Why do you want this fucking war?'

I was flabbergasted, unable to believe that he actually thought that the West had started the conflict. Foolishly, I tried to answer, 'We didn't start the war. Iraq invaded Kuwait.'

This prompted a blistering attack on the West, George Bush, Margaret Thatcher, John Major and anybody else he could think of. The tirade only ended when he turned on his heel and walked off in disgust, there obviously being more worthy patients in need of his attention.

I was left alone with my two minders for quite a while; no one else seemed particularly interested in my presence or plight. At one stage a young soldier moved over next to me and began speaking in surprisingly good English, 'We have shot down many of your bombers this week.' I remained silent, watching him intently. 'Last night alone, 25 were destroyed. Soon you will have none left.'

'Your soldiers are very good shots,' I replied, not knowing what else to say. I certainly wasn't going to provoke another outburst by saying that I thought his statistics were bullshit. However, his next statement chilled me and I could feel the blood drain from my face.

'You are the survivor from the soldiers in the north. The others were killed.' It was a matter-of-fact statement, said without emotion and was very convincing.

My mind raced once more. I had to try and get more information from this man. Had everyone else died? I suppose there were enough rounds flying around that night, and there were most certainly enough bloody Iraqis about the place.

'How many bodies were found?' I asked tentatively, expecting a harsh rebuke or slap for my impertinence.

'Four,' he replied without hesitation. My heart sank, what the fuck had happened?

'There are two others in hospital,' he continued. 'Your helicopter rescue was shot down as well. Another eight bodies were found in the wreckage.'

What did that mean? That two others from the patrol were in hospital, or that two from the crashed helicopter were? Either way, it was depressing news. The young soldier chatted away for a few more minutes, but I didn't really take in what he was saying; it was mostly rhetoric on how great the Iraqi armed forces were and what a fantastic job they were doing. My mind was elsewhere, dwelling on the loss of my mates. I suddenly felt terribly alone. Seeing that my responses had dried up, the young soldier moved off in search of another new companion, leaving me alone with my guards and my thoughts.

* * *

Time passed slowly, and I was largely ignored in the hustle and bustle of hospital activity around me. After what seemed like hours, an orderly appeared and questioned my minders. Then the three of them wheeled me off along a series of corridors and double doors until we reached a small, clean operating theatre. After the orderly left, it wasn't long before the doctors appeared, and the guards were ordered to the back of the room. One of the doctors, the anaesthetist I assume, took an instant dislike to me. He was in his 50s, rather fat and only about 5 ft 6 in. tall, but for all that he was extremely passionate in his hatred of the West, and I, lying there before him, provided a perfect opportunity for him to vent that animosity. Taking me completely by surprise, he launched a series of blows at my head that I was helpless to avoid, all the while screaming in Arabic at me. Not satisfied with this, he picked up a syringe with a long needle attached and placed it next to my right eye, making gestures as to what he was about to do. I was petrified. Getting beaten by a geriatric was bearable, but to have him remove an eyeball in the process took him out of the medical league and into Gestapo territory.

His companion, who must have been the surgeon, saw that things were getting out of hand and came to my rescue, calming the irate anaesthetist down. My guards found the whole situation rather amusing; they were leaning against the wall chuckling away to each other. Satisfied that the situation was under control, the surgeon returned to my leg and began to remove the packing that had been stuffed into the wound.

I screamed in pain and my unrestrained leg convulsed, giving him a good kick in the head. Surprisingly, he didn't turn on me but hurled a tirade of abuse at his partner for not having given me the anaesthetic. This was quickly rectified. I watched with horror as the anaesthetist began pumping vial after vial of a murky yellow substance through the plastic shunt still fixed in the crook of my arm. I counted three shots before succumbing to the drug, my last conscious thought, 'I'm a dead man, he's going to give me an overdose.'

* * *

My brain was registering a kaleidoscopic maze of smoky colours. It felt as if I were floating outside of my body. All pain and anxiety had vanished. 'If this is death, then it ain't so bad.' This thought flashed briefly in my head before a stinging sensation began penetrating my consciousness. Slowly I fumbled my way back to the present, like a drunk emerging with a severe hangover, and the source of the pain became clear. Someone was slapping me around the face.

At last my eyes opened and there before me stood another group of suited men, one of whom was using the beating of his hands against my head as a morning-after remedy. No sooner had my eyes focused than the questioning started. The policemen were making the most of a golden opportunity to pry open a confused mind.

'Mr Michael,' one began. 'What are you doing in Iraq?'

Still in no condition to respond, I looked up, confused and dumb, at the man. My lack of response only infuriated the policeman further and I instantly received another slap round the head to aid my memory. This copper wanted to assert his authority from the very start; he was no Mr Nice Guy.

'What are you doing in Iraq?' he shouted in my face.

Suddenly I felt a wave of nausea well up from within, as my body reacted violently against the drugs that had been administered. Now unrestrained, I sat bolt upright in the bed and grabbed a half-empty water pitcher off the table next to me. The policeman took a step back, realising immediately what was about to happen, obviously worried that he was about to wear the contents of my guts all over his cheap suit. I began retching violently, but yellow bile was the only substance my empty stomach was able to regurgitate. Nigh on four days had now passed since I had last eaten, yet strangely I still felt little hunger.

Happy that the convulsions had finished, the policeman resumed his questioning, from a suitable distance.

'Why are you in Iraq?'

'I am here to help pilots that have been shot down,' I answered simply.

'Rubbish!' he yelled at me straightaway. 'You are not English. You were hundreds of kilometres from the American and British lines. You were very close to the Syrian border and not that far from Israel. Who are you working for?'

'Here we go again,' I thought to myself. 'They still aren't bored with this.'

My reply was almost by rote now. 'I am a soldier in the British Army. I am not a spy. I don't work for the Israelis.'

'You are not British. You are a mercenary. Admit it. Why are you in Iraq?'

On and on we continued, the same theme ever-present. It was easy to deny, and hardly any effort was needed to lie. As long as they kept on with this line of questioning, and as long as I could convince them that I wasn't a spy, mercenary, Israeli agent or any other type of clandestine operative, I felt confident that my cover was safe. It was a dangerous game, though acting like the dumbest private that ever walked the earth helped matters immeasurably. However, it was a fine line between frustrating the inquisitors enough, but not too much.

Thirty minutes of questioning was sufficient for this lot, even the head-slap routine had become tiresome. The group quit the room in disgust, leaving me alone once more with my guards.

Now able to concentrate freely, I tried to get a good look at my leg, which was partially covered by a bandaged back-cast up to the knee. I could see my right foot, which was still a grotesquely swollen yellow colour, and any attempt at moving the ankle joint caused intense pain. Yet there was a worrying lack of sensation in the foot itself, as if it were detached from the main limb.

I dwelled on the cause of this – no doubt seriously damaged nerve endings – as I examined my new quarters. They were surprisingly plush. A modern-looking room with four new hospital beds, all empty apart from the one that I now occupied. It was spotlessly clean and brightly decorated, brown and yellow Arabic mosaics adorning the walls. I somehow suspected that these would not remain my lodgings for very long.

I moved uncomfortably on the bed, as rashes that had appeared on my back initially from webbing rub had now become infected and were turning into full-blown bedsores. I needed a wash badly. For the first time I noticed that I was still wearing my DPMs; nobody had thought to try and change the bloodstained, filthy articles. Not that this bothered me, for it meant that I still had an escape map, compass and, more importantly, my belt with the gold attached.

One of the guards moved over and offered me a plate of dates. The hunger that had thus far been largely ignored suddenly surfaced with a vengeance and I accepted the small morsel gratefully. I was just into my third date when a new bunch of visitors arrived. Guiltily, the guards snatched the dates away and moved themselves off into a far corner.

The new men, six of them, were dressed in a mixture of expensive silk suits, military garb and white doctors' coats. They crowded around the foot of my bed, mumbling and nodding their heads amongst one another. One of their number, a distinguished-looking man in his late 50s, finally spoke up. The amount of gold on his uniformed shoulders indicated a man of considerable rank, probably a general.

'Your wound has been excised successfully and we will prescribe a course of antibiotics for you.' His manner and bearing immediately gave the impression that he was used to people taking note when he talked.

'Thank you,' I replied, not really knowing what else to say.

He gave me a slight nod before continuing. 'You will not be able to walk for some time, and even then you will have a noticeable limp. The leg has lost a considerable amount of articulation in the ankle and foot. The bullet destroyed most of the small bones that allow inversion and eversion to occur. Do you understand?'

I nodded my head and replied, 'Yes, sir.'

'Only time will tell how much it will recover. The débridement of the wound was fairly straightforward and there appears to be no trace of infection at this juncture.' He paused briefly, looking at me over the top of a pair of half-mooned glasses. 'I must say that you can count yourself extremely lucky that you were not more seriously injured.'

I didn't need to be told that. I knew I was extremely lucky to be lying in the bed still breathing.

He waved an arm to his right, not really looking at where he was pointing. 'Colonel Al-Bayeth will continue to look after you. He will visit as time permits.'

I studied the assembled faces once again and this time picked out the doctor's tall, stocky frame, now clothed in a military uniform. The uniform and the fact that I hadn't expected him down here in Baghdad had thrown me.

With that last comment, the 'General' and his entourage about-faced and left the room, disappearing as quickly as they had arrived. Their departure was timely, to say the least, as my bladder had begun to throb with the mounting pressure.

'Toilet, toilet?' I asked my guards, pointing towards my crotch at the same time.

Recognising my plight immediately, one of the soldiers shot out of the room, returning seconds later with a receptacle in which I could relieve myself. As I struggled to manoeuvre on the bed, one of the guards innocently tried to help matters by undoing my belt buckle and loosening my trousers. This simple action revealed one of my treasured secrets. On lifting the belt, he froze – it was far too heavy an accessory for securing pants. Turning the belt over, he saw the encircling masking tape that both hid and attached the gold. The belt was pulled from me and the masking tape partially unwound. The look of consternation, followed by recognition as a gold sovereign dropped into his palm, was priceless.

Whipping the belt under an armpit, he thrust the sovereign into his near-toothless mouth and bit on the newly discovered coin. The joy that spread across his face was instant. He turned to his partner and began jabbering to him triumphantly. My toilet needs were now long forgotten. I had no idea how the two of them would take this discovery. It could be difficult to explain why a dumb private was carrying a small fortune in gold around his waist. Though a mercenary certainly might.

As it happened, I had no need to worry: these two lads had no intention of telling their superiors that they had stumbled across £2,000 worth of gold. They were already divvying it up. I received a thumbs-up and another exhibition of coin-biting, with lots of associated smiles and head-bobbing. I just grinned and nodded with them. There was not a lot I could do about it now anyway. The sad thing was that, had the guard not attempted to help me, the gold would never have been found – my clothing was never touched again.

Late afternoon saw the end of my five-star hospital accommodation. Accompanied as usual by the guards, two orderlies collected my trolley and wheeled me through the hospital, this time, however, leaving the building via a service entrance. The trolley clattered and bounced its way across an open gravel parking area, all the while heading for a huge red-brick building, its walls painted with numerous multicoloured children's murals.

As we approached the building, we turned right and moved down a wide concrete-paved alleyway that ran in between the building and what I first thought was simply a grass bank. However, a closer inspection revealed that the bank was in fact a cell block. The bunker-type construction had numerous small rooms, all of which had a single-barred window facing out into the alley. Several grey-uniformed soldiers were lounging about, sitting in small groups smoking and laughing, not paying me much attention as I was trundled past.

The orderlies stopped about halfway along the line and wheeled the trolley into a doorless foyer. To my left, I saw a room with two beds; a wrinkled old Arab was lying on one, coughing non-stop and looking just about ready for the morgue. A younger man, perhaps in his 40s, sat on the other, staring bleakly at me as I was pushed into the opposite room.

Although I was expecting to be put in a cell at some time, I never imagined that the conditions would be like these. Obviously the hospital prison enclosure, it was the most disgustingly filthy place I had ever seen. I was lifted onto an old hospital bed, one that had neither seen the light of day nor a clean since it had arrived, by the look of it. The mattress was black with stains of dried blood, the floor in an even worse condition.

Their responsibility finished, both my guards and the orderlies bade me farewell and left me in the care of my new keepers, one of whom was hovering in the background, eager to claim his latest guest. My new guardian moved on over and handcuffed me to the iron railing of the bed. The shackle was given a violent tug for good measure, an action that nearly separated my arm from its socket in the process. Satisfied that I wasn't going anywhere, he finally smiled and gave me a parting wave before the door was swung to, bolted and locked.

Over the ensuing weeks, Grumpy, as I named him, would be my senior gaoler and a face that I would wake up to day after day. In his late 40s, he was a veteran of the Iran–Iraq war and was seeing out the remainder of his time before retirement.

Our association didn't get off to the best of starts. He was very suspicious of me – after all, I represented the enemy that was bombing his city night and day. But as the weeks progressed, he lightened up a little, and by the end of my internment he would often come in and exchange Arabic greetings, tell me of the occasional Iraqi victory in his broken English, or pass on a piece of fruit – a delicious luxury.

CHAPTER 16

THE STRETCH

As the door to my cell clanged shut, it suddenly dawned on me that this was it. The roller-coaster ride of excitement that I had been on, basically since arriving in the UK seven months previously, had come to an unexpected screaming halt.

The last few months had been so hectic and rushed; the events over the past week a whirlwind of action. Only now, lying alone, wounded and at the mercy of my captors, was I able to fully digest the scale of my predicament. These four walls would be my home for how long? A deep and dark depression began to engulf me, something I had to battle against more and more as my captivity progressed and the days turned into weeks. Not for the first time, nor for the last, those unanswerable questions came back to plague me, bouncing around my head.

How long will the war last? Does anyone know that I am still alive? Are any of the others alive? Am I the only one to be captured? Why hadn't help arrived after we contacted the jet pilot? Are the others OK? What will happen when they find out that I've been lying? When will prisoners be released? Could I be another Terry Waite? I felt on the verge of tears, such was the self-pity that washed over me.

I was stressed and confused and didn't know whether to blame myself or others for our failure. Foremost in my thoughts, however, were two pressing questions, ones that surfaced constantly over and over again: What the fuck happened to the chopper? Why didn't AWACS answer our calls? When an SAS patrol is in the shit and calls for assistance, someone comes, that is part of the ethos behind the regiment's operations. If you are intent on sending people hundreds of kilometres behind enemy lines, you have to offer some kind of back-up in case it all turns pear-shaped. No matter what, at some stage any patrol will need support of one kind or another. So that led to other questions: Why had the system failed on this occasion? Had we got it so badly wrong that we were beyond help? And if so, why?

Sleep would be the only respite from this constant struggle within, from the battle to maintain my sanity and self-belief. I knew I had to refocus, to occupy my mind or I would surely go mad. Memories of the two combat survival courses, and more particularly stories recounted by former POWs, sprung to mind. Their experiences in similar, and on many occasions worse, conditions provided inspiration on how to cope with my situation. These men had managed to survive, one as long as seven years – so would I. One such story epitomised the importance of finding something to focus on, especially if you find yourself in solitary.

An American major, a former pilot, had told us about being shot down on a bombing mission over North Vietnam. Captured and tortured by the North Vietnamese, he was on the brink of suicide when he managed to find something to inspire his faith and maintain his sanity. He began the process of designing and building a dream home from scratch in his head. He drew up the plans, prepared the site, dug every footing, poured every foot of concrete, raised each wall and hammered every nail. Each point of design and construction was re-created in his mind. He was released after four years in solitary, not having seen a single white face in all that time. On returning to the States, he built that dream home.

It would be difficult to remain positive, optimistic and focused, but the alternative was not an option. It was a matter of survival.

So I began my mental conditioning, starting with the systematic surveying of my new surroundings. A small, barred, still partially glazed window faced out into the alley. The light that gained access through it cast particular angled shadows around the room; shadows that I would come to interpret as a crude sundial. My guards often lounged beneath its aperture chatting, taking coffee or banging their dominoes on a hard wooden table.

The room itself was about three by five metres. Its faded, stained and peeling lime-green walls often provided a form of escapism where I could imagine images, shapes or figures concealed amongst the deteriorating plaster and paint work.

The off-white ceiling was a mass of divots where lumps of plaster had come free over the passage of time, exposing a seriously suspect concrete roof above. A single light bulb hung precariously from its torn fixture in the centre; the live wires were exposed and corroded. The light rarely worked when switched on, forever shorting. The guards gave up in the end and resorted to torch light.

The door, hinged on the left and inwards opening, was a plain metal fixture devoid of any real features save those that secured it. It fastened shut using two bolts on its outer side and they, in turn, were locked using two padlocks. The jangle of the gaoler's keys and the sliding of the bolts would become a feature of my every waking day, a way of determining the approximate time, an indication of the arrival of a meal – or something possibly more sinister.

I slid my handcuffed arm along the side of the bed, testing how much movement I could expect. The end shackled to the underside of the bed allowed about a half a metre of play, though this was of little comfort in my present state. More of a concern right now was the fact that the end shackled to my arm was overtight; already the wrist was throbbing and causing me considerable discomfort. I would need to persuade Grumpy to ease the pressure as soon as possible, but unfortunately, the opportunity would not arise for hours.

As the day progressed, and word got around, an almost uninterrupted procession of curious Iraqi soldiers appeared at the window, all eager to get a glimpse of the new 'devil Westerner'. Often the sight of me would elicit the throat-slitting motion or a high-pitched victory scream accompanied by the smacking of the tops of their heads.

Over the weeks, the worst of these 'screenings' would often involve the aiming of rifles or pistols through the window at me and the firing of the weapon's action. A huge burst of laughter would follow the look of fear and automatic cringe as the hammer or firing pin fell on an empty chamber. These men weren't the most proficient of soldiers and I didn't really trust in their ability to play Russian roulette, especially at my expense. While the guards never allowed any of my tormentors into the cell, they certainly did nothing to discourage them on the outside of it.

Long, low shadows were being thrown across the left side of the wall by the time that the rattle of key in lock and scraping of withdrawn bolts announced Grumpy's entry. By now, not only were my wrist and swollen hand completely numb, but my bladder and bowels had joined in the act and were at bursting point.

Grumpy marched on in with a bowl of brown rice and a piece of bread in hand, what would from now on be my staple diet, and was immediately assaulted with 'Toilet, toilet!' I hoped that this simple request would be enough to alleviate both of my current problems.

He hesitated for a second, before placing the food on the floor of all places. Grumpy exited the cell, returning moments later with a plastic sandal that he placed on my bare uninjured foot before unshackling my wrist. That done, he moved into a position so that I might use his shoulder as a crutch.

The effects of gravity on my injury taught a swift, sharp lesson the instant I swung the leg off the bed. The sudden rush of blood to the wounded area caused such pain that I was forced to sit straight back down again, raise my leg and reassess the situation. The solution turned out to be to kick my right leg backwards as if doing a standing leg extension, and keep it in that position. It was neither ideal nor comfortable, but it worked.

So, with my arm round Grumpy's shoulders, and his about my waist, we hopped and walked our way through the cell door. Once in the foyer, we made a right turn and the frightening sight that was the toilet was revealed. The smell that wafted occasionally into my room should have served as a warning, but even so, the scene that unfolded before me came as a shock. With almost morbid fascination I stared at the tiny open cubicle that housed a small oblong hole, overflowing with stagnant faeces and urine.

Grumpy helped me as far as the doorless gap, allowing me to steady myself against the frame before retreating to the safety of the main foyer entrance no more than three metres away. I stood rigidly still, grasping the doorframe for dear life, trying to assess the best way to attack the problem without ending up as part of the putrid mess that lined the floor. Visions of slipping or falling arse-first into the middle of it didn't bear thinking about.

The bog was of typical Arab construction, a porcelain hole in the floor with a slightly raised footrest on either side. Its water reservoir was high on the wall behind and a rusty metal pipe ran down its length to join the bowl at the bottom.

I worked out a plan of action, summoned up the courage and went for it. My body would not tolerate the indecision much longer. Hopping into the cubicle itself, I managed to avoid the worst of the over-spill and get my good foot onto one of the rests, at the same time using the standpipe to steady myself. Standing in this position, I dropped what was left of my DPM trousers (the right leg had been cut away up to mid-thigh). Thrusting my injured leg out in front of me, I slowly lowered myself down into a squat, all the while holding onto the pipe for grim death.

It didn't matter that I wasn't comfortable, nature took its course mercifully quickly and I was able to complete the procedure in seconds. However, to my horror, I suddenly realised that one important ingredient was missing: toilet paper. I looked about in vain, and then my eyes fell upon the small piece of hose fitted to a tap at the base of the wall.

'Oh shit,' I cursed inwardly, 'I am going to have to wipe my arse using water and my hand while doing a fucking balancing act, fucking great.' This was assuming, of course, that there was water available. Much to my relief, water gushed from the end of the hose – an end that it wasn't wise to think much about – and I somehow managed to finish the procedure. By the end of my captivity, I could complete this necessary exercise in total darkness with confidence. An unusual claim to fame.

Quickly re-dressing, I hopped over to a small basin that was situated in the foyer. Grumpy was nowhere in sight. A few broken pieces of soap were lying about and I made full use of them as I tried to disinfect my hands as much as possible. As if on cue, Grumpy reappeared to help me back into the cell and onto the bed, allowing my wrist to remain unshackled so I could eat the evening meal.

After that experience, I made sure that I was never again unprepared for such a visit. By secreting small, torn pieces of the bed sheet in my pockets and behind the water standpipe to use as toilet paper, I ensured that my hand and arse would make the least amount of contact possible. Diarrhoea, or something worse, was a condition I most certainly did not want or need to encourage. My body and immune system had enough problems to cope with, without the added complications of a bowel disorder.

A small table had now been placed next to the bed, and upon it sat a pitcher of water and a plastic cup. Grumpy placed four multi-coloured tablets in my palm and ordered me to take them. It was obviously his responsibility to see that I did so, and he took that charge seriously. I obliged by putting the tablets in my mouth and went through the motions of swallowing them with a cup of water, all the while hiding the tablets under my tongue.

Satisfied that his duty had been done, Grumpy left me unshackled to consume my fare of rice and bread, closing and bolting the door on his way out. As soon as I deemed it safe, I spat the tablets into my hand to examine them, hoping for some indication as to their origin or purpose. But none was apparent; two were white and red capsules, the others white and yellow. I was none the wiser for my efforts.

'Well, if they wanted to kill me they would have done it by now,' I reasoned, and swallowed the lot, hoping desperately that they were in fact antibiotics.

Settling down to eat the rice turned out to be an interesting exercise in itself, and one that taught me a lesson that would not be forgotten. Nothing in Iraq was proving to be straightforward.

I attacked my first spoonful with some gusto, as my body craved nourishment; but it almost proved to be a disaster. As I chewed hard on the boiled brown morsels, my teeth clattered, jarred and almost fractured on numerous small, unyielding objects that felt decidedly like stones. Spitting the mouthful back into the bowl, I used a finger to inspect the inside of my mouth for any broken or chipped teeth; it certainly felt as if I had damaged some. Nothing came to light and I began to sift through the soggy, half-chewed pieces of rice. Sure enough, half a dozen tiny round polished stones were hidden amongst it all – the culprits that had nearly destroyed my dental work. I did not think that they had been put there on purpose; a more likely explanation for their presence being that they were the dregs from the pot in which the rice had been boiled originally. From that moment on, every spoonful of food that went into my mouth was meticulously sifted and vetted to ensure that I could eat without breaking my teeth.

Grumpy returned about an hour later to retrieve the empty bowl and to reattach the handcuff, this time taking care not to fix it too tightly. He left the room, securing the door as normal behind him, as the setting sun began to rob the room of the last vestiges of light. Within the hour, the cell was in complete darkness.

I lay there staring at the blackened ceiling, finally feeling able to relax as the night, the old ally, wrapped me once more in its comforting embrace. In the weeks ahead, I would yearn for the solace that the night brought, an escape from the realities that bombarded me from all directions during the day. It was only on very rare occasions that the guards disturbed me during the night – they enjoyed their own company, and I my solitude.

There was unfortunately one drawback that accompanied the onset of darkness, and it was a major one. Night heralded the arrival of swarms of Allied bombers, the same massed formations that I had seen while waiting for our Chinook to be refuelled only days earlier. Tornadoes, Jaguars, Stealths and numerous other warplanes would sneak in under cover of darkness, all eager to deposit their thousands of pounds of ordnance upon the Iraqi capital and other unsuspecting targets.

No sooner had night descended than the air-raid warning sirens would begin their incessant wail and batteries of anti-aircraft artillery across Baghdad would commence their desperate booming search for the hated planes.

One of these batteries was situated directly above my room: a sand-bagged emplacement dug into the top of the bank, I assumed. The first time it activated its deadly armament it scared the life out of me. I had never expected a Triple A position to be sited within the hospital grounds, let alone right on top of me. I doubt that the placement was accidental; the Iraqis were cunning enough to know that the bombers wouldn't attack a military position so close to a known hospital.

Off and on, throughout the night, the sounds and vibrations of countless tons of bombs could be heard and felt from my room. Often some came closer than I would wish. This posed the question whether or not my own side would make me the unintentional victim of friendly fire. Would a wayward Allied bomb, after all that I had been through, undo me in the end?

These first 24 hours taught me 90 per cent of the lessons that I would need to know in order to survive my stay in captivity. The smallest and most insignificant things could often mean so much, and after a few weeks of this routine, they most certainly did.

* * *

Days passed interminably slowly to begin with. Not long after first light, the jangle of Grumpy's keys would signal his entrance. His first task was to empty the jug of urine that I would have filled to the brim during the night, immediately followed by our little tango to the toilet.

On returning to the cell, he would bring my breakfast that consisted of a half baguette and a tiny glass filled with thick, sweet, minted tea. Occasionally, as a real treat, I would also receive a large dollop of margarine, wrapped in tin foil, to add to the bread. Once again, a lesson was learnt and quickly heeded: if I didn't use all the margarine, it would be taken from me and perhaps a week or more would pass before I received any again. Hence, to keep hold of the delicacy and to prolong the enjoyment of its taste, I would use the margarine sparingly, tearing off a piece of foil to wrap and cache the remainder under my mattress for a future occasion.

A day or so after my arrival, Grumpy must have decided that the floor was too dirty even for my miserable existence, which instigated a spring clean of sorts. He came in and threw several buckets of water smelling of disinfectant about the place, which he then proceeded to move about the floor with the aid of a squeegee. This then became a weekly occurrence, and before long the floor actually looked half-decent.

Unfortunately, the same couldn't be said of the toilet, which was a lost cause and treated with similar disdain. Grumpy would do his best to flush the toilet through with several bucketloads of water, from a good distance of course, but never with the regularity that it required. I couldn't blame him for his efforts, and, to be fair, I wouldn't have wished the job on anyone.

Not long into the stretch, another gaoler appeared on the scene; his responsibility was to relieve Grumpy from early evening to first light. A small, thin man in his early 30s, his character was the complete opposite to that of his comrade. From the day I laid eyes on him till the day I left the hospital cell, his cheerful, moustached face was never without a smile upon it. Doubtless he was not equipped with a full deck of cards, but I am sure that it was not in his nature to show ill will or malice toward anyone – a strange attribute for a prison guard.

His name was Djamel, something he confided in me within hours of our first meeting, though secretly I named him Dopey. It had been a toss-up between that and Happy, but what tipped it was the fact that he did have that 'lights on but nobody home' look about him, and it did no disservice to his cartoon namesake.

So between Grumpy, Dopey and myself, we established a daily routine that became almost ritual in its regularity, Grumpy welcoming in the morning and Dopey seeing out the night.

I became so proficient at predicting the hour through the use of the makeshift sundial pictured upon the cell walls that when my bowls of rice arrived late I would be champing at the bit, mentally banging my fist on a table demanding my food.

Within days of arriving at the centre, a vehicle was brought into the alley and parked under a reed lean-to opposite my cell. Each morning one of the guards would jump in and start it up, revving the engine maniacally until a high-pitched scream was achieved, the exhaust pumping plumes of thick blue smoke to flood and choke the air about. This obviously satisfied all that the vehicle was in good working order. However, on some mornings the starter motor refused to play ball, forcing the assembled guards to spend half an hour pushing the obstinate vehicle up and down the alley in an effort to jump-start it. The shouts of success once the engine burst into life were such that you would have thought Iraq had just won the World Cup.

* * *

After a week of bed rest and regular food, my strength returned enough for me to contemplate ways of doing exercise. Not wishing to hint that I might be feeling better or stronger than I appeared, I would sneak my exercise at night. This would consist of hundreds of leg raises, followed by hundreds of modified press-ups and tricep dips. Getting myself into a position to practise the dips was not a problem, but to do the press-ups was another performance in itself.

I would slide my shackled arm as far down the bed as it could go, tuck my legs up and feed them under the right arm then lower myself quietly to the floor. In that position, using the bed as a bench and with my injured leg curled up to my backside, I would start to perform incline press-ups, pausing every couple of minutes to ensure that no guards were near enough to hear.

It wasn't much of an exercise regime, but it gave me an incredible morale boost to think that: a) I was getting one over on my captors; b) I was doing something off my own bat to aid my recovery; and c) I was providing myself with a goal, something to look forward to during the day. It was a way of breaking up the monotony and a release for all the pent-up physical energy and frustration.

The nightly air raids usually had little effect other than to rob me of a few hours' sleep, though they sometimes seemed more threatening. I knew things were getting a little dodgy when the guards would mysteriously disappear and the firing of the artillery above would suddenly become frantic. The booms of not-too-distant bombs impacting in the vicinity would catapult lumps of ceiling or wall in my direction, lumps which disintegrated on either the floor or my head. I wouldn't hear the guards again for hours, not till they felt secure enough to return, when they would shine a torch in through my window to see if I was still in one piece.

But that was nothing compared with a couple of incidents when the concussive force of a 2,000-lb bomb, dropped within hundreds of metres of the block, blew in the remnants of my small glass window and blew me out of the bed. Shaken and cowering under the flimsy iron frame and mattress, I remained in that position for most of the night until I was sure that the planes had returned to their bases. On these occasions the guards would refuse to return to their stations until first light and I, unpatriotically, didn't sing many praises to the pilots above.

However, through experience, I learned to judge very quickly when it was time to quit the top of the bed and take refuge underneath. When the guards felt it wise to do a runner, I took note and promptly made a move. The bed didn't offer much in the way of protection, but it was better than nothing.

From very early on in the piece, I was able to play on Dopey's good nature to my advantage, making a great show of massaging my wrist each time he released the handcuff at the evening meal time. After this exhibition, he then would always ask me if the shackle was too tight or not when replacing it for the night. In this way, I was able to have the ratchet of the handcuff very loose on my wrist, and that combined with the freezing temperatures allowed sufficient leeway for me to actually slip my hand out of the shackle.

Having a degree of 'freedom' during the night, I then began to form a contingency plan to aid my escape should the chance arise. The most likely source of help would come from the Allied air raids. A stray bomb could take out part of the cell, and my guards at the same time, though this wouldn't be of much use in the condition I was in. I could barely hop from my bed to the toilet, let alone walk or run. There was no way that I would be able to get very far under my own steam, but at some stage my mobility would improve.

I then decided that the next thing to do would be to acquire an Arab dish-dash, the perfect disguise for wandering lost about the streets of Baghdad. I still had my escape map and button compass, and so wouldn't be entirely blind. The final objective would be to steal a vehicle and head south across the desert to the Saudi border, avoiding the marauding tanks and planes at the same time.

So, all I needed was a direct hit from a bomb that blew down the door or a wall, killed all the guards and left the car outside intact. The guards would have to be obliging enough to leave the keys inside and I would have to be in a condition to take advantage of it. Amidst all the confusion, it would be a simple case of driving out of the hospital grounds and off into the night, my escape assured – what could be easier?

It wasn't much of a plan, but then I had little else to go on at this stage. I was pretty certain that Grumpy and Dopey wouldn't be too enthusiastic about lending me a dish-dash and helping me hop to Saudi.

* * *

The longer I remained in the cell, the more secure I felt about the Iraqis' not wishing to kill me. I couldn't quite understand why, but I most certainly appreciated it. Everything about their dictatorial society pointed towards a total lack of human compassion for those they considered enemies of the state, and I definitely fell into that category. Little did I know that Saddam Hussein had placed a large bounty on the heads of any Westerners captured alive, and was in fact intending to use any captives as bargaining chips if things went horribly wrong.

From time to time, a Republican Guard commando sergeant, whom I nicknamed Rambo, visited me. About the same size as myself, he would waltz on in with his tan-and-green-coloured uniform immaculately presented and a maroon beret firmly planted pancake-fashion upon his head. His English was very good and he took great pride in recounting stories of recent Iraqi victories to me. Guaranteed to be smoking a cigarette, he would suddenly appear as if standing guard outside my door all along. 'Good morning, Mr Michael,' was his usual opening line (Arabic names start with the surname first and then the given names follow), followed by a polite question about my health.

We would exchange pleasantries for a while; he would offer me a cigarette on each visit even though I always refused, and then the propaganda would be trotted out. 'Last night 27 American planes were shot down.' For some reason, the casualties only ever appeared to be Americans. 'And we have taken many prisoners in several successful operations in the south.' I would nod my head and offer congratulations, looking most impressed with the dubious statistics.

On one occasion I tried to get him to bring me a toothbrush. My teeth had never been in that great a condition – due to too much neglect in my youth – but two weeks with no care whatsoever was giving me cause for concern. I had resorted to pulling pieces of cotton out of my blanket or sheet to use as a dental floss substitute. Although he promised to bring me a toothbrush, it never appeared.

Around this period I discovered that I was not alone in my cell; I had in fact acquired some unwanted bed-mates, who were intent on making my life as uncomfortable and unpleasant as possible. I awoke one morning in a fit of scratching, small bites scattered across my shoulders and neck. An inspection of the immediate area soon revealed numerous large lice inhabiting my hairline. I assumed the warmth from my body had awakened them from their dormant state within either the mattress or blanket. Without treatment, there was no way I would be able to rid myself of the annoying parasites, and so I had to make do with a daily search of my head to catch and crush those I could find.

* * *

No more than three weeks into my stay, the imaginary shell into which I had withdrawn was shattered; my false sense of security at having conned the system was revealed as a pipe dream.

Late one afternoon my adrenaline began pumping as I heard numerous pairs of feet come to a halt outside my door. The jangle of key in lock and the scraping of the securing bolts being opened, way out of routine, was enough to get me all hyped up, ready for something out of the ordinary. I wasn't to be disappointed.

In stepped Grumpy and immediately after him marched two cheaply dressed men who could only have been emissaries from the secret police. The three of them held a brief discussion in Arabic – I suspected to confirm that the policemen had the right person – before Grumpy discreetly exited the room, leaving me to my new visitors.

I had been interrogated by so many different faces that I couldn't tell whether or not I had seen them before. One was holding a clipboard – I wondered if that was a sign of authority here – and he opened the proceedings.

'You are Michael Coh-bun?' he asked in heavily accented English, having terrible trouble trying to pronounce my surname.

'Yes,' I replied.

He moved to the side of the bed, next to my shackled wrist, and looked me up and down. Wham. The back of his clipboard landed slap-bang in my face. The stinging blow instantly brought tears to my eyes and produced a slow drip of blood from my rather prominent nose, which had taken most of the impact.

I was more surprised than hurt, astounded that the totally unexpected attack had been provoked simply by answering yes to my name. The reasoning behind the assault was soon to become apparent.

'Mr Michael,' he continued, 'you have been lying to us. You are veerry dangerous man.' Had the circumstances been different, I may have burst out laughing at this comment and the way he emphasised the 'veerry dangerous' bit. He had to be joking. At that moment in time I represented the most pitiful example of a dangerous man that ever existed.

'What is your unit?'

'I am a medic.' Whack! The same again, only this time the wooden board definitely hurt.

Surprisingly, a wave of violent anger rose from within that was so intense it took a considerable amount of self-control to suppress what would have been a suicidal reaction. The temptation to smack the Iraqi in the head with my unshackled left arm was overwhelming; but I knew it would probably be the last thing I would ever do. The slightest hint of what I was thinking could prove just as disastrous.

I tried not to look at him, all the while thinking to myself, 'You fucking little shit. I could smack you over even with a knackered leg.' It didn't occur to me until afterwards that this sudden bravado must have been the result of an improvement in my condition. That was one battle I was winning.

'Mr Michael,' he started again in his thick, guttural accent, 'we know everything. You flew into Iraq in two Chinook helicopters, which we heard; you were dropped next to the northern MSR, in the wrong position. There were eight of you.' Once again, he stopped and looked at me. Suddenly my bravado had disappeared, replaced by shock. My mouth went dry, a cold chill went down my spine. I suppose I had expected them to find out eventually, but I thought that would be from my own mouth, not in this manner. I was up shit creek without a paddle.

'Someone else has been caught.' My mind raced. The implications of that slowly became apparent. If my story differed from theirs even slightly, my goose would be well and truly cooked.

'I am sorry, sir,' I replied, trying to gain time and think of a way to talk myself out of this one. 'I cannot answer that question.'

It only took a minute or so to persuade me otherwise, his fists and clipboard showing the displeasure he felt at my answer. As my lips began to swell, I pleaded inwardly, 'Please don't hit my leg.' He was getting great satisfaction out of rearranging my face, but the injured ankle would provide a far simpler and effective solution. At this stage, the policeman was completely ignoring it, but for how long?

Stepping back to survey his handiwork, he continued, 'Andy McNab, Vince Phillips, Bob Consiglio, Steve Lane . . .'; his pronunciation was atrocious as the names of all the patrol members, mine included, were read out. 'We have been told everything. Everyone is happy now, all your friends are well looked after. You see, you cannot lie to us anymore.'

I stared at him in shocked silence, my mind a blank. I had run out of options. 'Oh fuck!' I thought to myself. 'What's going to happen now?'

'You are in the SAS. You are a commando, an assassin in Iraq. You are here to find our missiles and to call American planes to destroy them. Also, to blow up fibre-optic cables. This is the truth, isn't it!' The 'it' was spat in my face for emphasis.

I needed time to think, to digest all this new information and work out a plausible response, but time was one thing that I didn't have, and the policeman appeared to already know all the answers. No matter which way my frantic mind searched, the door was always barred. There was no easy way out of this one – I was well and truly fucked.

'Yes,' I mumbled, all the fight gone. Three weeks down the track, how valuable was any information I might have anyway? Of little importance, I reasoned, and certainly not worth getting another ten barrels of shit kicked out of me.

'Ah, you see,' he replied in a reasonable voice, as if talking to an errant child, 'this is much better. So, you admit to being one of the Bravo Two Zero, yes?'

'Yes,' I confirmed once more. If they had been told everything, which certainly appeared to be the case, there would be little I could add.

'That is good. We have three of your friends in another prison.' My spirits suddenly lifted at this news, but I had no time to dwell on it, for now the real questioning commenced in earnest.

'How many of your SAS are operating in Iraq?'

'I have no idea,' I replied honestly.

'You must have some idea, they are your regiment. You are not helping!' His voice became angry and his arm drew back, threatening to lash out at me with the back of his hand.

'Listen,' I began quickly, 'I am a private. What do you expect a private to know? I only joined the regiment a couple of months ago and am still a trainee. I have very little knowledge of the SAS.'

He paused and thought about that a moment. For the first time, the other policeman got his ten cents' worth in, prompting his companion in Arabic to ask another question.

'How many tanks are the SAS using? What types are they?'

'Bloody hell,' I swore to myself. 'Now what is he on about?' The regiment didn't use tanks, although some of the wagons had some serious artillery on board. I had a quick think. If the Iraqis believed that the boys were racing around in tanks, I wasn't going to try and dissuade them.

'I don't know how many are in use, but they are Scorpions.' Not being an avid tank-spotter, I had very limited knowledge on the subject and thus little to fall back on. I somehow suspected that they wouldn't believe that the regiment were mounting ops in Russian T62s, and the lightly armoured Scorpion reconnaissance tanks seemed to fit the bill perfectly.

This answer provoked an excited conversation between the two. 'How many SAS troops do you think might be operating in Iraq?'

'Hard to say,' I lied. 'Two hundred, maybe even more.' I was happy to spread some 'disinformation'.

'And planes?'

I was really warming to the task now, but still needed to keep my answers within the realms of credibility. 'Lots of planes, bombers, fighters, helicopters. They have everything.'

Now that I was 'co-operating', the policemen were quite genial. The questioning continued for about another ten minutes, often taking a bizarre tack. Where they got their ideas from, God only knows. Drawing the interrogation to a close, the main inquisitor suddenly asked, 'Would you like to be moved to the same prison cell as your friends?'

This surprised me somewhat. I would have thought that it was a bad idea to have a bunch of known 'dangerous men' housed together in the same place. Naturally, I replied that I would like that very much. The copper nodded, his parting words, 'We will see if it is possible.'

After they left the cell, Grumpy immediately took their place, as if to make sure they hadn't walked out with me hidden under a jacket or something. He looked a little embarrassed at the way I had been treated, and later that afternoon came in to give me an orange – perhaps a token of apology, as if it were his fault.

Lying back on the bed alone once more, and able to think freely undisturbed, I found a conflicting mixture of emotions running through my head. First, unless something terrible had happened, Andy and two others at least were alive and well somewhere, I assumed, in Baghdad. But what about the remaining four? He had mentioned another name during the conversation, but as his accent had been so bad, I had not been able to decipher it.

'Thank fuck I'm not the only one to have been caught.' The thought flashed selfishly in my head, immediately followed by a guilty conscience. I had no right to be pleased that others were sharing my fate. Any one, or even all of them, could have been in a worse condition than I was.

The truth of the matter was that I had no desire to be kept in an Iraqi prison cell by myself for ever and a day, and the knowledge that some of my mates were here in Baghdad as well was, ironically, quite a morale boost. If the Iraqis were prepared to place me in with Andy and the others, that would make life all the easier to bear, and if the policeman kept his word, I could be back with them very shortly. This was unfortunately wishful thinking. I was not reunited with any of the others till the day of my release.

* * *

Now that the cat was out of the bag and my secret common knowledge, I fully expected to be on the receiving end of more maltreatment. Being a medic was one thing, an 'assassin commando' was something altogether different. The first evidence of this change, not that it resulted in any beatings, was Rambo's arrival the day following the interrogation. He was looking even more immaculate than usual.

'So, Mr Michael,' he began, drawing himself up erect before my bed. 'You are not a medic but actually a commando!'

I looked up at him, shrugging my shoulders, nodding in agreement at the same time.

'You know, here in Iraq we have the Republican Guard, the best commandos in the world. We have to train very hard, you understand?' Once again I nodded, allowing him to continue.

'I will tell you, for example, our training. We have to run 40 kilometres with a pack, swim the Euphrates with the "Klash" over our heads, then finally run another 20 kilometres to do battle.'

Throughout his speech I nodded solemnly, not allowing a trace of disbelief to surface. He finished with a question. 'Your training, it is like this?' It was of course a challenge, and one that I wasn't going to rise to.

'No,' I replied, 'our training is nowhere near as hard as that. Nobody would be able to pass it.'

He seemed very pleased with this answer. 'Yes, the Iraqi Republican Guards are elite. Your troops will find out if they come up against us. They cannot win, we cannot be defeated.'

After the PR rhetoric, he did offer a piece of information that made my ears prick up. 'Another of your commandos is still in hospital. Like you, he can now be proud to have Iraqi blood.' I had picked up on titbits of information about another wounded Westerner since arriving, and this was the strongest confirmation of that yet. But the unanswered question remained: who was it?

Rambo departed, leaving me pondering that point. When the question was finally resolved on my release, the answer astonished me.

* * *

One of my favourite fantasies when things were getting pretty bad was to dream that the boys would come bursting into my cell, guns blazing, and whisk me off to a chopper, ready and waiting to fly me the hell out of Iraq and back to safety.

On one night, not long after the last interrogation, I awoke after such a dream to the sound of the city racked by sustained small-arms fire and thought that perhaps my dream had in fact turned into reality. I soon learned that this was not the case when a torch was shone in through the window, accompanied by a hand holding a pistol. The soldier drew back the slide and prepared to shoot, only to be stopped at the last minute by one of his companions. As they argued in Arabic, I lay there cringing pathetically on the bed waiting for that sickening impact that would signal my being shot again. This was most definitely not a game. The weapon was finally withdrawn and as the two of them ran off I listened, lying there breathing heavily, heart pumping and shitting myself – what the fuck was going on?

All around the gun battle raged and continued throughout the night, never too close, but not that far away either. It was serious enough for the guards to disappear until the firing had ceased; they were either fearful for their own lives, or they were needed as reinforcements. To complicate matters further, the air raids continued unabated, though the Triple A was very sporadic.

At the time, I tried to find an explanation for what I had heard. Perhaps it was an attempt to take the capital by the coalition forces. The attempt to shoot me justified this theory – my captors would prefer that I was dead rather than repatriated – but the lack of heavier weapon fire didn't support this. It could have been a hostage rescue attempt, but the gunfire appeared to be coming from every direction. An operation of that type would more than likely have had only one or possibly two targets, certainly not so many as to get bogged down in a major house-to-house scrap.

The next morning my guards were skulking about the place very subdued and talking in hushed voices. Grumpy never said a word to me when he brought in the breakfast, and on this morning, and the following one, all I received was a cup of hot, sweet tea. Whatever had occurred the night before had spooked the lot of them.

Not till long after my release did I learn that it was in fact a coup attempt by some of the disaffected generals in Saddam's regime, a desperate bid to topple the despot and save Iraq from a war that was destroying the country. Needless to say, the coup failed, suppressed ruthlessly by the Republican Guard at Saddam's behest. Those generals who instigated it, and some that were thought to be involved, were not seen again.

* * *

The remaining days of my confinement proved to be somewhat uneventful after all that had happened. The routine returned basically to normal, though Grumpy became more approachable, often electing to leave my handcuff off for hours on end. A week or so before my release, he also took it upon himself to become my personal physiotherapist. I doubted that he had any official qualification in this profession, but perhaps he had had a lot of experience.

Every morning, after breakfast, he would come into the cell and begin manipulating my injured foot up and down, attempting to prevent the newly forming cartilage seizing up the ankle joint.

To bring this into perspective, when I eventually returned to Hereford, I was immediately put under the supervision of the camp physio, who assigned me two sessions of therapy each day for weeks. These appointments entailed manipulations of my ankle so painful that copious amounts of Volterol had to be taken an hour or so before each session. This still did not really do much to ease the distress; it simply dulled it, tears of pain inevitably pouring from my eyes during every forced articulation.

Two minutes with Grumpy the physio was a form of torture in itself and enough to leave me in a state for hours after – I swear my hand imprints are still imbedded in the steel frame of that hospital bed.

* * *

Just over a week before my release, the bombing of the city intensified considerably. Cruise missiles rained in every couple of hours during the day, and the waves of air raids during the night were almost uninterrupted. Though I had no idea at the time, this all coincided with the beginning of the ground war, the week of all-out attack on the Iraqi capital aimed at destroying morale and reducing the operational cohesiveness of Baghdad to almost nil.

After a week, this intensive bombardment suddenly stopped without any apparent reason. The first day and night without the wailing sirens or the booms of Triple A were uncommonly silent, and a strange air of disquiet descended over the cellblock. The following morning, Grumpy marched into my room and announced full of pride that a great war had been averted, that both sides had pulled back from the brink at the last moment thanks to the unyielding leadership of Saddam Hussein.

I queried this – 'The war is over?' – trying desperately not to get my hopes up.

'Yes, yes,' Grumpy replied. 'Finished, Insha-Allah.'

I found this information very doubtful, though lying there afterwards, no longer cuffed to the bed, I conjectured that perhaps the Iraqis had finally decided to evacuate Kuwait of their own volition. That night I listened long and hard for some indication that the campaign was ongoing, but nothing occurred.

The next day Grumpy came in and gave me the news, 'Five days, you go.' He made an upward motion with his hand, 'It is over.'

I dared not think that he was telling the truth. Surely, I couldn't be repatriated so soon. It would take months of diplomacy and negotiation to secure any POW releases.

An hour later another entourage visited me, this time a medical one, headed up by my old friend Dr Al-Bayeth.

'How are you feeling this morning, Michael?' he asked genially, at the same time inspecting my ankle. 'Ah, these stitches should have been removed weeks ago.' He turned to one of his companions and rattled something off in Arabic, before turning back to me. 'There is no infection, but I will have the wound cleaned.' This was the first time that my foot had been attended to since I entered the hospital cell some five weeks earlier.

Finally I spoke up. 'I have no feeling in my toes. Does that mean I will not walk properly?'

'You will have a limp, for sure. But the lack of feeling should return eventually as your nerve endings regenerate.' He paused for a second, 'You know the war is over.' It wasn't a question, but a statement. 'Now we will have to begin the process of rebuilding Iraq.'

We chatted for a few minutes longer, most of the conversation revolving around what the likely effects of my injury would be. The doctor had considerable experience in dealing with gunshot wounds and their eventual outcome. 'You will not run again.' It was simply said.

This was the comment that hurt. I was somewhat of a fitness fanatic and enjoyed a lot of sports: triathlons, rugby, basketball and many others. Did this signal the end of that?

The last comment he made before leaving the room caught me totally unawares and made me slightly embarrassed. 'Would you like a girlfriend?'

'Pardon?' I asked, totally confused.

'The nurse who helped me with your operation at the clinic, she would like to be your girlfriend,' he explained. 'She will be going to London soon to study.'

'Shit!' I swore to myself. The last thing I wanted to do was upset or offend anyone when my release was so near. 'That is very kind but I already have a fiancée.' There was no way I was ever going to tell Sue about this one.

'Oh, well, no problem. I will write up some notes for you to take away. I wish you goodbye and a speedy recovery.'

I thanked him and returned the farewell, sighing with relief as he left the room. 'Bloody hell! From being smacked over to nearly married, talk about a contradiction. What are these people like!'

I never saw Dr Al-Bayeth again, but I am sure he is the person I must thank for still having a foot, and the mobility I enjoy now.

* * *

I was no longer shackled, nor was the door to my cell closed – a total transformation had taken place. Though still wary of the good news, I could not help but be optimistic about what would happen over the next few days. After all, five more to endure was nothing – provided the situation didn't change.

For a short time the following day, I thought my release was no longer imminent, as great booms resounded across Baghdad. For a good ten minutes the sounds of jet engines and after-burners screamed over the city, but the loud blasts were strangely not accompanied by any shock wave.

Grumpy came into the cell later and explained that the noise was actually Iraqi jets doing victory rolls and fly-bys over the capital. The majority of the Iraqi air force had fled to Iran at the beginning of the war, out of harm's way, and now the heroic pilots and their aircraft had returned to reclaim their right to fly the Iraqi skies. Grumpy went on to explain how many victories the Iraqis had achieved in the air, the scores of American planes shot down by the superior Iraqi pilots, and so on, but I had stopped listening. I was so relieved that the whole shebang hadn't kicked off again that I couldn't care less what crap Saddam was dishing out to his people.

That night, between midnight and one o'clock in the morning, I was woken by Dopey, two plain-clothed civilians carrying AK47s, and another man entering my cell. Immediately on guard, still not entirely convinced that no more harm would come to me, I viewed the new arrivals with mounting dread, my eyes flicking nervously between the unknown faces.

The one not carrying a weapon pulled out a piece of paper and began to read from it by torchlight. 'You are Michael Coburn?'

'Yes,' I answered, becoming more agitated by the minute.

'I am the representative from the Red Crescent. I am here to check your details, then you are to be moved. Do you understand?'

My mouth went suddenly dry, my heart thumped. Why was I being transferred in the middle of the night if the war was over? I didn't like this one bit.

'Yes,' I replied hesitantly.

An exchange began in Arabic between Dopey and the rest, and before I knew it I was being hustled out of bed and into a blacked-out van that sat waiting in the alley. Things were getting worse by the minute.

The back doors were closed and locked, with me lying on a stretcher, and off it drove. For over half an hour the van twisted and turned through the streets and thoroughfares of the capital. The ride was far too similar to my initial excursion from the Syrian border and all those feelings of helplessness and vulnerability came rushing back. Why was I being moved in such a secret manner? It did not bode well.

The van lurched to a halt suddenly and excited voices began assaulting the vehicle from all directions, hands banging on its sides.

As I had not been restrained, I sat up and looked fearfully at the rear doors as they were pulled open. The dim light from a couple of incandescent bulbs perched high upon an internal security wall next to which the van was parked added to the sense of menace. The illumination actually revealed a group of multi-uniformed soldiers, not a matching set of military clothing between them, all straining to get a look at the new prisoner.

Not a recognisable face was amongst them, and it dawned on me how much I had come to appreciate my 'family' surroundings at the hospital. By knowing intimately the idiosyncrasies and characteristics of my previous captors, Grumpy and Dopey, I had in effect taken a good deal of the fear of the unknown out of my detention, but this was no longer the case. I was back to square one.

Several pairs of hands reached into the vehicle and dragged me from it, though not in a rough manner, eager to get hold of their prize. I was held up by two of the soldiers, who proceeded to support and guide me toward a doorway with a huge metal door.

Once through the door, it soon became apparent this most definitely wasn't a holiday resort. The concrete floors beneath me had been worn smooth over the passage of time by many thousands of pairs of incarcerated feet. As I was moved past a series of small metal doors that lined a long corridor on either side, it became starkly evident this was a prison.

'Commando?' one of the soldiers walking next to me asked.

'Yeah,' I answered simply. This provoked an immediate rendition of the high-pitched victory chant, accompanied by the masochistic head-slapping routine. Why anyone felt it necessary to beat his own head in this manner was totally beyond me, but he could do it as long as he liked, if it stopped him from trying it on mine.

We finally stopped outside a cell near the end of the hall, and next to the pungent-smelling ablution block. A glimpse of the toilet facilities gave me the impression it was an improvement on what I was used to, but only just. My guards helped me in through the open doorway and laid me down on top of a small reed mat, the only comfort in the tiny cell. The door clanged shut and I was left in darkness, listening to the hollowing echoes of receding footsteps.

The first rays of the morning light were not long in coming, finding a route into the cell through a tiny rectangular hole in the far upper right-hand corner of the enclosure. Propped up against one wall, I examined the depressing reality of my new quarters. To call the cell spartan would have been kind. The thin reed mat, worn through in places, was the only protection between my body and the hard cold floor beneath. The room was about two by one and a half by three metres, a rectangular box, constructed entirely of concrete apart from the sturdy metal door, which looked as if it could have withstood an attack by a squadron of tanks.

Next to me was a blue plastic bowl with a metal cup inside it: my eating utensils. At the bottom of the room, in the right-hand corner underneath the window, a concrete trough only a couple of inches deep slid under the wall, obviously there to use as a toilet.

'Fucking arseholes.' I hurled my silent abuse at the four walls, cursing those that led me to believe that I was to be released – some release. The frustration brought me to the verge of tears. To have the glimpse of freedom offered, then snatched away, was a crushing defeat for my morale. I found myself longing for the solitude and familiar faces that had surrounded me in the hospital facility – anything to drag me away from this nightmare.

Once again, lectures from my combat survival courses rang true: 'The decision to escape must be taken at the first available opportunity. The further down the chain that you are sent, the deeper into enemy territory you will find yourself. Your guards will appear more professional (for that is their role), and the construction of the detention centres will be much more secure. All of this will combine to ensure that the options left open to you are very limited, an escape all the more difficult to engineer.'

This prophecy was now coming true, for here in this cell, I could see no way out. It would be a matter of having to psych myself up again, to readjust and concentrate on the primary objective: survival.

PART IV
RELEASE

CHAPTER 17

FREEDOM

For a couple of hours I just sat there, staring at the wall, trying not to ponder my fate, but without success. The clanging of opening and closing doors brought me out of my reverie. With each creak open and slam shut, the noise became louder. I could imagine the guards working their way down through the cells to the last, my own.

A scrape of metal on metal signified my turn as four locks were in turn opened. 'That's a bit over the top,' I thought to myself. 'Bloody takes ten minutes to open the door and that's if you have the keys!'

I looked morosely at the guard who stood in the doorway as he signalled for me to hand him my plate and cup. 'What crap will you serve here, then?' I asked myself as the bowl was passed to him. The guard moved out of the cell for a second, then returned with both a bowl full of delicious-looking food, and a steaming hot mug of black tea. I was gobsmacked. The door slammed shut, only one of the locks was re-secured, and I was left staring in bewilderment at my breakfast.

Two boiled eggs, some salt, a good-sized baguette, butter, date jam and an orange – this was heaven. I devoured the meal in double-quick time, fearful that someone would come to take it off me, and then sat licking every inch of the bowl afterward, regretting terribly that I had not savoured the food longer.

No more than half an hour later, the door opened once more and an elderly looking gentleman stepped in, several documents in hand. 'You are Mr Michael Coburn?' he asked in a very stressed-out manner, almost breathless.

'Yes.'

'Today we are sending you home. You will change into these, please.'

I was passed a yellow canvas suit, jacket and trousers, with POW emblazoned on the jacket front.

Once again the door clanged shut and I sat there dazed and confused. What the fuck was going on? This was almost surreal. Was I having a dream? Would I wake up to the sound of Grumpy opening the door? Not daring to hope too much that this was in fact a reality and I was about to be released, I quickly traded my stinking DPM shirt for the yellow jacket, but left the trousers on the floor. I couldn't pull them up over the foot of the back-cast, the legs were too narrow.

Within a few minutes the door opened once again and in stepped an ancient, grubby-looking man carrying a bowl of filthy water and an old safety razor. I saw in an instant what was about to happen and tried desperately to avoid what turned out to be a compulsory shave.

Now it was not that I was against shaving, but being someone who naturally has a heavy beard growth, one had to bear in mind that my beard had not been either cleaned or touched for over 50 days. The razor was unappealing, to say the least, in that it was totally clogged up with the facial hair of the other prisoners who had been fortunate enough to use it before me.

With mounting horror, I watched as the old man worked up a lather with a brush, then tried to apply it, basically dry, to my face. He then took the completely blunt instrument and attacked my beard with fervour, tears of pain streaming down my face as each individual facial hair was plucked rather than cut. The secret police could learn a thing or two from this boy.

The whole process took several minutes to complete, leaving my chin and throat a raw and bleeding mess. He made a show of trying to clean the razor before turning to me once more and saying, 'Moustache?'

A great wide mass of hair that could have been called a moustache of sorts sat under my nose and covered a serious amount of my face. Still, there was no way I was going to give this guy a second chance. 'No, no. It's OK,' I said forcefully, holding my hands up at the same time. He got the message and packed up, leaving me alone in the cell once more.

My mood had changed dramatically from the hour before, and there was no suppressing my excitement at the prospect of being released. It was unbelievable. Had there been any hitches, it would have been devastating.

I could hear all the doors being opened and dozens of pairs of shuffling feet moving about in the corridor. I looked expectantly at the door, waiting desperately for my turn to be helped out. The scrape of metal on metal signalled its opening and was immediately followed by the entrance of the official, papers still in hand. He stopped and regarded my leg, alerted to the fact that I was not wearing the full POW uniform.

'Why are you not wearing the trousers?' he demanded.

'I can't get them on over the cast, they are too tight,' I replied. 'I need a knife or scissors to cut them.' The last thing I wanted was to have to remain in prison because there were no trousers big enough to pull over my leg.

The official shouted something in Arabic and a guard promptly appeared, knife in hand. An incision was made and the material ripped up to the groin. I then removed my DPM trousers, escape map and button compass still secreted within, and pulled on the yellow replacements. It was not much of a trade, but that was the last thing on my mind. I was getting the fuck out of there!

'The moustache suits you,' the official said genially as I changed. 'You should keep it.'

I didn't bother to answer. I think just about every male I had seen in Iraq was moustache mad – they all wore them.

Once I'd changed, a guard moved in and helped me to my feet. Hopping unsteadily, I was manoeuvred out of the narrow doorway and into the corridor, where I received my first view of a white face in weeks. Lined up against the far wall were 20 or so other prisoners, all looking the worse for wear, and I was added to their number. The guard abandoned me as soon as I was able to steady myself; a roll-call had already begun.

I was so busy scanning the faces that I nearly missed my own name being read out, but recovered quickly enough to answer 'Yes', avoiding the hassle of a second reading. Desperately, I searched for a familiar face, but none was recognisable.

The roll-call finished, the assembled prisoners were led toward the main door in single file in complete silence. With an outstretched arm steadying me against the wall, I tried to hop after them and was left well behind. One of the guards grabbed another of the prisoners, and he returned to prop up my shoulder.

'Are you all right there?' he asked in a friendly, American-accented voice. 'Here, let me give you a hand.'

'Cheers, mate,' I replied, before the guard got the no-talking order in.

We caught up with the remainder at the entrance to the main prison block, a slight queue having formed as one by one the prisoners were transferred onto two large coaches. As we waited, an Iraqi moved down the line with a puff-spray perfume bottle, squirting the most hideously strong smelling aftershave on us that I had ever smelt – but then I guess we didn't smell too good either.

At last it was my turn to move out into the early morning light and fresh air. Even the short hop to the coach from the doorway was absolute bliss. Moving down the coach, I scanned the faces once more, seeing that everyone was in the same boat as me, their eyes pleading that this be for real and not a wind-up. Suddenly I paused. Was that Andy sitting in one of the window seats, staring blankly ahead oblivious to everything? I tried to catch his eye as I shuffled on past but he appeared either not to notice or recognise me. I don't know that I would have recognised myself either.

Two plain-clothed guards jumped on the bus last of all, both of whom carried AKs. A great show was made of drawing all the curtains inside the coach, more to prevent people seeing us than us seeing Baghdad, I suspected. Hydraulics hissed as the coach's double doors closed and the engine roared into life. We were off.

No one spoke as the coach slowly made its way through the early morning traffic, not a head moved lest it draw unwanted attention from a guard and cause a halt to proceedings. Through the corner of my eye I caught the occasional glimpse of life outside, but the curtained windows made a good survey of the city nigh on impossible, not without appearing blatantly obvious anyway.

It was not very long, 15 or 20 minutes at most, before we pulled off the main road and came to a halt. The doors opened and one of our minders dived off, the other standing guard at the door. For the first time, heads began to move, curtains were pulled back and the sight that greeted my eyes was a surprise indeed. We had stopped in the parking area of a large, modern hotel.

The guard at the door called for everyone to stand up, then motioned for everyone to exit the bus, counting us off as we did so. As soon as I hopped off the bus, a young woman, wearing a badge that identified her as a member of the International Red Cross, came to my aid and offered her shoulder as a crutch. 'Please, let me help you,' she said, already steadying my body. 'I am Louise, a doctor with the IRC.'

As I looked about I noticed that there were numerous others mingling amongst the prisoners, offering encouragement and support, telling everyone that it was all going to be OK. One of their number, a tall distinguished gentleman, raised his voice above all the others and announced, 'Gentlemen, if I could please have your attention.' His slightly accented English was immaculate. 'You have just been formally handed over to the International Red Cross. If you could make your way into the hotel, we will begin the administration process necessary to complete your repatriation to Saudi Arabia.'

There was no stress or urgency in the way he spoke, and his manner injected a sense of calm and reassurance over the assembled people, the Iraqis included. Delicacy and tact were needed to complete the transfer from Iraqi hands, not bullish demands or harsh words. He had the measure of the situation exactly right.

I was already being steered toward the hotel entrance by the woman helping me even as the chief negotiator gave his speech, and within seconds I was inside the building. We passed two plain-clothed Iraqis in the foyer, manning a desk that guarded the main entrance.

'Who are they?' I asked. I knew the answer already.

'Iraqi secret police. There is a strong possibility that they are going to try and snatch one of you as a hostage, so we actually have Iraqi commandos surrounding the perimeter of the hotel for our protection. It's a very delicate situation here at the moment.'

She led me past the main reception desk, a huge black polished marble affair, and into a reception room where rows of other prisoners were laid alongside one another on stretchers. I was helped to an empty one and I lay down on it gratefully. 'Thank you, Louise,' I said, slightly embarrassed that I needed the help of a woman.

'It was my pleasure, we are here to help. But please,' she continued, 'do not attempt to move about the hotel without one of us present, even to the toilet. The fit prisoners have been moved up to the third floor for their safety, but we cannot move the stretcher-cases up there. We are taking the hostage threat seriously and you are more at risk of kidnap down here.'

I nodded. 'Don't worry, I won't be moving anywhere without help.'

Louise continued, 'At least one of us will be in the room at all times, and if you need the toilet, which is outside by reception, then we will find someone to accompany you, OK?' She said all this quite matter-of-factly, as if it were an everyday occurrence that a young female doctor should be in Baghdad helping injured POWs escape the clutches of the Iraqi secret police.

'Has this woman, have these people no concern for their own safety?' I thought to myself. Somehow I suspected that the Iraqis didn't really give a shit about the neutrality of the Swiss or their IRC organisation. I watched Louise as she moved off talking to those others lying on stretchers, a kind word here, a supporting hand there, and marvelled at the bravery. To place all your trust and confidence in the concept that no one would dare interfere with the goings on of the IRC – well, she had more faith than I.

Lying back, staring up at the high ornate ceiling complete with crystal chandeliers, I began to wonder what had happened to the rest of the guys. I looked across to my left and saw a thin pale figure lying there with a horrendous-looking leg injury, metal pins protruding out of it along its length. An unruly moustache covered his face, much like my own, I suspected, and as we looked at one another it suddenly dawned on me that I knew this man.

'Mac?' I asked hesitantly, 'is that you?'

'Mike?' he replied. 'God, we thought you were dead.'

I couldn't believe this, my A Squadron sergeant major, the man who had sent me over to B Squadron, was lying next to me, a shadow of his former self.

'Bloody hell, Mac, you look like shit.'

'You should take a look at yourself, mate!'

I hadn't thought about that. I probably didn't look much like the man who had left Saudi two months earlier either.

'What the hell happened to you?'

'I was doing a target recce of an Iraqi installation when we got bumped. Jocky tried to drive out of it but we ended up in a huge field of low-wire entanglement that wrapped itself around the axles. While we were trying to extricate ourselves, the wagon was shot up and I took a hit through the skin of the rover and into the back of my leg. It smashed the leg to fuck. Keith and Jocky abandoned the pinkie, carrying me in the process, hoping to lose them in the darkness.'

I tried to imagine Jocky and Keith, not exactly the biggest guys in the world, trying to lug Mac's 15-stone bulk out of a contact.

'When John was trying to carry me, my arms were still touching the fucking ground!' We both had a laugh at that; it was easy to do so now.

'Anyway,' he continued, 'we were getting nowhere, and the Iraqi follow-up was gaining on us big style, so I ordered them to leave me.'

He paused for a second, allowing me to contemplate the situation. You needed some balls to make that decision.

'Jocky asked me if I wanted him to top me. Nice of him to offer but I preferred to take my chances with the Iraqis.'

'Yeah, I can see it now,' I answered. 'No, it's OK, Jocky, I'll just stay here and bleed a while.' We had another laugh.

'We applied a tourniquet to my leg, then I told them to fuck off. The Iraqis found me at first light, and here I am.'

'Did the secret police get hold of you?' I asked morbidly, keen to know more detail.

'Yeah, I was lying in a field hospital, drips all over the place, and they walked in, pushed the doctor out of the way and ripped all the drips out. Then they simply said answer our questions or we let you bleed to death.

So I told them what they wanted to know, none of it was secret and they had a pinkie there to look at.'

'Basically the same happened to me,' I replied, and told him the patrol's and my own story, as far as I knew it.

'We received a message on the 319 about ten days after you deployed to say that you were MIA and to keep an eye out, but your area of operations was a hundred clicks or more away from us.'

'Fucking ten days!' I couldn't believe that. 'Why didn't they warn you off straightaway?'

Mac shrugged his shoulders at that one.

We chatted on for a while. He explained that the general who had performed the operation on his leg had practised in Harley Street. Both of us had to agree that the medical attention, when it was finally given, was very good.

I stopped Louise as she was walking by, curious to see if it was Andy I had seen. 'I will send a message upstairs and see if your friend is there,' she replied, continuing on with her Florence Nightingale duties.

Within minutes Andy appeared, still sporting his green duvet jacket. How he had managed to keep that without it being confiscated by an interested Iraqi soldier, I don't know.

'All right, Kiwi,' he chirped in his broad cockney twang as he shook my hand. 'I thought you were dead.' I supposed that this was possible, I had hit the deck pretty quick, but that was before the soldiers had opened fire.

Andy turned and recognised Mac. 'Fucking hell, Mac, what are you doing here?' They shook hands and Mac recounted his story once more for Andy's benefit.

I interrupted as soon as it was convenient, dying to know what had happened to the others. 'What about Dinger, Bob, Mal and the rest, where are they?'

This stopped Andy in mid-waffle, but not for long. 'Bloody Dinger and Mal were released yesterday, weren't they, jammy bastards.'

'So they are all right, then, in one piece?' I questioned yet again.

'Yeah, yeah. They're fine. Probably pissing it up back in Hereford now.'

I doubted that very much somehow, but let Andy continue.

'Anyway, I saw you hit the deck and bomb burst into the wadi.'

'That's when you figured I was dead, then?' I interrupted.

'Yeah, that's it,' he answered before continuing. 'So I shot down the wadi a 100 metres, turned north again and crossed the road. Can't have been that far from the border when it started to get light so I looked for a LUP, found a small culvert and hid in it, waiting for last light.' He paused for a second before returning to his spiel.

'Fucking ragheads found me first, though, didn't they? Dragged me out of the culvert and took me to a garrison on the border. That's where I saw that they had caught Dinger as well.'

'What about Bob or Legs?' I interrupted once more.

'Don't know. Dinger was with Legs when he was picked up and said that Legs was in a bad way. Anyway, they started beating up on me, trying to get me to talk, but I held out for a week or so. By that time, I knew they had Mal as well and all of us were getting severe hidings.'

I was mentally ticking off the names as Andy rattled on: Dinger, Mal, Legs, himself – three still unaccounted for.

'I made the decision to tell them everything. It wasn't worth one of us getting beaten to death for.' This made sense; none of us had information that merited a posthumous MID (mention in dispatches), Mac included.

'The Iraqi comms must be well-knackered because it took them near on three weeks to click that I was part of the patrol,' I said, picking up the thread of the story. 'I thought that I had bluffed my way out of it, the old secret police certainly weren't too happy when they realised that I had been lying to them all along.'

Andy started once more. 'When we arrived in Baghdad, the guards here let us all stay in the same cell.'

'What, the three of you were together most of the time, then?' I questioned almost disbelievingly. 'Bloody lucky bastards. You want to try doing a bit of solitary like Mac here, mate, and me.'

Louise interrupted our reunion with some bad news, immediately putting a damper on proceedings. 'I am sorry, but the weather is too bad to fly you out today. The flight has been postponed till tomorrow, as long as the conditions are right.'

'What about the Iraqis?' I asked. 'Is that going to cause problems with them?' I had visions of the soldiers bursting into the hotel and dragging everyone back to prison for the night.

'We want everyone who is able to move up to the third floor,' Louise replied, in a not-too-confident-sounding voice. This was obviously something they had not planned; the repatriation was to happen speedily before there was time for second thoughts. This now gave those opposed to the release of prisoners an opportunity to mount an attack against that decision.

'Three of us will stay and sleep down here with the injured tonight.' Louise's voice was upbeat but her face betrayed the underlying stress. This was a dangerous situation for all concerned. A final smile and she departed, relaying the news to those who hadn't heard.

'Well, I'm off upstairs, then,' Andy chirped, rising to make a move.

'See you two later.' And with that parting comment, he was gone, seemingly oblivious to it all.

The remainder of the day passed uneventfully, the mood more subdued than before, now that a storm had prevented the chartered aircraft from landing. Louise and a male companion sat in the middle of the room, either quietly chatting or reading, ready to offer assistance if needed.

I had the dubious honour of having to help Mac go to the toilet. He had been struck down with diarrhoea for the last few days and in his present condition was in no state to either move or help himself. What was called for was a bedpan, naturally an item unlikely to be present in the hotel, so I improvised and removed the top of one of the ashtray/rubbish bin stands. This basically gave us a 'potty' that Mac was able to place under his backside, which he filled immediately, much to his relief. After returning the full receptacle to me, I placed it as far away as possible from our stretchers and delegated responsibility for its emptying to Louise, which she accordingly did without comment. Better her than me.

No one expected to have to cater for all the prisoners for the night, so there was very little in the way of food available. The Iraqis kindly agreed to send in some bread and rice, which was distributed amongst those who wished to continue the diet they had enjoyed as guests of the Iraqis.

* * *

The spare hours gave the IRC personnel plenty of time to complete all the administration necessary for our transfer out of Iraq and into Saudi. We were issued with IRC identity cards, our only means of identification, and a list of names was compiled then checked off against the list of MIAs given by the coalition forces.

Louise came around once more with a list of those not accounted for that was shown to all the prisoners present. Any light that could be shed on their whereabouts or condition would be of invaluable aid to the Red Cross when questioning the Iraqis.

I read the list of names; those who were accounted for were struck through in red. I saw my own name first, perhaps subconsciously drawn to it, and then others began appearing out of the long list: Consiglio, Robert; Phillips, Vincent; Lane, Stephen – their names were unmarked. Those of us present, those released, Mal and Dinger, all our names were struck through. I gave the list a couple of reads before suddenly realising that Geordie's name was missing. What did that mean?

I passed the list back to Louise, only able to confirm that Bob, Vince and Legs had certainly been in Iraq, and that perhaps she needed to add Geordie's name to the list. The very thought that we might be leaving Iraq without knowing what had happened to the others was an extremely unappealing one.

Despite the tension, the night passed uneventfully, but unfortunately morning brought no respite from the bad weather. A more practical cause for concern, apart from the kidnap threat, had now begun to raise its ugly head. The men with injuries, many a lot more serious than mine, were in need of serious medical assistance. The IRC didn't have either the supplies or the facilities within the hotel to cope with this situation.

People milled around the large reception room, occasionally peering out the huge draped windows at the patrolling Iraqi soldiers or to see if there was any change in the grey, wind-blown skies above. One of the pilots lying next to me had only been shot down two days previously and was recounting how the Iraqi Army had taken flight the moment the ground war commenced. It was almost impossible to believe that such a huge force could be routed in this manner, but I sure as hell wasn't going to complain about their lack of fighting ability.

As the day progressed, the gods began to look more kindly on our predicament and the high winds dropped, allowing a window of opportunity.

'We have had confirmation from Riyadh that the planes are now on their way,' Louise told everyone excitedly. 'The international press have got wind of it and are lined up all round the hotel. You are celebrities now.'

I turned to Mac. 'This is going to be a problem, isn't it?'

'We'll have to see if they can sneak us out the back or something,' Mac replied. 'Anything rather than being spread across the front page of *The Sun.*'

The arrangements were that two buses would be used, as before, to ferry the prisoners from the hotel to the airport. The distance from the hotel entrance to where they would be parked wasn't that great, but it was certainly enough to give the assembled world media a good look at everybody.

Andy had returned by now, along with a couple of the RAF Tornado crew members. 'We're riding in an ambulance anyway, aren't we?' I said to the IRC co-ordinator. 'So why don't you just bring it to a side entrance or something, and we'll use the exit of the rest to hide our own.'

'Yes, and we can put jackets or shirts over our heads to divert attention away from the ambulance as well,' one of the pilots offered, enjoying the drama intensely.

The IRC representative didn't really see the need for the secrecy, but nevertheless was prepared to help if that was what we wanted.

The hour of departure arrived. The hotel foyer was packed with the assembled POWs and their IRC escorts. The suppressed excitement and anticipation in the air was almost tangible. Everyone present was dying to get out of Iraq as quickly as possible, to leave the nightmare behind and be reunited with friends and family, but still dreading the possibility that at any moment it could all go wrong.

The waiting buses opened their doors, signalling the exodus; we ducked out via a service entrance. Two of the IRC reps carried Mac's stretcher and Andy helped me along the corridor to the exit, then straight into the waiting ambulance. Mac was quickly installed in place, the curtains were drawn and the rear doors closed. As the engine was gunned into life, I thought to myself, 'Dear God, please let this be true.' It wasn't the first time I had resorted to prayer since my capture. Though I'm not a religious man, strangely enough I did find that prayer gave me some comfort in my darkest hours of need. I had certainly promised the head man an IOU if He managed to get me out of this one.

Meanwhile, true to their word, three of our intrepid RAF friends were performing an Oscar-winning rendition of 'the men who did not wish to be identified'. With jackets thrown over bowed heads, they drew all the attention of the assembled media onto themselves and away from our vehicle.

Within minutes we were off, driving quickly through the main streets of the capital and chased by carloads of photographers, reporters and cameramen. I kept a constant eye on the events outside, peeking around the side of the curtain that shielded us from the paparazzi, and was amazed at the lack of destruction about. I had expected the city to be a bombed-out mess, reminiscent of the Blitz. But all the damage I saw was the odd destroyed building here and there, normally with its neighbour totally unscathed.

We continued along like this for the 20-minute drive to the airport, constantly pursued by the press.

At the airport entrance, however, they were forced to abandon their quarry and watch miserably from the perimeter as we proceeded to drive up to the two awaiting Swiss 727s.

I so desperately wanted to get on that plane that I was almost salivating, my pulse racing at the thought that probably within half an hour I would be lifting off into the sky and saying farewell to Iraq for good. The doors opened and Andy jumped out, helping me do the same. Mac was so keen to follow that he almost tried to do the same himself, but the IRC rep prevented him from doing so till he had more hands available. I was well-installed in the rear of the aircraft by the time Mac was carried aboard.

As one would expect, it took only a few minutes to load the plane with its impatient cargo. Our jet was mostly filled with Brits and Americans, the other with Kuwaitis and other members of the Arab coalition.

The head IRC co-ordinator came down the plane and shook all our hands, wishing us the best of luck. Until that moment, I had not realised that they were not travelling with us, but there were still over 300 Kuwaitis to be repatriated. Their job was far from over.

As the doors were finally sealed and the turbines kicked into life, I thought of the unassuming humility and confidence in their work that these people had. To place themselves in the hands of known tyrants, to help and protect complete strangers – strangers who had not so long before been the architects of something they totally detested – was an act of complete selflessness.

The aircraft trundled down the runway and taxied to the furthest point before turning to prepare for take-off. As the thrust increased and the plane shot forward, I saw the last images of Iraq before we were consumed by grey cloud. Baghdad, once a hive of activity and a jewel of the Middle East, now disappeared beneath the aircraft, a sad and broken shell of its former self. Its people had borne the wrath of the West, and Saddam Hussein would remain aloof and seemingly invincible, still a man to be feared.

Seconds later the city was completely lost from view and now the tense wait began. Everyone on board was thinking or worrying along the same lines. It would be so easy for the Iraqis to send a SAM (surface to air missile) hurtling towards the aircraft. We had a lot of territory to cover before the safety of the Saudi border was achieved. The minutes ticked by ever so slowly and although there was plenty of conversation, it was noticeably subdued, as if everyone was counting down.

Then, without warning, a pair of American F16s appeared on our starboard side. One of the pilots manoeuvred his aircraft so that it actually sat right over the wing itself. He jostled in as close as he dared, ripped the oxygen mask from his face and punched his left hand over and over in the air. Suddenly the aircraft lifted well above the plane, though still in sight, and performed a 360 sideways roll to the right, at the same time blowing off chaff in all directions. It then returned to its original position over the wing, so close I could easily make out the young pilot's screaming, happy face. Over and over this move was repeated, the pilot trying to achieve a more perfect result each time. The message was loud and clear: 'Don't worry, boys, no Iraqi can fuck with you now. We're taking you home.' Two Tornados appeared on the opposite wing. They also nudged right up to the fuselage, their pilots a little more reserved but no less ecstatic, with smiles beaming from ear to ear. Looking from wing to wing, I felt myself unashamedly well up with tears as the tension was finally released. In this fashion, as we crossed the Saudi border in two passenger jets nursed by a fighter escort on either side, I knew I was at last free.

CHAPTER 18

HOMEWARD BOUND

The atmosphere aboard the plane was absolutely euphoric, with raucous conversations taking place from one end to the other. It could have been the beginning of an organised holiday tour, such was the party mood that now existed.

Before landing at Riyadh, an American lieutenant colonel, the senior officer on board, told everyone that they would be exiting according to rank, though naturally those Kuwaitis with us would take pole position. Andy, Mac and I decided that the three of us at the rear would not be playing that game and that we would remain on the aircraft till representatives from our unit arrived to spirit us away. The offended colonel marched down to our end of the plane to have a word, but on realising that he was actually dealing with three Special Forces operatives, two of whom were injured, his attitude changed completely.

'I just want to tell you guys,' he began in a strong Texan drawl, 'that I think the work you do is fantastic. It is an honour and a privilege to shake your hands.'

At first I thought he was being sarcastic, but as he continued talking I realised that he was genuinely proud to meet us. It was an open demonstration of emotion that those of us from more conservative backgrounds are not really accustomed to. He stayed and chatted for a good ten minutes until the plane's rapid descent signalled our imminent arrival and forced him to return to his seat.

Riyadh's international airport was jam-packed with dignitaries and media representing all those countries that had participated in the ousting of Saddam's army from Kuwait, and countless others who had observed from the sidelines. The plane had barely come to a standstill before the stairs were in place and the forward door flung open. As the now-former POWs began to disembark, I could see the full red-carpet treatment was being deservedly laid on, especially for those Kuwaitis who exited first, their arms raised in triumph.

Andy, Mac and I would never be able to participate in such a public welcome. Our work and identities needed to be kept secret due to the sensitivity of previous, current and future operations that perhaps only a small minority of people would ever get to hear about.

While the attention of the world was focused on those leaving the aircraft via the front, an ambulance was discreetly pulled up to the rear exit under the tail. The three of us were then quietly removed unobserved from the plane and expeditiously spirited away to a C130 that was waiting for us on the far side of the airport.

Once aboard the Hercules, we were immediately flown a short distance to another airfield and transferred once more, this time to a RAF 727 medivac plane, destination Akrotiri Air Force Base, Cyprus. A reception committee was waiting for us on the 727, and each of the POWs had been allocated a peer to act as minder for him. Mick, a mate with whom I had completed selection was mine, though I have to admit that I thought Pete or Ken would have been present, but that didn't wipe the grin off my face.

Now, back amongst our own, we were able to truly relax, allowing those about us to do the worrying. After a quick check-up by the medical staff aboard, I was allowed to go forward and sit with the blokes, while Mac unfortunately was relegated to a stretcher in the rear of the aircraft. Whisky and cigarettes were freely distributed, but when the first decent meal in months arrived it was greeted with derisory boos of disapproval. Chicken curry in a bed of rice, of all things! Still, it was pure luxury to be able to attack a meal without fear of fracturing my dental work.

It was then that I found out that Geordie had managed to walk out of Iraq all the way to Syria. He was the only survivor of the patrol that the regiment had been aware of up until a couple of days before. It was an excellent achievement considering no one else had made it, though when I spoke to him later he admitted that the NVA was the thing that saved his arse!

The fact that any of us had been captured was only revealed when Dinger and Mal were seen live on *Sky News* being handed over to the Jordanians. Apparently one of the wives put the regiment in the picture. Consequently everybody was caught napping, and there was nothing in place to shield the identities of Dinger and Mal from the world's media.

I was later informed that one of the first preconditions for a ceasefire when the Iraqi military surrendered was that all prisoners must be returned immediately. The Americans had obviously learnt a painful lesson in Vietnam and were determined that that would never be repeated. George Bush and Norman Schwarzkopf received my full vote of confidence on that stand.

I later met General Schwarzkopf in Hereford, after the patrol had given him a brief on our mission in Iraq, and I was personally able to pass on my gratitude. I have to say that he is one of the most charismatic men I have ever met. He thanked us for our bravery and commitment, and his genuine appreciation of our plight, the way he shook my hand and said thank you for what we did, has stayed with me always. It was an honour to meet him.

* * *

Cyprus was only a few hours' flight away and before we knew it the famous tourist island resort was in sight. Ambulances transported all of us from the airfield to the base hospital in Akrotiri, where hordes of bored nurses and doctors were lying in wait. A huge medical and casualty reception centre had been established, ready and waiting to cater for all the war wounded that were supposed to be processed through the centre before being passed fit enough to travel home.

A British Red Cross nurse who had accompanied us on the journey from Saudi ferried me in a wheelchair through the labyrinth of hospital corridors, finally coming to a halt in a doubled-bedded room reserved for Andy and me. Within minutes, news of our arrival spread through the near-empty wards, and suddenly Dinger was at the door, his now acutely thin, haggard face bursting into a wondrous smile on seeing me. Moving on over, he gave me a hug. 'How are you, mate?' he asked in a voice full of genuine warmth. 'I thought you were dead.'

'Thought I was as well, mate,' I answered. 'It was a close thing.'

Mal then popped in through the doorway and the scene was repeated over again, the big Aussie nearly crushing me in his embrace.

'What happened to the leg, Mike?' Mal asked once he finally let go of me.

'Didn't run fast enough, mate,' I replied, lightening up the situation. We would all be in tears any second now at this rate.

'You Kiwis always needed to brush up on your soldiering skills,' Dinger jumped in. 'Come on over to B Squadron and I'll teach you a thing or two.' This was more like it – a good slagging match would get us all in a much better frame of mind. We carried on like that for a couple of minutes before unanswered questions were forced to the surface. Knowing that Dinger and Mal had been here for a couple of days already, I asked the burning question: 'What about Legs, Bob and Vince?'

Instantly Dinger's mood changed, pain written all across his face. 'Legs is dead,' he said simply. 'I am sure of it. I don't know about Bob.'

I lay there in stunned silence, not really knowing what to say as the reality hit home.

'The same with Vince,' Mal added. 'Though we have no confirmation from the Iraqis.'

No one said a word for a minute. Each man was lost in his own thoughts, thinking about a missing comrade. What the hell had gone wrong?

I didn't get a chance to discuss the question, as Andy came waltzing in, a small bag full of knick-knacks in hand.

'All right, guys,' he began, throwing the bag on his bed. 'You want to get one of these, Kiwi? – Walkman, watch, shaving gear, heaps of stuff in them. I've scored a couple.'

Dinger and Mal looked over at Andy and shook his hand. Obviously they had only seen each other a couple of days before.

'Listen up, then,' Andy continued, 'the spooks want to give us all a debrief now; Hereford is demanding one straightaway. I'll go first, and then the rest of you file on through, OK?'

'Andy, before any of that crap, can you go and ask the nurse or someone to find me two tons of disinfectant and something to kill head lice with? Cheers, mate.'

'Sure, Kiwi, don't worry about it,' and off he went on his mission.

I turned to Dinger. 'What happened, mate?'

Dinger looked hard at me for a moment, considering his reply. 'When that last contact blew up, we had shit flying in from all directions and I lost sight of the rest of you completely. We hit a bunch of Iraqis almost straightaway. I emptied the Minimi into the lot of them from about five feet, bloody brilliant it was. Anyway, Legs and I bomb-burst down towards the river, expecting to have Bob and the rest of you somewhere behind in tow, but once we got there we realised that we were alone. We began to move up the bank towards the north when we heard a follow-up squad behind us, shooting up everything and anything that moved. Our only option left was the river. There was a small boat chained to the bank but we couldn't release it without drawing attention to ourselves – shooting the padlock off would have had them on us in seconds. I wasn't sure about jumping in, I mean we had all just about gone down with hypothermia only a few hours before, you know? But Legs was positive, he made the decision, so we ditched all our kit and waded on in into the water.'

'Bloody hell, Dinger,' I exclaimed, shaking my head in wonder. 'The Euphrates is over 600 metres wide there. It must have been like an arctic swim in those conditions.'

'It was worse, mate, believe me,' Dinger continued on. 'At first we swam out only about 60 or 70 metres, then hit high ground. Not being able to see a thing, we thought initially that maybe the river had narrowed there and we had made it across. Of course it turned out to be a small island, too small to hide on, so we had to go back in again. I didn't want to, I was shattered, but Legs sorted me out and we jumped back in again. God it was cold, the current was so strong we were swept well downstream.

'We tried to stay next to each other as much as possible, talking and encouraging one another across, but about 50 or so metres from the far bank, Legs stopped talking. I managed to get a hold of him and drag the two of us to the bank, but he could hardly stand up. I wasn't in a much better condition myself.'

I could envisage the scene easily, the two of them struggling out of the water, dragging themselves up a muddy bank, clothes soaking wet and weighing a ton, frozen to the core. I had looked at that great swollen mass of river and said to myself 'No way!', but these two had done it – what balls.

'Anyway, we managed to get ourselves out of the water and into a small farmer's shed nearby. Both of us were in rag order, but Legs was becoming really lethargic. Hypothermia was setting in. For the remainder of the night, I tried as best I could to keep him and myself warm, lying on top of one another and that, but it was so fucking cold, you know?' I could see the pain in Dinger's face as he was recounting the story. He had felt as helpless as me.

'Anyway, come morning, Legs was totally incoherent, verging on unconsciousness. He was slipping away, I knew it. The only thing I could do for him now was to get him to a hospital. There were some farmers working in the fields about, so I dragged Legs out of the shed and got their attention. They dropped their farm tools and buggered off somewhere, looking for the soldiers, I suppose. Legs couldn't understand me, but I tried to tell him I was sorry, that I couldn't help him any more and that he needed to get to hospital. Before I knew it, they were all over us; I couldn't have made a break even had I wanted to. The rest of it's history.'

'What about Legs, mate?' I asked quietly.

'Last I saw of him, he was being loaded into the back of an ambulance on a stretcher. After that, I was getting so much of a kicking that I wasn't able to take a lot of notice.'

'But you don't think he made it?' I prompted again.

'He would be with us now, if he had,' Dinger replied, shaking his head.

Of course, this was now common knowledge amongst Andy, Dinger and Mal, but to me it came as a complete shock. For some reason I had always taken an optimistic view of the eventual outcome. I don't know if this was wishful thinking, or just the mind refusing to allow itself to believe anything to the contrary. But now, as I absorbed Dinger's story, I could feel a cold emptiness within. This wasn't an exercise where people came back to life once the umpire with the white armband turned up. This was permanent.

'We still don't know for sure,' Mal said, breaking the silence. But it wasn't said with much conviction.

I needed to know the full story, why the patrol had split, what had happened to Mal, Vince and Geordie. I needed to understand how this disaster had come about, but it required more facts to do so.

'Go on then, Mal,' I said. 'Give me the rest.'

'Well,' Mal began, 'where do I start? Half an hour, I suppose, must have passed before we actually realised that the split had occurred, and by then it was miles too late. Geordie scanned the area with the NVA, tried the TACBE, and we waited where we were for another half-hour in the vain hope that the rest of you might come along, but still nothing. So we made the decision to carry on north, Geordie leading with Vince and me following. Perhaps all of us would meet up again; it wasn't that unlikely, our bearings would have been pretty close.

'Before first light, we laid up in a shallow trench, all freezing but still OK; that was until that bloody snow turned up. By last light, we were all in a bad way and to a certain extent were now operating on automatic.

'As darkness descended, and we made ready to move, it became apparent that Vince was clearly suffering; in fact, with the benefit of hindsight, I would say he was probably already hypothermic. He couldn't even hold his weapon properly. Geordie was also struggling; I was probably the least affected. Nevertheless we continued northwards, staggering on into the howling blizzard; there really was no alternative. I took the lead, navigating, whilst Geordie followed on with Vince. The further north we moved, the more the weather deteriorated, and with it the visibility. All the while, unbeknown to me, or Geordie for that matter, Vince was slipping away. You know, Vince was always such a big hard bastard, I guess we just didn't expect that the day spent exposed to the elements could have done him such damage.

'Anyway, the sleet and cold were bad enough, but it was the wind that really proved to be the killer – we just couldn't get away from it. So we carried on, trying to keep moving, trying to keep warm and alert. It was a nightmare.

'Then it happened, somehow . . . I don't know. Vince became separated, we weren't paying enough attention, our minds numbed with cold and not thinking clearly.

'Geordie yelled at me that he couldn't see Vince. Initially, I wasn't concerned; this had happened a couple of times and on each occasion we would simply stop, retrace our steps and within a minute or so there he would be, trudging on behind. But this time was different. We stopped and began to search, but with no result. Panic began to set in, things were getting desperate. We had to find him; the conditions were so bad we were stumbling about all over the place, near as good as blind.

'Thirty minutes passed before Geordie made the decision, saying we had to go on otherwise the two of us would be history as well. We had a brief discussion, an argument of sorts, I guess, but at the end of the day he was senior. No matter how I look at it, I didn't stand my ground, and that moment is something I will have to live with for the rest of my days. I haven't seen Vince since.'

There was a long pause as I absorbed this information. I broke the silence with a question, to which the answer was readily known. 'Do you think he could have made it through the night?'

'He was going down, mate, that's why he stumbled off in another direction, losing us. I can't see him having lasted more than half an hour in those conditions.'

Mal's face registered the guilt he felt, but there was nothing he could do to alter the situation. Perhaps there would have been three hypothermia cases instead of one had they blundered around all night looking for Vince. Just as with Legs, it was a hard call to make.

Now eager to continue, Mal ploughed on. 'We carried on all through that night, me in the lead navigating with Geordie following, until first light when we LUPd. The day passed pretty uneventfully at first; that was until another fucking goatherder stumbled onto us.'

'I don't believe this,' I interrupted once again. 'You were compromised by another goatherder? The Iraq desert must be bloody saturated with them!'

'Well,' Mal carried on, 'Geordie decided we should kill the goatherder but I was having none of it. Seniority or no, it was mindless to kill the bloke aimlessly and this time I stood my ground. In any case, Geordie was in a shit state. He was hypothermic and had real trouble walking; I guess his feet were all cut up from his ill-fitting boots. I honestly felt I was a better judge of this situation.

'It was obvious we wouldn't survive another night like that so I decided to try to speak to the herder, gain as much information as possible so we could make a more informed decision – even if it meant killing him after that. As it was, I didn't give Geordie much of a chance to argue and simply began speaking to the old man. Communicating was a drama but by drawing in the sand, pointing and so on, he indicated to me that there was a habitation with a vehicle nearby.

'Armed with this, I decided to follow the herder. I figured that if he led me to the habitation I could assess the situation from there and hopefully find some way or means to better our situation. Then it would simply be a matter of returning to get Geordie, which would be no problem as there was an excellent reference point on the map.

'After a heated discussion, this reasoning was reluctantly accepted. I gave Geordie my belt order, hid my M16 under my shirt as best I could and followed the herder at a distance.

'We walked for a couple of hours, moving very slowly with me always a fair distance behind. Then I decided to move ahead of him and not long after – bingo, I saw a small house in the distance with two white 4x4s parked to one side. I thought all my Christmases had come at once. At least now there was hope.

'With my weapon still hidden, I approached the house just as the owner of the vehicle was coming out. He saw me, yelled at someone inside and made a run for one of the vehicles. As I pulled my weapon and dropped to the ground, soldiers began appearing from the house. First of all, I shot the guy trying to drive off in the 4x4, followed by the first three soldiers that had exited the house. Unfortunately, that was about the time I ran out of ammo. As quick as I could, I crawled into the vehicle nearest to me, only to find the keys missing. There was a horrible silence as the firing stopped and then the barrel of an AK47 was pointing at me through the broken windscreen. But the guy didn't fire.'

I stared at Mal in disbelief. 'You killed some of their mates and the soldiers let you live?'

'They made up for that by using me as a football for an hour or so,' Mal answered.

I still couldn't believe it. 'I'm not surprised!'

'Yes, another life used! I reckon that was the second one on this mission. Anyway, I ended up at the interrogation centre run by the secret police and the Republican Guard. Pulled the pilot rescue routine – told them I was a dentist not a soldier and that my helicopter had crashed in the desert somewhere. Got a hell of a time; they thought I was lying and that I was part of the eight-man patrol from the north. Each day they threatened me that lying would end in mutilation and death. They brought in a dentist and a doctor to test my story and they confirmed that my credentials were bona fide.

'Then, after about nine days' interrogation, with my physical condition going down rapidly, it suddenly all stopped. My story was accepted, my interrogators apologised for the mistreatment and explained that they were not really bad people but this was war. My situation improved immensely; medics tended my injuries and I was given food. I thought I was home and hosed, as long as my cover story held.

'For a couple of days everything was fine, relatively speaking; that was until they burst in with the full story of the patrol. I was well and truly rumbled and they were not impressed. The lies had been exposed and the soldiers took their anger out on me with a beating that lasted most of the night.

'By morning, they decided to stop, probably concerned that they had just about beaten me to death. A doctor came in and commented that he thought I had a fractured skull, though I have to say the dentist in me was more concerned about the state of my teeth. Anyway, what really surprised me was that there then appeared to be a genuine concern for my welfare and the mistreatment stopped completely. But that was definitely life number three.'

'It's no wonder they were so pissed off with you,' I said. 'They probably sent platoons of troops out into the desert looking for a non-existent helicopter.'

'Well, whatever, they obviously decided to forgive and forget. I reckon they were happy that the last bit of their jigsaw was in place. I was taken from the interrogation cell to a military prison and allowed to move into the cell with Andy and Dinger.

'That's how we stayed until Dinger and I were released on the Jordanian border a couple of days ago. Apart from the news conference, it was all rosy after that.'

'News conference?' I asked, looking at Dinger at the same time. 'What do you mean, news conference?'

Dinger answered the question. 'The Jordanians held a news conference with all the released POWs in attendance. We were forced to sit at a table in front of the world's media, basically paraded for them.'

'What a nightmare,' I thought to myself. Wanting so desperately to be free, then suddenly finding that your identity was going to be blown all over the world; I had got off lightly.

Suddenly, a bizarre thought flashed into my head and I looked at Mal once more. 'Oi, you,' I began. 'What happened to that bloody camera?'

Mal looked a little confused at first, then comprehension dawned, a great smile breaking out across his face. 'Hey, of course,' he laughed, 'the Iraqis will be able to get a nice blow-up of you taking a dump!'

Dinger, ignorant of the camera incident, spoke up. 'What are you two on about?'

A quick explanation had all of us chuckling, enough to ease the strain of the last few minutes. By recounting their stories so soon after the event, they were in fact reliving them. The expressions on their faces and the unvaried, matter-of-fact tone of their voices revealed their suppressed emotions. I suppose I must have sounded like them when I filled the two of them in on my own adventures.

Our tête-à-tête was broken up by Andy's arrival. With him was a nurse carrying various bottles of disinfectant for my use. Surprisingly, I felt the need to be on my own again, to be able to digest all the information I had just received and try and make some sense of it all – to understand why and how it all happened.

Turning to Andy, I said, 'Right, mate, you can wheel me down to the bathroom and then I can run a bath and fill it up with this stuff.' I intended to annihilate the lice and anything else that might be trying to grow on me at the same time. A good soak for an hour in the bath would be just what my battered and abused body needed.

Andy stayed to help me into the bath, then disappeared to start his debrief. I immersed myself in the scalding hot water, which was red with disinfectant and chemicals. The first wash for over two months was absolute bliss. At the first dunking, the water nearly turned black with gunk and grime, and a huge plug of scab detached itself from the underside of my foot, where the bullet had exited. Three times I ran and emptied the bath, until the water remained crystal clear and I was certain all the parasites that had taken refuge on my person were well and truly gone.

With a towel wrapped around my waist, I wheeled myself back to my room over an hour later and put on the new set of clothes that had been brought for me. My discarded yellow prison garb sat at the foot of my bed, a crumpled heap of cheap, bad-smelling material. I thought about throwing it away, but perhaps it would be better to keep it as a poignant memento, a reminder of all that had passed over the last few months. I placed it in a plastic bag and put it next to my bed. Whether I wanted a reminder of the past or not was something I was not too sure about at that time.

* * *

Seven weeks after having my initial operation, the stitches were finally removed from my ankle. But the news I was so desperate to hear – How would I heal? Would I be able to run again? What would be the end result? – none of this was any clearer; only time would tell. As for my arm, it had healed nicely despite the fact that the Iraqis had never even bothered to treat it. All that remained was a shiny pink scar where the bullet had passed through.

The ensuing days were filled with debriefs, tests of every description, calls to families and loved ones and endless meals of gloriously rich food.

The debriefs themselves took place within the first 36 hours, the pressure to inform Hereford of the patrol's actions mounting with every hour that passed. While they were being conducted, the camp psychiatrist, especially flown in from the UK, was hovering in the background dying to get his hands on us, intent on making the most of this opportunity to 'study' post-traumatic stress disorder.

From the very start, I had made it clear that I had no desire to talk to a psychiatrist. As far as I was concerned, it was none of his business how I felt or what I thought. The only psychological debrief I needed would be done with a few close mates over a pint of beer down at the local. That is what I wanted, and I let him know this was the case. After our initial interview, one that lasted all of five minutes, he did not bother with me again.

It was during this time that we finally received confirmation of the fate of Legs, Vince and Bob. Legs and Vince had indeed succumbed to the effects of hypothermia, while Bob had died from a single gunshot wound to the upper chest. Their coffins were sent to Saudi, the bodies well-presented and embalmed by the Iraqis. From there they were flown directly on to the UK for family identification and post-mortems. The news left me confused: one minute I felt ecstatic about my release; the next, I felt guilty to be so happy when my mates had died. Even though I knew all along that it was likely they had not survived, while they remained MIA there was always a chance that they had just been missed and were languishing in some hospital or prison in Iraq. That vain hope had now been quashed for good.

All the POWs were becoming restless. There were friends and families waiting who had, in some cases, not heard news of their loved ones in months. It would not be long before impatience turned to anger.

With this in mind, someone finally came to their senses and ordered the 727 to be fired up. Enough tests had been completed. The psychiatrist was told to pack his bags, and any more debriefs could wait. It was time to get home.

* * *

The weather in England was so bad that the ground didn't appear till just prior to touchdown. Rain was battering the aircraft on all sides. The 727 kicked into reverse thrust, the frame shuddering as it strained to come to a halt. Staring out the window once again as the tarmac and buildings flashed past, I spotted the regiment's two Augusta 109s, ready and waiting to shuttle us back to Hereford. The 727 pilot ignored the base terminal and manoeuvred the aircraft to within 50 metres of where the helicopters were standing. The transfer from aircraft to aircraft was completed within minutes, and suddenly we were on the final leg, a 20-minute flight back to Stirling Lines.

CHAPTER 19

22 SAS REGIMENTAL HEADQUARTERS, STIRLING LINES, MARCH 1991

I sat on the edge of my seat, crutches and leg thrust out before me, and let my eyes wander about the sparsely furnished room. There was a huge polished desk that dominated the opposite end to where we were seated. The walls were adorned with nothing but the occasional plaque, painting or piece of regimental memorabilia. I shouldn't have been nervous but the sense of having been in this situation before, in a similar office before a man of the same rank, was hovering in the background. I had to force myself to remember that I was on friendly territory.

'Good afternoon, men.' The CO strode in purposefully from an unseen doorway, adorned in his camouflaged DPMs with blue regimental stable belt. A large man, over 6 ft tall with an unruly mass of dark black hair, he moved on over to where we were seated. I began to rise with Andy, Dinger and Mal, but he insisted I remained seated while he shook our hands.

From the door through which we had entered an assistant appeared carrying a tray with a bottle of champagne and five tall, thin glasses. The tray deposited, the man disappeared discreetly, closing the office door behind him. Pulling a chair over to sit in the opposite corner, the colonel delivered his opening line, a comment that will live with me for the rest of my days: 'Well, gentlemen, before we start I want you to all know that you are not going to be court-martialled.'

The silence was deafening, the blood drained from my face and I felt my jaw drop on hearing those words. What the fuck was he talking about? Court-martialled? I looked at the man carefully to see if this was some kind of joke, but he simply stared back at me, showing no emotion whatsoever. I flicked a quick glance at the others, all of whom were wearing the same incredulous expression. 'He's got to be winding us up,' I thought to myself. 'This guy can't even begin to imagine what we've been through!'

He reached over to the small table and began to pour the champagne, passing a glass to each of us in turn as if what he had just said had never occurred. Everyone ready, he raised his glass, toasted our return and drank. The somewhat shell-shocked remainder of us followed suit.

As I raised my glass, my mind flashed back to weeks before. Images of the fear and the pain of being shot, of the beatings I had received, of the loneliness of the prison cell, of the feelings of desperation and doubt, of Bob, Vince and Legs. The glass rested on my lips but I did not drink.

'I want to clear the air right away,' he continued, 'so if you have any questions about what went on, fire away.'

I looked at Andy for a lead, expecting him to bombard the colonel with some of the million and one questions that I had been tormenting myself with over the last two months, but he said nothing – possibly conscious that he may be skating on thin ice and therefore shouldn't be the first to rock the boat.

Dinger, direct as ever, had no such reservations. 'Sir, what happened with our comms?'

'You were given the wrong frequencies,' he replied bluntly. 'They couldn't work that far north. I am investigating how that was allowed to happen. As for your SATCOM, we have no answer for that one.'

'What about the TACBEs?' Mal immediately responded. 'Why didn't the AWACS ever answer our calls for help?'

'You were 300 kilometres out of range. AWACS only operated in the southern regions, Saudi, Kuwait. I don't know who told you that there would be coverage that far up but it was wrong. You weren't supposed to be heading for Syria anyway.'

Andy finally woke up. 'But that was the plan, sir, the whole patrol was there when the OC told us Syria would be the E & E destination.'

'I am aware of that and it has been addressed.'

The temperature in the room was beginning to rise. The patrol's E & E plan had, contrary to what we had been told, actually taken us away from our vital support element. This admission showed an incredible breakdown in communication between the command elements of the regiment, and one that was certainly too late to address now.

'What happened to the lost comms procedure?' Dinger questioned again. 'Why wasn't a new set brought in to us?'

'With those S60s around, I was not going to send any aircraft to your location till we had confirmation of exactly what was going on.' He continued, 'I had few air frames available to me and four half-squadron groups to support. I couldn't risk them until the situation was clarified.'

Not satisfied with that answer, I carried on. 'In that case, why didn't you send a chopper with the QRF when you received our compromise message? Our ERV was miles away from those S60s.'

His reply was direct and to the point, needing neither further elaboration nor comment. 'Listen, at that stage of the war Scuds were being launched at Israel practically on a nightly basis. I would have sacrificed a squadron of men for a Scud. Stopping them was the priority, end of story.'

A momentary silence once again ensued, as the enormity of that statement sunk in. If the SAS hierarchy were prepared to sacrifice scores of men for the sake of a Scud, then our call for help was insignificant in the scheme of things, and that immediately cast the patrol in an entirely different light.

* * *

My questions were now over, I had the answer I needed and the uncertainty would burn no more. The fault was not our own, nor had it ever been. Our fate had been sealed by those in charge, from the comfort of a secure location. Ill-equipped and poorly briefed, we had always been sent out there on our own; it was just that no one had thought it necessary to tell us. 'Expendable' might be an unpalatable description, particularly amongst elite soldiers, but I now had no doubt in my mind that in our case it was an accurate one.

'This was war and hard decisions needed to be made,' the CO continued. 'It may seem difficult to justify now, but at the time that was the reality of the situation.'

But it was difficult to justify, particularly given the coalition's celebrated total air superiority and the Americans' 24-hour CSAR capability. Under these conditions, even the excuse of no available air frames sounded unconvincing. More importantly, however, the reality of the situation was that these decisions, the lack of action or support when the patrol was in need, eventually contributed to the death of three men and the capture and torture of four others.

As the magnitude of the commanding officer's remarks sank in, I realised that I would no longer see the regiment in the same light; the pedestal upon which I had placed it had been kicked from under it. It wasn't the fighting men that were the problem; they were outstanding. You couldn't ask for more dedicated or committed soldiers – they had to be, to get where they were. It was my faith in the system that had been shattered, a system with an unwritten code that says you can expect to be backed up when things go wrong.

The moment the statement had left the CO's mouth, I lost my Kiwi naivety and those who commanded the regiment forfeited my trust. Loyalty and trust are things that are not given lightly and should not be taken for granted; they must be earned. To receive such gifts, and they are gifts, one must reciprocate them, nurture them and never ever abuse them. As far as I was concerned, no matter who had made the decision to ignore our plea for help, it was an abuse of our loyalty and trust, and I would never allow that to happen again.

My mind now drifted in and out of the present, as the CO answered more questions from the others. I had lost all interest in the conversation now, I just wanted to get out of the room. If I dwelled too long on the answers I had heard, in my present frame of mind it would have either reduced me to tears of frustration or into a flying rage. I had castigated myself over the whole term of my imprisonment. I was certain that my incompetence was responsible for the patrol's failure and my capture. I never ever considered, even in my darkest hour, that we had been abandoned.

Dinger jumped in with a question that brought me back to life: 'Why didn't you just send a jet over our location to check us out?' I could hear the edge of anger in his voice now.

'I never thought of that,' the CO replied.

'What about the American pilot who we contacted by TACBE?' Andy asked.

'He forgot to file a report on the transmission. It was three days later that he remembered to tell anyone and for you, of course, that was too late.'

We shook our heads in amazement. Fundamental mistakes up and down the chain of command, particularly after the patrol's deployment, had sealed our fate.

The discussion carried on for about 40 or so minutes before the colonel called a halt to the proceedings. I had to give him his due, he had not tried to pass the blame on to others but had let any accusations fall square on his shoulders. He held the highest rank in the regiment, the buck stopped there.

There were no apologies made; it was simply a case of exchanging facts as they happened. However, the fact that the CO admitted mistakes had been made did not absolve him of his responsibility.

'Right,' the colonel summed up, 'I intend to hold an open debrief for the regiment on what happened to Bravo Two Zero. I expect you all to complete a comprehensive written account of what occurred, to be handed in within a couple of weeks.' He stood up, the audience over.

We shuffled out of the room in total silence, each man lost in his own thoughts, all attempting to reconcile the enormity of the CO's revelations with what we thought had gone wrong. But in light of critical matters such as the lack of Landrovers and equipment shortages, ineffective enemy, ground and weather intelligence, incorrect frequencies, rushed planning, poor passage of information, poor decision-making and pure bad luck, our self-criticism had been excessive and largely inappropriate. These external factors, coupled with the contingencies of war, had combined to thwart the patrol at every turn.

The regimental debrief should have been the final, official chapter in the Bravo Two Zero story, but it did little to address the issues at hand.

As it transpired, the process would take many years to complete, as every now and then a new piece of the jigsaw, previously unknown or seemingly irrelevant, fell into place. Some of these pieces prompted the writing of this book.

* * *

The 20-minute drive northwards out of Hereford took no time at all and before I knew it the driver was pulling up at the front door of the picturesque country cottage. Blue and Gail were standing there ready to greet me. I swung myself out of the vehicle and hobbled over on my crutches, stopping to clasp Blue's outstretched hand. 'All right, Mike?' Blue asked, a modest smile on his face. 'Welcome back.'

It was one of the reunion scenes that I had re-enacted time and time again when in prison; for some reason, I often felt that I was carrying out the act from my cell. When these events actually happened, in exactly the manner that I had pictured, I realised that in a way it was my imprisoned mind trying to tell me that everything would be all right; that getting back to Hereford and seeing my friends once more would signal a definitive end to the nightmare that I had been through.

Looking back at this period, I can now see that I was suffering. A great gaping hole had been cleaved through my soul and it was in desperate need of healing. Though Pete, Ken and other close friends gave support and encouragement, I knew there was only one place that I really wanted, desperately needed, to be: back home in New Zealand. This is where I could lay my demons to rest and let the process of healing begin.

* * *

It was a cold, sunny spring morning as the coffins, borne by immaculately uniformed men of B Squadron 22 SAS, were carried at a slow march into St Martin's.

The church was packed to overflowing, full of past and present SAS soldiers, all of whom had come to pay their final respects. A regimental belt, beret and medals lay atop each flag-draped coffin as they slowly paraded down the aisle towards the pulpit, heads turning to watch in solemn silence, the men present reminded of their own mortality.

Eulogies were read and hymns were sung in an atmosphere that was so electrically charged with emotion that one could not but be moved by it. But it was not just an emotional outpouring of grief, for there was also a real groundswell of anger amongst those recently returned from the Gulf, a feeling that this service should not have been necessary.

Once outside, the piercing cracks of the honour guard's rifles fell silent, a lone bugler began the 'Last Post', its eerie lament a final salute to those who had fallen.

Standing there in the regimental cemetery, I suddenly felt very detached and alone – it could so easily have been me that the shots and bugle rang out for. Tears of pain and loss flowed freely, unashamedly, as each man passed the graves, bowed their heads and paid their last respects.

* * *

Several months after our return from Iraq, representatives from the UN arrived in Stirling Lines to see those of us who had been POWs; their aim, to take down statements on the way in which we had been treated whilst in Iraqi hands. A commission had been set up to try and recover damages from the Iraqi Government, compensation for the maltreatment of both civilians and military personnel.

The SAS ex-POWs were each allocated numbers for these proceedings in order to maintain our security and protect our identities; my designation was Soldier Five.

EPILOGUE

Crump. The sound of a huge bomb exploding somewhere in the city centre could be easily heard from my elevated rooftop position. The spiralling black smoke was evidence of expended explosive and material fire, a rough indicator of the location of the explosion.

No longer did I wear camouflaged DPMs or carry a rifle; these had been traded in two months earlier for a smart $600 suit and a Motorola hand-held radio. I was a civilian now. Seven years after the Gulf War, I had finally decided to leave the regiment, and now toured the world in my capacity as a security consultant.

'What do you think, Kiwi?' Mike, the boss of Stirling Security, asked me, conscious of the high-profile clients we had with us in the villa.

I lowered the binoculars from my eyes and surveyed the deceptively picturesque view to my front. Fundamentalist terrorists had just detonated another bomb, the fourth blast in just over an hour, a concentrated attack in the run-up to elections two weeks hence.

'I think we should stay put till the situation has calmed a little,' I replied. 'It's only a short hop back to the hotel, and with our escort we'll do that in under ten minutes.'

'Sounds good to me,' Mike replied in his naturally informal manner. 'I'll get the escort boys to go out and get us some pizzas.'

Our clients joined us at the villa's balcony, concern etched on their faces. They were civilians, men and women not accustomed to being subjected to this kind of threat, but then that is why they contracted people such as Mike and myself to assess the viability of remaining and continuing their business here. There was a point where the pursuit of money and the risk to one's own life collided; we were here to ensure that never happened.

As I continued to scan the rambling skyline, rows upon rows of off-white housing and apartment blocks, the huge natural harbour that stretched out into the almost limitless horizon, I pondered the events that had brought me to this point.

I had left the regiment, but not the job. This was just another posting, another trip, not unlike Northern Ireland, South America or Bosnia. The only difference was that now the huge green machine that had been my life blood for the past 13 years was no longer with me – but its training and lessons most certainly were.

After the Gulf, I had been all but ready to walk out the gate, confused, disappointed and let down. Then Sue walked back into my life. She was the medicinal cure my abused self needed. Within days of my return, we were back together, and with her at my side most of my troubles paled into insignificance. Her attitude to what had happened was totally the opposite to what I would have expected. Forever making fun of my injury, trying to lighten my mood, she would threaten every time we were out without my crutches to hire a skateboard and tow me along behind. Without complaint, she would spend hours each night massaging my injured ankle, trying to relieve the pain or just provide comfort. Her constant support and love convinced me that this was the woman that I wanted to spend the rest of my life with, and we were eventually married.

A month after my release, I was given the time off to return to New Zealand and see the friends and family that I had yearned for. It was an extremely emotional time for all concerned, but the most poignant part of the trip was the couple of days I spent back with the Kiwi unit in Papakura. These were men of my own ilk, men who could understand where I was coming from and, most importantly of all, men I could trust. I drank too much, talked too much and shed a few tears with mates that I regarded as brothers. By the time I boarded the flight back to the UK, I was well on the way to becoming my own self again. It was many, many months before the nightmares finally subsided, but that trip to New Zealand laid the firm foundation for my future recovery.

My rehabilitation took over a year to complete, countless visits to the Forces Rehab centre at Headly Court and a further operation on the ankle delaying my full return to work. However, the biggest incentive I received occurred before I had even begun the intensive rehabilitative process.

Not long after my return to Hereford, I was summoned once again to the CO's office. After offering me a seat beside his desk, the CO came straight to the point. 'I've read your medical assessment and I think that you should leave the armed forces and go back to New Zealand, take a medical discharge.'

I was stunned, literally speechless. I didn't know how I was supposed to reply to that. What did he expect me to say? 'Thank you for your decision, I really appreciate you kicking me out'? I sat there in silence, my mind racing to find a suitable reply. Perhaps he was testing my resolve, to see whether my heart was still in the job.

'I don't really want to do that, sir,' I replied. Although I had contemplated leaving myself, I never expected to be pushed.

'OK, then,' he continued, 'we will see how you progress. But you must realise that your days in a Sabre Squadron are over.'

I nodded my head in acknowledgment, fuming to myself. 'I'll bloody show him what I can and cannot do, and I will be the one to decide when I want to quit.' That conversation did more to put me on track than any amount of pep talks could ever have done.

When, nearly 14 months after my initial injury, I finally passed the army's BFT (battle fitness test) well within the allotted time, it was as if I had passed selection for the third time. More importantly, however, I had proved the sceptics wrong.

Even then the doctors still held reservations regarding my return to operational SAS duties. It took a fair amount of persuasion and cajoling on my part to get them to finally agree to allow me to return to work. We compromised by saying that I understood that there would be certain caveats placed on the type of soldiering I would be allowed to participate in – though how they ever thought they could monitor this, God only knows.

On reflection, the doctors and others had severely underestimated the powers of recuperation that a young, fit body and positive mind could summon up.

'We will have to fuse the ankle, it will be the only way to stop your pain,' the surgeons had said. Pain was something I could live and work with, I had already resigned myself to that; and if it was to be the choice between pain and function, or no pain and no function, there was no choice.

Perhaps the most persuasive argument for carrying on in the regiment came once my rehabilitation and return to work were assured. With a now much wiser head on my shoulders, I was able to see that what I had been through was in no way unique. Over and over again the regiment, as with other units, had gone into battle ill-prepared and over-enthusiastic, relying on the guts and determination of those men on the ground to pull off the spectacular success that was required.

It was only through experience, through lessons hard learnt in the field of battle, lessons to be remembered, that disasters like Bravo Two Zero would be avoided in the future. As a survivor, I owed it to myself, to the regiment, and to Bob, Legs and Vince, to pass on the experience gained to others. I kept this ethos within me for the remaining years that I served with 22 SAS.

As for the Iraqis, I bear them no ill will or grudge. They were only doing their job, just as I was in their country doing mine. Had the situations been reversed, had it been my capital, my friends, my family being bombed day in and day out, what is there to say that I would have acted any differently? One thing is for sure, Dr Al-Bayeth prevented my ankle from deteriorating and perhaps even saved my foot from being amputated. For that one act, I am grateful.

* * *

When I finally left the regiment in 1997, I had no real idea of what the future held for me. I had no job, no income, simply a desire to quit the life I had led for so many years.

What finally prompted me to leave? I felt the regiment had nothing left to offer, and, in all honesty, I no longer had the commitment or desire to try and make a difference.

In such a career as this, at a certain age there comes a time when a crossroads is reached, where an extremely important decision needs to be made. At 33 years of age, I arrived at that point and I decided that it was time to move on, time to start a new life and career while I was still young enough and fit enough to do so.

EPILOGUE

In a letter to the then commanding officer, I explained my reasons for leaving and also the way I felt about the Gulf. Time is a great healer and over the years I had come to live with what had happened to the patrol, though that did not mean for one second that it was ever forgotten. I did not regret going to war, for that was one of the very reasons I left New Zealand and joined 22 SAS, just as I did not hold the regiment itself responsible for the patrol's fate.

Nevertheless, should blame need to be apportioned, one would think that those ultimately responsible would have both the character and the fortitude to stand up and be counted. Leaders up and down the chain of command make mistakes; the sign of a good leader is one who can admit this and learn from them. To date, this has certainly never happened.

Bravo Two Zero aside, I had for the most part thoroughly enjoyed my service with the regiment and even now sometimes still yearn for those exciting days.

BREAKING RANKS

In early 1998, I made a deliberate decision that the time had come to correctly record the events that had occurred during the Bravo Two Zero mission. This decision came as a direct result of the books and films surrounding Bravo Two Zero, publications that were allowed by the MoD and publications that ultimately generated much negative speculation and commentary. The latter had continued unchecked to the extent that the patrol had become so misrepresented that I, and Mal for that matter, felt that silence was no longer an option.

To make matters worse, the British MoD's 'no comment' stance on the UK Special Forces (UKSF) only served to fuel the controversy. Significantly, it emerged at my High Court civil trial, where the British Government tried to prevent publication of *Soldier Five*, that the MoD had received advance copies of the manuscripts of *Storm Command* by General Peter de la Billiere, *Bravo Two Zero* by Andy McNabb and *The One That Got Away* by Chris Ryan, all of which contained new information pertaining to Bravo Two Zero. Alterations were made by the MoD to these books and then publication permitted, thereby allowing a selected version of the patrol's story, edited by the MoD, to be released into the public domain.

The MoD's own internal memos were referred to during the court trial hearing regarding the vetting process for *Soldier Five*, and in particular that of *Bravo Two Zero* and *The One That Got Away*. For the book *Bravo Two Zero*, one memo dated 2 August 1993 stated in part:

> Although I see no reason why we should give this clearance priority over other more important tasks, we ought nevertheless to press ahead and try to be as helpful as possible.

As for Ryan's book, *The One That Got Away*, a minute dated 14 June 1995 to the Armed Forces Minister and other MoD personnel stated in part in relation to the proposed serialisation of the book:

> . . . In this case there are no major problems . . . because the material has already appeared in one form or another in the public domain . . .
>
> In the course of the book, Ryan levels criticism at Vince Phillips, a patrol member who did not survive. Action will be taken to warn Mr Phillips' family of the impending publication.

The last comment made with reference to Ryan's book, I found particularly galling. The MoD had recognised the offending nature of some of Ryan's commentary and the effect it would have on the Phillips family, but very little was done to prevent the impact of this criticism. Further, the failure to take effective action did not engender loyalty amongst the SAS soldiers. The High Court trial judge in his decision referred to:

> The fact of the publication of these books and the content of them both caused great upset amongst SAS members in general and the remaining members of the Bravo Two Zero patrol in particular. The concern of the remaining members was that both books exaggerated the role of their authors and contained quite fictitious incidents. In particular, there was deep concern that the author of *The One That Got Away* blamed the compromising of the patrol on a member who later died of exposure. The defendant gave evidence that the desire to correct what he regarded as this wrongful slur on the reputation of a dead man later became one of the principal motivations for the writing of his account.
>
> The upset caused to SAS members in general, and to the members of the patrol in particular, was exacerbated when films of the books were released. Efforts were made by the three surviving members who had not written books to persuade the regiment to make some public comment. Although a public statement was

issued by the Ministry of Defence (MoD), it was regarded by the
defendant as rather bland and he felt disappointed and angry at
the lack of support shown to patrol members.

As opposed to enforcing their 'no comment' policy, the MoD in not
attempting to stop publication of these books aided in undermining it.
Such a policy may be for the best in truly confidential circumstances,
but I, and others, class the story of Bravo Two Zero as the exception,
given its wide public dissemination. In this instance, 'no comment' was
never the right policy, not for the families of the deceased, the surviving
patrol members who maintained their silence and, most of all, not for
the good of the SAS community as a whole.

The decision made, I realised that in breaking my long-held silence I
would be embarking upon a route that would officially ostracise me
from a community that I had given up the best part of my adult life for.
However, this was a sacrifice I was prepared to make; to place the
important accountability that should be made in the right context, to do
right by a dead comrade and his family – something that should have
occurred a long time before – and to properly correct that which had
been over-exaggerated and fictionalised.

My aim was to let the truth be known and allow the public to make
an informed judgment with the proper facts before them.

* * *

After six intense weeks of writing, the first draft was complete, my
thoughts transformed into pages of typescript that flowed like a
ruptured dam. By mid-September of the same year, the manuscript was
in a near-final form and ready to be presented to the necessary parties
for consideration. Foremost amongst those were the NZSAS and the
UK MoD, and the responses from the two aforementioned
organisations could not have been more at odds with one another.

For the NZSAS's part, the then commanding officer wrote: '. . . it
[*Soldier Five*] is a largely innocuous document and one from which the
NZSAS has emerged, as you had hoped, in good standing.'

The UK MoD's response, on the other hand, could not have been
in more stark contrast. Within days of receiving the manuscript, the

MoD had threatened court proceedings against the UK sub-licensed publisher, Hodder & Stoughton, and in the same breath began applying similar pressure to the proposed New Zealand publisher Reed Publications.

It was arranged for Hodder & Stoughton to send the manuscript to the UK MoD for comment well in advance of any publication, in conjunction with Reed doing the same with the New Zealand SAS; however, the only response received, via the publishers themselves, was the immediate threat of court action should publication proceed. The MoD relied upon a confidentiality contract I considered I was directed and pressured into signing in 1996 as the basis for their action.

The contract itself, alleged to have been introduced in an effort to curb revelations by 'SAS insiders' regarding Special Forces operations, was compulsory for serving SF members – failure to sign resulted in RTU (return to unit – construed by SAS soldiers themselves as being sacked by the regiment). Legal advice was not made available, the signatory was not permitted to retain or show a copy to any outside adviser, and wide distrust prevailed over the contract's real purpose and objective within the regiments, both SAS and SBS.

To further complicate matters, the UK MoD now bound all those they came in contact with into an all-encompassing confidentiality undertaking that denied anyone the ability to discuss, outside an MoD-dictated forum, what all the fuss was about.

Initially this tactic was rather confusing, though it soon became very apparent that the MoD's plan of attack was to first of all stop publication at all cost, regardless of the merits of the book, and second, isolate me to the extent that I would not be in a position to challenge them legally or practically.

This divide-and-conquer strategy found some initial success: Hodder & Stoughton were subdued relatively quickly and Reed were obliged to undertake not to publish.

Yet despite all these manoeuvrings, I still had no idea what the MoD's problem was with the book, aside from the fact that the 'whole thing' was supposedly confidential, a ridiculous proposition given I had been particularly conscious to avoid disclosing confidential information (all that I considered necessary for compliance with the Official Secrets Act and confidentiality contract obligations) when writing and that numerous other accounts had already entered the public domain.

Surely common sense dictated the reason for giving the manuscript to the MoD in the first place was to allow them the opportunity to come back with what they were unhappy about. This had been the procedure in the past and, remarkably, still continues to be the procedure today, as exemplified by the vetting by the MoD, and release for publication in the UK four days before my civil trial in New Zealand was about to start, of the book *Eye of the Storm* authored by an ex-SAS RSM Peter Ratcliffe.

Finally, a delegation from the MoD's NZ solicitors, and from the UK's NZ High Commission arrived at Reed's Auckland headquarters, armed with documents and affidavits that were designed to impress upon Reed's management that this book was the most serious breach of UK national security since the discovery and arrest of MI5 double agent George Blake.

Suffice to say, Reed were unimpressed. More importantly, however, behind this imposing veil of national security, unbeknown to my legal advisors, the publishers or me, memos were flying about London that did not support this claim at all. These memos were disclosed as part of the High Court trial process that began in Auckland in September 2000 and they undermined the MoD rationale and position.

In one memo dated 25 September 1998, written to the SAS Colonel Commandant, it was stated in part in relation to my proposed book that:

> . . . due to the nature of the book's contents and the full reporting of Bravo Two Zero's experiences in previous publications, we will be unable to argue that damage results from publication of material in this book which is demonstratively and specifically damaging to national security.

However, after that memo, in a subsequent letter from the same SAS Colonel Commandant dated 20 October 1998 to the Prime Minister, Tony Blair, it was stated that my proposed book was the first breach of the confidentiality contract and that it should be pursued vigorously through the courts in the United Kingdom and New Zealand. Conveniently, there was no mention of the earlier internal memo of 25 September 1998 regarding the lack of any specific damage to national security that would result from publication of material in my book. If anything, it suggested the opposite when it stated:

> The result of not taking firm action will be further and more damaging publications . . .

The inference, as contained in this letter, was that my book would be damaging, even though the MoD's internal assessment indicated no specific damage to national security.

Perhaps a more accurate summation of the circumstances and detail of *Soldier Five* at this stage would have saved the British MoD many years of litigation and, not least of all, millions of pounds in taxpayers' money.

At this point, the MoD's blanket moratorium on the book and refusal to identify what was the problem was really giving me cause for concern, so I instructed my English solicitors to write to the Treasury Solicitor to try and draw them out. In the letter of 8 October 1998, the following was communicated:

> . . . it seems a more constructive approach would be . . . to invite you to continue the vetting process envisaged by the contract . . . and to identify to us . . . those passages in the book which are causing you difficulty, and the reasons they are doing so. We can then consider with our client, and discuss with you, how the book can be edited so as to make it acceptable to you.

Not only was this offer never taken up, the MoD did not even give the letter the dignity of a decent reply. This was particularly frustrating, as I also pointed out that the motive for writing the book was to set the record straight, something one would have thought the MoD would have appreciated given the historical controversy surrounding Bravo Two Zero.

The actual MoD response was to summon my solicitor to London, where he was forced to sign a confidentiality undertaking before being allowed to participate in their meeting, one that stated he must not divulge any of the discussions or material that he was shown to anyone, myself included!

The gagging order aside, what could be relayed to me was that the MoD had drawn up a series of permanent, lifelong undertakings that they demanded I sign. I would not be allowed to see these in advance, further I would have to sign an undertaking not to disclose the nature of the permanent undertakings to anyone, ever, particularly my wife. I was expected to present myself at Whitehall, sign the non-disclosure undertaking, then the permanent undertakings would be placed before me and I would read and sign those, not being allowed to keep a copy of either document.

The feeling of déjà vu was so strong I had to pinch myself. This situation was uncannily similar to 1996 and the signing of my confidentiality contract in Hereford; incredibly, they were trying to pull the same stunt all over again. Now there was a major difference, though: I was no longer part of their armed forces and there was no way they could force me to sign against my will. This time I had the right and freedom to choose as I pleased – and I chose refusal.

Unfortunately, this bullying attitude was succeeding in other quarters, particularly with the publishers concerned. In fact, at this point I have no doubt the grey men in Whitehall thought the whole thing would be wrapped up and over before Christmas.

But what the MoD had not counted on was the deep-seated feeling of moral righteousness that burned within me. A feeling that this needed to be done, the book needed to be published, the real story, as far as I was concerned, needed to be heard. It was, and still is, this passion that has sustained both my wife and myself throughout our ordeal.

Weeks began to turn into months, with still no resolution in sight. The MoD had by now come back with a statement saying that the entire book was confidential and would be subject to injunction proceedings save for those chapters that concerned my New Zealand service and the introduction.

By mid-December 1998, court proceedings were looming for Reed Publishing and consequently they were no longer as enthusiastic about the project as had once been the case. They saw a long uphill battle before them, despite a recent Television New Zealand win in both the High and Appeal courts of New Zealand against the MoD on subject material relating to my book. Eventually TVNZ televised a documentary on the whole saga.

I travelled to New Zealand in late February 1999, keen to find out for myself exactly what the situation was first-hand, communication with Reed management becoming suspiciously ever more difficult from the UK. While there, a meeting with Reed was arranged and there was an obvious tension in the air. I was informed that a High Court hearing date had been set down for early March between Reed and the MoD.

However, a few days prior to the hearing, at which Reed were to represent me as the co-defendant, I was informed by phone that Reed had withdrawn from proceedings, and with it publication, and that I was on my own.

Now, as anyone who has been involved in litigation will know, dealing with lawyers at the best of times is no inexpensive thing, and in a case as complex and diverse as this, particularly one that was looking to be fought in two countries, the costs involved were increasingly enormous. Certainly, without some form of support, I would be either bankrupt, as had been threatened, or at best forced to capitulate through lack of funding – something that I am sure was one of the MoD's primary objectives. As it was, my own source of funding, i.e. our life savings, was almost exhausted and, faced with the unlimited resources the British MoD could summon, the future looked very bleak.

At the eleventh hour, though, help came from an unexpected quarter. By either good luck or grand design, I was referred to an Auckland-based barrister and, following a phone conversation, a meeting was arranged at his chambers.

* * *

Southern Cross Barristers' Chambers is situated on the corner of High and Victoria streets in central Auckland. The twelfth floor is the domain of various legal entities, and Warren Templeton occupied a strategic northern corner office with views through the tower blocks to Auckland's Rangitoto Channel – ideal for spotting the America's Cup yachts as they passed by en route for practice and competition in the Hauraki Gulf.

Despite all the legal wrangling over the past six months, I had as yet not actually met a single lawyer in person and so was not really sure what I would be confronted with.

I suspect had I been presented with an uncertain individual, no matter how competent, I would probably have given up the ghost. As it was, Warren turned out to be just the opposite. Fit, middle-aged, with dark hair running to grey, he had an engaging open personality that at once relaxed and reassured, and gave me strength and confidence – traits that were put to good use over the ensuing four and a half years, particularly when I was under enormous pressure from the MoD litigation. A keen sportsman, one of Warren's passions was the state of New Zealand rugby, a passion not at all tainted by his one-eyed Cantabrian heritage.

He was not intimidated by the thought of a major opponent and was quite happy to meet what was going to be a difficult challenge. As our relationship grew over the ensuing years, his passion for his Crusader rugby team in the Super Twelve Competition was only matched by my passion for the Auckland Blues team. Consequently many of our late-night telephone conversations, initially discussing some aspects of the legal case, generally degenerated into passionate arguments over the states of the two teams we respectively supported. I think, on balance, we may have spent as much time debating rugby issues as we did legal ones.

As we made our introductions, Warren's secretary came in with a copy of my confidentiality contract and passed it over. Without further ado, Warren began to scan the document, offering me a seat opposite him in the process.

Silence ensued as he examined the document minutely, reading and re-reading the text, flicking the pages to and fro as he scanned their contents. Finally, after what was to me a very nerve-racking and seemingly endless wait, he grabbed a marker from his desk drawer and began highlighting various passages of the neat typescript with slashes of colour. Finished, he handed the contract back to me and stated, 'Look at those points. Besides being draconian, they are legally very questionable.'

I examined all that he had highlighted then looked up, still confused and a little anxious. The words looked the same to me: was this a good or bad thing? Was he going to say my case was hopeless or the opposite? Before expanding further, Warren asked me to tell him the whole story, 'Everything, from the beginning.'

The next couple of hours flew by as I recounted my story, piece-by-piece, from the Gulf War till the present, Warren interrupting as necessary to clarify a particular point or question an incident until he had a complete grasp of the event. By the end of it, I was mentally exhausted, still not sure where all this was going.

Warren sat back in his chair and looked across at me over a pair of rimless spectacles, marshalling his thoughts before saying:

'My impression is that you have good legal grounds to challenge the contract and the process by which it was signed. There are features to your case which are unique and while I will, of course, need to ponder the facts more carefully, I consider you have strong arguments. Further, the morality and merit are on your side and will hold you in good stead. I know that you cannot afford much right now and we can sort all that out later, but this is something you should fight.'

A wave of relief swept across me and, had I noticed, I probably would have found myself holding my breath. I had always thought that the contract was suspect, but it was the first time anyone had actually said that was the case. Now here it was, the statement I had been dying to hear for months. At last I had some positive, constructive direction to follow. More importantly for me, however, Warren listened with understanding and an air of confidence that was in itself a refreshing change to the contradictory messages that had gone before. He did not try to shy away from the issues at hand, simply analysed them and gave a considered opinion.

That meeting did more to reassure me and put my mind at ease than all the previous advice I had received. Warren's support and commitment were exactly what was needed to refocus and put me back on track. He saw an inherent injustice being perpetrated, a fellow Kiwi in desperate straits and in need of help, and, perhaps most important of all, he saw that there was a fundamental moral right in what I was trying to achieve.

Warren continued, 'The first thing we need to get you to do is move back to New Zealand. You are too exposed in the UK, and, tactically, you need to ensure the principal legal battle is fought here. It will also give you the opportunity to file for Legal Aid, and, if granted, it will remove a considerable part of the financial burden and stress. The fact that Legal Aid could be granted would also send a signal that you had a reasonably sound case.'

Coincidentally, both my wife and I had already been discussing leaving the UK; New Zealand or Europe were at that time the two options open to us. We felt that, with the controversy surrounding me, it was impossible to continue to live in Hereford, where I bumped into regiment personnel on a daily basis. Not that the majority of them would not talk to me – indeed, I was made aware that many supported the morality of my stand, but I felt uncomfortable at placing them in that position. After all, it was my fight, my problem and no one else need be marked by association.

This was really just the prompt we needed to get out. I flew back to the UK two days later, confident that Warren had my interests, the hearing and everything else well in hand. Within six weeks we had the house in Hereford sold, and Sue and the girls were en route to Auckland. I was forced to remain in the UK a little longer to tidy up some loose ends, but was more than happy to see my family safely away.

* * *

Life back in New Zealand was certainly a refreshing change and, of course, for Sue and the girls a wonderfully new experience. They quickly adapted to their new country – an idyllic place to raise children – and the relaxed lifestyle, oblivious to the machinations of the MoD that continued behind the scenes.

In the meantime, Warren had also been busy researching and preparing our defence. Coupled with this, he put forward my case to the Legal Aid board (later known as Legal Services Agency) and, after much debate and deliberation, it was granted. That in itself was no small feat and ultimately made a huge difference not only to how my case was run but also to the tactics that were applied in defending the court proceedings.

A tactical decision Warren advised early on was the withdrawal of the undertaking I had given whilst in the UK (not to publish or disclose the contents of *Soldier Five* without giving the MoD 24 hours' advance notice). The reasoning behind this was twofold: 1) to force the MoD to reinitiate their proceedings with myself as the main defendant and 2) to get the MoD to commit to a New Zealand procedural process.

Warren communicated this to London by fax on 21 June 1999. In that fax he gave notice that, though I had no immediate plans to publish, 'I am instructed to advise that any undertaking (to the extent that it may still be valid) is of no effect, and you are now given 24 hours' notice of this position.'

The reaction to that fax was described to me as 'nuclear'. Somewhere, someone or something exploded in Whitehall and fresh ex parte injunction proceedings were filed in both the UK and New Zealand. However, this was expected. Warren immediately contacted the MoD's NZ lawyers, stating there was a duplication of process and, as we had no intention of moving to the UK, they must elect which proceedings they intended to fight. After some debate, the UK proceedings were stayed and New Zealand given primacy, thus placing the battleground firmly in our backyard.

* * *

As the weeks turned to months, anything and everything was a problem for the MoD. Just getting access to the affidavits sworn against me was a major operational exercise. Access to these documents, already filed in court under a confidentiality caveat, was denied by the MoD and in particular those documents that now apparently detailed the specific breaches of confidentiality I had long been seeking. The restriction in getting access to these items had the implication that they were so 'hot' one needed to view them under guard.

Warren was told he would only be permitted by the MoD lawyers to inspect the documents on his own, at their offices. He could not make copies nor show me any of the detail of the alleged breaches. This demand was rejected and resulted in Warren making an application to the High Court for proper and reasonable access. After a defended hearing, the judge agreed, and the MoD were ordered to hand over copies of their 'secret' material, which could be kept at Warren's chambers where we both could assess the material in our own time.

This officious and heavy-handed attitude was typical of the MoD throughout the litigation process. More importantly, however, now the MoD's 'confidential' items were finally known (confined to 23 instances, as opposed to the whole book) we were able to set about disproving their claim.

Over a period of several months I managed to compile a schedule, painstakingly cross-referenced by Warren, that countered around 95 per cent of what the MoD was alleging was not in the public domain. But we realised that this might not be sufficient for the court, given the MoD's security allegations, and therefore Warren decided an independent military expert would be invaluable in corroborating our findings. He had to obtain special court permission to allow the expert to have access to the court documents.

Dr Christopher Pugsley, a New Zealander and a military historian and lecturer at the University of New England (UNE), Australia, was flown over to make an assessment. Working from Warren's home, Dr Pugsley was provided with the analysis that we had compiled, along with the 20-odd SAS books I had referred to, and a copy of the manuscript. During the course of a weekend, Dr Pugsley satisfied himself that we were essentially right and that the so-called confidential contents of the book were already in the public domain in one form or another. This done, he returned to Australia promising a report to corroborate his findings in the near future.

However, within a few weeks of this meeting, Dr Pugsley became strangely difficult to contact and, more disturbingly, was not returning Warren's telephone calls. The next we knew was that he had been offered a position at one of the MoD's military colleges in the UK. The circumstances of his obtaining this new position I found both remarkably coincidental and very concerning, though the more pressing issue was that Dr Pugsley could no longer be our expert witness due to a conflict of interest.

Thus, with less than three months to go before trial, we were left desperately searching for another specialist to corroborate our non-confidential position. Warren scoured the length and breadth of New Zealand and finally came up with an excellent alternative, Dr Jim Rolfe, a former NZ Army intelligence officer.

Dr Rolfe was presented with all the material that we had compiled and over the ensuing weeks he verified our findings, and in some areas even expanded on them. Dr Rolfe's value was proven at trial, where he provided expert testimony on several crucial, sensitive technical issues, the quality of his assessment being accepted by the trial judge ahead of the MoD's own expert.

Disclosure of the MoD's documents was yet another major point of contention and a constant source of frustration for us. Papers that we knew should have existed failed to materialise, time and time again. In particular, Warren and I had been 'tipped off' as to the existence of two crucial documents that proved important in casting doubt on the MoD's position, i.e. that their contract was valid, signed without issue, and that my book was a major national security breach. Their reluctance to acknowledge these documents resulted in further court hearings, until finally, months after the initial request, the items in question surfaced. The first of these documents was a letter dated 8 November 1996 from the then Commanding Officer of the SBS (Special Boat Service) to DSF (Director Special Forces) raising, amongst other things, questions over the implementation of the Special Forces confidentiality contract. The Special Boat Squadron is part of the UK Special Forces and its personnel were also directed to sign the same contract under similar conditions to SAS personnel. The SBS letter from the then Commanding Officer, which was referred to during the trial, included in part the following:

> There is a deeply held general mistrust over the aim of the contract . . . This perception is given weight through the MoD's refusal to downgrade the Explanatory Notes to enable independent legal advice to be sought prior to signature.

> I have some concern about the possibility that the MoD may be cited as having either coerced the ranks into signing, or have some Constructive Dismissal liability arising from those men who have lost money . . .

The second produced document, a resumé of a presentation given to SAS personnel at Stirling Lines in mid-December 1998, and delivered by the man responsible for the initial damage assessment on my book, stated:

> In common with the Colonel [CO 22 SAS], I have no issue with what Kiwi [Coburn] has to say about the Bravo Two Zero experience, and this aspect of the issue is indeed beside the point.

Interestingly, however, this document also revealed another reason behind the introduction of the UKSF confidentiality contracts, one that had little to do with the MoD's near-paranoiac view on national security but more to do with maximising UKSF's employability in the face of increasing competition from other agencies; i.e. in commercial terms, secrecy effectively protected the SAS lead vis-à-vis its market position. The MoD minders present at trial were most concerned with Warren's line of cross-examination on this point, recounted below from the court transcript:

> WT: In your view, this case is all about enforcing the contract to safeguard the employability of the regiment, keeping ahead of its competition within the UK and to protect your customer base . . .
> ST: Yes, the reason I hesitate to answer it kind of is putting a market spin on this . . .
> WT: They are your words in your cross brief document . . .
> ST: Which words?
> WT: Employability, customer base, protecting the market, competition . . .
> ST: Yes.

As if all this wasn't enough, the MoD's solicitors also challenged the right of Warren and I to enlarge our legal team to assist in what were complex, groundbreaking legal issues.

With each new member Warren tried to enlist, a fresh application to the court had to be submitted. Non-disclosure undertakings were required from these people, all contributing to the illusory 'national security' blanket that the MoD was trying to cast over the entire proceeding.

The legal team grew, regardless of these difficulties. Many people, both lawyers and non-lawyers, gave their time and moral support for little or no financial reward, for a cause that was not their own but which they felt was worthy of their participation. To receive their advice, counsel, personal time and effort really was to me quite a humbling and special experience and words will never be enough to express my gratitude. These people included Associate Professor Paul Rishworth and his colleague Professor Julie Maxton, both from the Auckland Law School; Grant Illingworth, barrister, teamed up with Warren as defence trial counsel; Raynor Asher QC, and Peter Twist, barrister, both of whom assisted with time and background research for the trial. To these and many others, particularly those based at Southern Cross Chambers, I am eternally grateful.

* * *

At long last, some two years after the MoD received my manuscript, the trial came to pass. Over a two-week period, the British Government tried, unsuccessfully, to spin the press, shroud the court in a veil of national security and, last but not least, undermine my credibility.

The MoD's security paranoia over its case and the trial in general translated into examples such as screens hiding their witnesses from the public, along with voice-overs to protect their identity from the TV audience, bodyguards, covert movements and selective reading aloud of 'sensitive material'. All this probably did more damage to the MoD's cause than good. Warren certainly saw it as counter-productive, a view confirmed by the press covering the trial. Warren insisted that our witnesses, myself included, would give evidence in the open for all to see, the only caveat being name-suppression and 'pixelation' of camera footage. When armed with the truth, there is nothing to hide. This procedure worked well to our advantage.

It was thanks in a large part to the competence and skill of Warren and Grant, coupled with the MoD witnesses' poor performance under cross examination, that the final result in our favour was put into perspective.

The MoD's spin doctor had so much bad publicity to deal with that, to quote one UK journalist's comment (who travelled to New Zealand to cover the trial), 'He ended up just spinning.'

Justice Salmon found that I signed the contract under duress and undue influence, without legal advice, and that the contract was invalid. Despite the MoD lawyers' attempts to challenge and discredit me during the trial, my testimony was accepted by the judge; and I, and my faith in my legal team, particularly Warren, was vindicated by the successful result.

The MoD's second cause of action, namely the alleged breach of confidentiality claim, was thrown out. This ruling was particularly satisfying given that Warren had pleaded to the court for the 18 months preceding the trial that the confidential material was substantially in the public domain. The MoD's list of 23 confidential items were, over that period, whittled down to 15, then 12, then during the trial itself, 9. Of these, the trial judge, Justice Salmon, found the material to be in the public domain and ruled only that some minor technical alterations be made to the text. The MoD never challenged this aspect further.

I doubt there are many that disagree with the concept of confidentiality in its proper place and format, but the MoD's contract, and the way it was implemented, was not the way to go about securing it.

However, this proved to be far from the end, as, shortly after the release of the High Court decision, the MOD signalled their intent to appeal, though many months would pass before this came to fruition.

* * *

Mid-2001 saw the MoD's appeal hearing before the New Zealand Court of Appeal in Wellington. The Court initially was going to hear the appeal with five judges until it came to light that one of the panel was the father of one of the MoD's trial lawyers. Unsurprisingly, my lawyers formally protested to the Appeal Court at this inclusion on the bench and that resulted not only in the withdrawal of the judge concerned, but also the reduction of the panel from five to three.

Over what was set down for a three-day hearing, the MoD's lawyers attempted to persuade the court of the legal right and enforceability of their confidentiality contract, and the absolute need for injunctive relief. We, of course, argued the opposite.

However, from the outset, I had the strong impression that the court was taking a less-than-favourable approach to Justice Salmon's judgment and at the end of the hearing I made my way back to Auckland a little stupefied as to the exact reasoning for the apparent hostility of the court to our submissions.

Nevertheless, we felt confident that once the court had the opportunity to fully review all the documentation from the High Court, the right of our case would once again be established. There were findings of fact that any appeal court would have to substantially overturn in order to produce a decision contrary to the original ruling, something that was both rare and difficult to do.

Weeks turned to months, with no hint of a decision on the horizon. While the case had several intricate points of law, it was reasonably assumed that three months would be about the right time frame to expect the court to give its decision.

* * *

A week short of the six-month mark, we were given notice that the decision would be released the next day. Following this news, Warren received a call from one of the opposition lawyers and in the ensuing discussion comment was passed to the effect that we would lose the contract argument but probably get through on grounds of Freedom of Expression (enshrined in the New Zealand Bill of Rights) and be allowed to publish.

Sure enough, as Sue, Warren and I sat around the computer reading the emailed judgment as it spewed forth, the prediction of the previous evening proved to be uncannily accurate. The Court of Appeal had seen fit to agree with the MoD case: that being, if the contract was valid and covered all information acquired from Special Forces work, this would also include information already in the public domain, and thus, if the contract was upheld, I should be stopped from publishing the book irrespective of 'public domain' information.

That the Court of Appeal could reinstate the contract as being valid when the High Court trial judge, who had the benefit of hearing all the witnesses over a two-week period, had firmly rejected the contract as being valid, was very puzzling to me.

This book is not the forum to go into the strange comments that permeated the appeal court's decision, though in a contradictory statement, out of tune with the rest of the judgment's commentary, the main author stated the following regarding the UKSF contract and its implementation:

> . . . there can be no doubt . . . that Coburn was under significant moral and economic pressure to sign. I do not wish to appear unduly critical of events, which took place within the constraints of service discipline. It is apparent, however, that the inherent pressure upon Coburn was compounded by the fact that he was told he could not take any form of outside advice, in particular, outside legal advice on whether he should sign and what his rights generally were. In a civilian situation to deprive a party to a proposed contract of that ability would seem highly objectionable . . . What remains, however, is the inherently coercive situation in which Coburn found himself and his inability to obtain independent advice once he fully realised the scope of the contract.

While the court agreed that these factors were present, it did not agree that they were sufficient to vitiate a contract entered into within the military. But this case was being tried on the basis of English common law, not military law, and one would have thought that the military context should have had no bearing on normal contract practice. And yet in spite of all this, the Court of Appeal agreed that injunctive relief preventing publication of *Soldier Five* was not justified, relying principally on our Freedom of Expression arguments for their justification.

As for the MoD, their response to this finding was different, to say the least. Millions of pounds had been thrown at the case by the MoD up to this point, and obstructive machinations employed en route, but when questioned three years later by the local media in London regarding the New Zealand Appeal Court decision to refuse an injunction, the MoD spokesperson was reported as simply stating that: 'He [Coburn] is entitled to his opinion.'

But in upholding the confidentiality contract, the Court created a new set of legal problems that made publication an interesting challenge and exercise, despite the court's decision to refuse injunctive relief, something that could result in further legal complications. That aside, I appealed the judgment on numerous points, to the next court, the Privy Council in London.

Strict rules govern leave to appeal to the Privy Council and Warren was required to persuade the New Zealand Attorney General's office that the appeal was warranted based on the grounds that there were exceptional legal questions of public importance involved. This success was hard won, as MoD opposition involved a further defended hearing for Warren to fight.

As 2002 progressed, further fuel was added to the fire from an unexpected quarter. Following the large public interest generated by the High Court trial, BBC *Panorama* producers had approached both Mal and myself regarding running an exposé on Bravo Two Zero with a view to highlighting the intrigue and incongruities that surrounded the story. As the BBC began to delve beneath the surface, in what proved to be a remarkable feat of journalism, bizarre and apparently contradicting facts came to light, so much so that the slant of the programme changed from one looking to tell the 'true' story, to another looking to reveal an apparent betrayal. *Panorama* uncovered the transcript from the Bravo Two Zero patrol logs, something that would normally have been classified secret. That transcript, extracts of which were eventually publicly televised, proved beyond doubt that the SAS hierarchy had received the patrol's calls for help, but had chosen to ignore them.

This proof was something that I, and the other patrol members, had long suspected, but until that disclosure had never really been absolutely certain of, as the SAS officers in charge at the time had claimed our transmissions came through corrupted and unintelligible. The MoD's comment regarding the release of the log transcript by *Panorama* was simply that: 'They appear to be authentic.'

Another revelation that would normally have been lost, given that the Gulf conflict had been confined to the history books, was that one of the conditions agreed to by the Special Forces hierarchy in discussions with General Schwarzkopf prior to the Special Forces being given the green light to deploy was that the SAS/SBS were on their own: a point the British military decided not to share with its men. This fact went some way to explain the reluctance of the SAS command to ask for US support when it was most desperately needed.

Not only had these facts been never previously disclosed, they were also made all the more unpalatable by the realisation that the patrol had been misled from the outset of the mission's inception, particularly regarding assistance on the ground, should we need it. This most certainly added weight to the view that the patrol was expendable.

The MoD refused to comment in any substantial way to the *Panorama* production, neither offering a countervailing view, nor incredibly – given their unrelenting battle to suppress my publishing efforts – trying to prevent its release. Perhaps they were getting a little exhausted by this time!

It was, in the end, left to the former RSM of the SAS, Peter Ratcliffe, to provide the quasi-official response to questions put forward by the *Panorama* team. He was allowed to publish his SAS book, which hit the shelves four days before my trial started. He was not a contract-signer but was serving in the SAS when the contracts were introduced in 1996. The fact he did not have to sign the contract was never satisfactorily explained by the MoD witnesses at the trial. The *Panorama* programme showed that his view, while reflecting the establishment position, did not cover the full story.

And so, February 2003 saw the final act in this longstanding legal battle play itself out, the wheel having turned full circle. We found ourselves before the Privy Council located opposite 10 Downing Street itself.

The MoD turned up with a veritable battalion of lawyers and observers, packing the chamber to overflowing. As in the Court of Appeal, Raynor Asher QC joined with Warren in presenting my argument to Their Lordships. While all received remuneration via the Legal Services Agency, Raynor's work again was invaluable, and both Warren and I appreciated his selfless support. In addition, both Paul Rishworth and Rick Bigwood from the Auckland University Law Faculty gave unstintingly of their time in helping in the preparation for the comprehensive written legal submissions that had to be filed to the hearing.

Their English Lordships appeared to be most perturbed by the fact that a case of such importance involving the Attorney General for England and Wales and challenging the British Government was heard through the New Zealand judicial system, as opposed to the English courts, ignoring the fact that it was the British Government that elected to follow that course in the first instance.

In their decision itself, Their Lordships said they were 'troubled' by the fact I was not given legal advice on the contract, even though I had requested it at the time. However, they did not go as far to say that they considered I was 'unduly influenced' or acting 'under duress' at the time, even though they accepted I was acting under some major pressure, as had the Court of Appeal.

The Privy Council saw fit to agree and uphold the NZ Court of Appeal decision but with a 4 to 1 majority decision. Lord Scott, the dissenter in the Council's majority decision, strongly disagreed with the other Lordships, stating that he agreed with the High Court trial judge's factual findings.

* * *

Now, five years on, we have once again reached the point of presenting *Soldier Five* to the public at large, the legal confusion vis-à-vis publication having been clarified at the Privy Council. However, the incongruity of it all is that the MoD had within them the power to limit the Bravo Two Zero disclosures from the outset, by using the Official Secrets Act, but chose not to.

One positive by-product of this whole legal process has been the acknowledgement by the MoD that Vince Phillips should never have been vilified, as seen in some previous publications. The Phillips family finally received official acknowledgement of this fact from the Secretary of State for Defence in early 2003, before the Privy Council hearing started. Why they chose to officially acknowledge this so long after the fact can only be a matter for speculation, but certainly it was something that should have occurred years before.

I remain a committed supporter of the SAS, having spent ten years of my life, in two different armies, as a soldier in this specialised unit. It is of critical importance that members of the SAS have total trust in each other and in all levels of command. That is a major part of the ethos within the unit, something that allows it to operate so effectively around the world.

When that crucial trust is broken, it is viewed as a betrayal and it is no coincidence that outsiders investigating events of the time have now tended to cast Bravo Two Zero in this light.

I, along with others in the SAS, objected strongly at the time the various publications, including films, were disclosed to the public with little or no action taken by the MoD to stop them. As is now obvious from this book, and the legal steps I have taken to fight for the right to set the record straight, the disclosures affected me strongly. I do not regret what I have done and would do it all again if I was placed in the same position today.

Although it is now over ten years since the first Gulf War, I still believe the principles that I fought to uphold are relevant today. I went to war, and nearly died, for the very freedoms that the British Government has done its utmost to suppress, and that is the saddest indictment of all.

* * *

Finally, to the families of Bob, Vince and Steve, for it is only fitting that this is where the book should end, and it was, after all, my desire to tell the correct story of Bravo Two Zero that set this ball in motion. You can hold your heads up high in the knowledge that your loved ones proved beyond doubt that they were men of courage and character, and they were soldiers I was proud to have served alongside. These three men paid the ultimate price for their loyalty; they gave their lives so that others might have freedom that they themselves can never again enjoy.

Lest we forget.

GLOSSARY

2IC: second in command
AAA or Triple A: anti-aircraft artillery
AO: area of operations
APC: armoured personnel carrier
APR: automatic parachute release
AWACS: airborne warning and control system
basher: bivouac
bergen: backpack
berm: sand barrier
BFT: battle fitness test
blade: general term for member of the SAS
bone: stupid
bowser: tanker used for refuelling aircraft on an airfield
CI: chief instructor
CIC: commander in chief
claymore: light, portable anti-personnel mine
click: kilometre
close target recce: covert reconnaissance of an objective to gain detailed
    information
CO: commanding officer
COMCEN: Communications Centre
contact drills: actions taken when a patrol comes under or initiates fire
crabs: slang term for the RAF
crow: term for new member of a squadron
CSAR: combat search and rescue
CTR: close target recce (see above)
CTT: counter-terrorist team, often just referred to as 'team'

cyalume: chemical lightstick activated by cracking

deconfliction: process of ensuring friendly forces do not encroach on each other's AO

DF: direction find

didi-mau: get the hell out – fast

dinkie: short wheelbase Landrover

DOP: drop-off point

DPM: disruptive pattern material (camouflage)

DS: directing staff

DSF: director special forces

DZ: drop zone

E & E: escape and evasion

EMU: electronic message unit

ERV: emergency rendezvous

FGA: fighter ground attack

falaise: term derived from French-speaking North African countries for the high ground where several wadis or dry watercourses converge

FARP: forward air refuelling point

FOB: forward operations base

FRV: final rendezvous

GPMG: general purpose machine-gun

GPS: global positioning system

GSW: gunshot wound

HAHO: high altitude, high opening

HALO: high altitude, low opening

hard-standing: military term for road, concreted area, etc.

head-shed: commanders

IR patrol: information reporting

LCD: liquid crystal display

loadies: loadmasters

locstat: locations statistics

LUP: lying-up place/point

LZ: landing zone

M203: M16 rifle with 40-mm grenade launcher underslung

MBT: main battle tank

MIA: missing in action

MID: mention in dispatches

Minimi: light machine-gun capable of using boxed or magazine-fed 5.56-mm ammunition

MoD: Ministry of Defence

MSR: main supply route

Navex: navigation exercise

NBC: nuclear, biological, chemical

NVA: night vision aid

OC: officer commanding

OP: observation point (same as IR, see above)

OPSEC: operational security

pinkie: 110 Landrover specifically designed for SAS use

PSI: permanent staff instructor

PTI: physical training instructor

PTSU: parachute training school unit

QRF: quick reaction force rescue team

RHQ: regimental headquarters

RICE: rest, ice, compression and elevation

RMO: regimental medical officer

RNZIR: Royal New Zealand Infantry Regiment

RSM: regimental sergeant major

RTA: road traffic accident

RTU: return to unit ('sacked')

RV: rendezvous

S60: 57-mm anti-aircraft gun

SAM: surface to air missile

SAS: Special Air Service

SATCOM: satellite communications, also referred to as TACSAT

SBS: Special Boat Service

SF: Special Forces

shamag: Arab headdress

SHQ: squadron headquarters

sitrep: situation report

slime: intelligence corps

SNCO: senior non-commissioned officer

SOP: standard operating procedure

squeezer: slang term for an Australian

SSM: squadron sergeant major

stag: sentry duty or sentry watch

TAB: tactical advance to battle, long tramp, carrying bergens

TACBE: tactical beacon – emergency voice and beacon transmitter

TACSAT: satellite communications, also referred to as SATCOM (see above)

TEL: transporter erector launcher

TOD: tour of duty

UKSF: UK Special Forces

VWs: voluntary withdrawals

wadi: watercourse (dry)

White Phos: phosphorous grenade